Red Hat Linux 6.0 Administration Tools

McGraw-Hill Tools Series Titles:

Maxwell	*UNIX Network Management Tools*	0-07-913782-2
Medinets	*UNIX Shell Programming Tools*	0-07-913790-3
Carasik	*UNIX Secure Shell*	0-07-134933-2
Ross	*UNIX System Security Tools*	0-07-913788-1
Medinets	*PHP3: Programming Browser-Based Applications*	0-07-135342-9

To order or receive additional information on these or any other McGraw-Hill titles, in the United States please call 1-800-722-4726, or visit us at www.computing.mcgraw-hill.com. In other countries, contact your McGraw-Hill representative.

Red Hat Linux 6.0 Administration Tools

Charles Fisher

McGraw-Hill

New York • San Francisco • Washington, D.C. • Auckland • Bogotá • Caracas
Lisbon • London • Madrid • Mexico City • Milan • Montreal • New Delhi
San Juan • Singapore • Sydney • Tokyo • Toronto

McGraw-Hill

A Division of The **McGraw-Hill** *Companies*

1 2 3 4 5 6 7 8 9 0 AGM/AGM 9 0 4 3 2 1 0 9

P/N 0-07-134744-5

Part of ISBN 0-07-134746-1

The sponsoring editor for this book was Simon Yates, and the production supervisor was Clare Stanley. It was set in Sabon by ***TIPS*** *Technical Publishing.*

Printed and bound by Quebecor/Martinsburg.

This book is printed on recycled, acid-free paper containing a minimum of 50% recycled, de-inked fiber.

Contents

Code Listings

Introduction

This is a book about Red Hat Linux. Linux is a "UNIX-like" operating system. The core software is maintained by Linus Torvalds, while Red Hat Software, Inc., collects supporting tools from around the Internet and packages the lot into their Linux distribution.

This is a practical book, and some knowledge of UNIX is assumed. Generalizations and theory are avoided to the maximum extent. The unique features of the Linux system are demonstrated with little regard to design fundamentals.

Who Should Use This Book?

This is a book mainly for UNIX users and administrators who are curious about the specific features of Linux. While this book draws from a number of development technologies (such as C, HTML, PHP, Perl, and the shell), the focus is upon system maintenance and administration.

This book is written for two audiences. The first includes technical users who have an immediate need for some feature available in Linux. The second includes those who are curious about the Red Hat Linux system, and who may someday exploit its features or direct others to do so. Favor is given to the first audience.

This book is also appropriate for use in a classroom environment, even though there are no formal problem sets. The creation of such activities is left as an exercise for the instructor.

How This Book Is Organized

An effort has been made to keep each subject entirely contained within a chapter. To a large extent, the material is not cumulative. It is conceivable that a reader could begin with a later chapter in the text, then return after some time (if at all) to the earlier material. There are only a few places within the text where this effort has not been maintained.

Conventions

The following conventions are used in this book:

- Code lines, keywords, and any text you see onscreen appear in a special `monospace` typeface.
- Filenames are also set in a `monospace` typeface.
- New terms are in *italics*.
- Case is very important in Linux administration. Always pay attention to uppercase and lowercase in commands and scripts.
- Commands and any text you must type appears in **boldface**. For example, "Type **ls -l**."

Linux, UNIX, and the Internet

Linux is an operating system of dazzling complexity, and it is easy to become diverted by its many features. The temptation to include much more in this text than is reasonable is very great—there is far more to Linux than what is contained here.

It has long been accepted that the Internet is driven by UNIX. Internet and UNIX standards have developed coequally for the life of both environments. The profound influence that the Berkley Software Distribution has had upon UNIX has been continued by powerful UNIX utilities such as `sendmail`, Sun Microsystem's `NFS`, NCSA/Apache `httpd`, `wu-ftpd`, and many other tools.

The Internet is now causing a vast social revolution. It has made resources and information from around the world available with a single click of a mouse. This text is, to some small extent, a point of entry into this broad new horizon. By mastering the material presented here, a reader can construct and maintain a global communication system.

You have purchased your ticket, and we are prepared to disembark. Linux awaits.

01

Installation

The most difficult step in the use of any significant computer application is undoubtedly the initial configuration. This is certainly true of Red Hat Linux. Despite a dramatically simplified installation program, the individual acting as the installer must provide extensive system information before a working Linux system can emerge.

The two areas that present the greatest difficulty for novice installers are disk partitioning and the configuration of the XWindow system. Red Hat has done some work to make both of these areas somewhat less daunting, but conditions easily arise that require extensive knowledge of these subjects, as well as specialized software tools.

This chapter aims to familiarize a Linux installer with the intricacies of installation, with a special focus on the problem areas. Reading through this chapter before installation will help you prepare for these problems and alert you to the types of information required.

Planning for Installation

A basic installation of Red Hat Linux requires relatively modest hardware. Red Hat Linux can be installed on a computer with an Intel 386 with 16MB of memory, a 120MB hard drive, and a 3.5" floppy drive. If a CD-ROM is not available, either a network install must be performed, or an image of the installation files must be placed on the hard drive. CD-ROM installs are *much* more straightforward, and are strongly recommended for the novice installer—even if it requires machine disassembly. If additional subsystems are installed (such as a web server, database server, or electronic mail server), more disk space and/or processor power will be required.

Understanding Disk Partitioning

A hard disk drive must be cut into partitions before Linux can be installed on it. Linux requires at least two partitions—one for file space (usually for an extended file system), and one for virtual memory (swap).

There can be up to four *primary* partitions on a hard drive. One of the primary partitions can be designated as an *extended* partition, which can then hold additional *logical* partitions. Linux can use up to fifteen logical partitions that are created within the extended partition.

On a running Linux system, both the drive as a whole and each partition on the drive are represented by Linux as files in the `/dev` directory. The files differ, depending on whether IDE or SCSI drives are in use.

On an IDE system, up to four drives are usually available. These drives are named /dev/hda, /dev/hdb, /dev/hdc, and /dev/hdd. The files exist, even if the corresponding drive is not physically present.

On a SCSI system, multiple drives across multiple controllers should be available. The *boot drive*, or the first available SCSI drive, is known as /dev/sda. Additional drives are known as /dev/sdb, /dev/sdc, etc. Additionally, SCSI CD-ROM devices are known as /dev/scd0 and above, and SCSI tapes are known as /dev/st0 or /dev/nst0 and above.

Caution

If an IDE hard drive is installed as /dev/hda, it *must* be the boot drive, and it will assume precedence over any available SCSI drives. Do not install a device as /dev/hda if you intend to boot from a SCSI device.

Each primary partition on a drive is represented by a device file. The four primary partitions on the IDE boot drive are /dev/hda1, /dev/hda2, /dev/hda3, and /dev/hda4. These files exist even if the partitions have not been created. If one of the primary partitions is of the extended type, the logical partitions it contains can be addressed starting with /dev/hda5 (and rising to /dev/hda6, /dev/hda7, /dev/hda8, etc.). A SCSI boot drive uses the device files /dev/sda1, /dev/sda2, /dev/sda3, and /dev/sda4 as its primary partitions, and /dev/sda5 and above as its extended partitions.

This arrangement can be further complicated by IDE CD-ROMS, which appear on the system as hard drives. Most PCs place the IDE CD-ROM drive as the master IDE device on the second channel, which makes it /dev/hdc. Attempts to run **fdisk** on the CD-ROM device will prove ineffective. After installation, it is generally wise to set a soft link from /dev/cdrom to /dev/hdc (or whatever IDE device has been used for the CD-ROM drive). Many programs require such a link to properly control the CD-ROM drive. Programs that play audio CDs specifically require this link, and they also require write permission to the device file (which is granted with a command of the form **chmod 666 /dev/hdc**).

Because of the geometry of modern hard disk drives, partitions near the outer edge of a disk provide much better performance than partitions near the center. The *swap* partition should be allocated in such a way that it lies on the outer edge of the disk, since swap performance can greatly influence overall system performance. Other areas of the disk that will see high usage should also be located near the outer edge. This is covered in more detail in "Using fdisk" on page 6.

Usually, if DOS or Windows has been previously installed on a computer, there is a single partition that spans the drive holding the FAT file system. This partition must be split before Linux can be installed. This can be done by destroying the single partition and repartitioning the drive, or by non-destructively separating an unused portion of the partition which can then be used for Linux.

Note

The `fips` tool found in the `dosutils` directory on the CD-ROM included with this text can be used for non-destructive repartitioning, but its use is entirely unsupported and it may cause data loss. Other commercial repartitioning tools are available, which may be more flexible than `fips`.

While Linux can recognize any combination of primary and logical partitions for its file systems, DOS/Windows only allows a single DOS FAT file system to exist in any of the four primary partitions. The DOS version of **fdisk** does not allow the creation of a second DOS FAT file system in a primary partition, and DOS will freeze on boot if Linux **fdisk** is used to create multiple DOS FAT file systems in the primary partitions. However, multiple DOS FAT file systems are allowed within the logical partitions.

Also, please note: there can be grave difficulties in using Linux `fdisk` to mark DOS FAT file systems, as this section from the `fdisk` manual page explains:

> The DOS 6.x **format** command looks for some information in the first sector of the data area of the partition, and treats this information as more reliable than the information in the partition table. DOS **format** expects DOS `fdisk` to clear the first 512 bytes of the data area of a partition whenever a size change occurs. DOS **format** looks at this extra information even if the /U flag is given—we consider this a bug in DOS **format** and DOS `fdisk`.

The bottom line is that if you use `cfdisk` or `fdisk` to change the size of a DOS partition table entry, then you must also use **dd** to zero the first 512 bytes of that partition before using DOS FORMAT to format the partition. If you are using `cfdisk`, for example, to make a DOS partition table entry for `/dev/hda1`, then (after exiting **fdisk** or **cfdisk** and rebooting Linux so that the partition table information is valid) you would use the command **dd if=/dev/zero of=/dev/hda1 bs=512 count=1** to zero the first 512 bytes of the partition.

BE EXTREMELY CAREFUL if you use the **dd** command, since a small typo can make all of the data on your disk useless.

For best results, you should always use an OS-specific partition table program. For example, you should make DOS partitions with the DOS FDISK program and Linux partitions with the Linux `fdisk` or `cfdisk` programs.

Filesystem Considerations for Partitions

As has been previously stated, Linux requires at least two partitions at installation (one for the root file system, and one for swap). It is usually desirable, however, to create additional file systems (and the partitions on which they reside) to isolate different areas of the Linux system. Each separate disk partition can hold a single native file system.

For example, it is usually a good idea to prepare the `/home` directory as a separate file system. This ensures that if `/home` fills, normal logging activity will continue on the root file system and many other system administration options will remain open.

The following are important directory locations which might do well when configured as separate file systems:

`/home`

Creating a separate `/home` file system isolates the system areas from non-privileged users. If more than a few trusted users will be accessing the system, the creation of a separate `/home` file system is highly recommended.

`/opt`

Commercial software is installed in `/opt` on most major UNIX variants. Red Hat does not create an `/opt` directory in the normal course of installation, but the Sybase Adaptive Server Enterprise SQL Server does create the directory. In this guide, however, it is recommended to install Sybase on `/home` to simplify the preparation of PHP. It is therefore suggested that `/opt` not be created as a separate file system, but that a soft link be set from `/opt` to `/home` at a later time. The installer is free to disregard this advice and allow `/opt` to be created in the root file system, or allocate a separate device for it.

`/usr`

The `/usr` directory holds binaries that are not critical for system administration. This directory can be a part of the root file system, or it can be separate. Some UNIX variants share this directory across multiple systems with NFS. This is much more difficult to maintain under Red Hat, as such an installation invalidates RPM.

`/var`

The `/var` directory holds system logs in `/var/log`. If the relevant subsystems are installed, /var will also contain electronic mail in `/var/spool/mail`, and news spools in `/var/spool/news`. Each of these separate areas of `/var` might require a separate file system, depending on the configuration and use of the system.

Using fdisk

Bearing the previous discussion of disk partitioning in mind, an example of a typical workstation `fdisk` session is shown Listing 1.1.

This workstation has a 3.5 gigabyte hard disk drive. A Windows operating system is installed on the drive, and has been configured to occupy a 2 gigabyte partition (which is the maximum allowable size for the older FAT file systems).

This `fdisk` session will be used later in the example installation of a new Red Hat Linux system. If a new drive were added to the computer, an `fdisk` partitioning session similar to the one below would be required before the new drive could be used under Linux.

Warning

Be extremely careful in running fdisk on drives with an installed operating system. It is extremely easy to make a mistake that wipes out a partition and the operating system on it. The value of backups in such a situation cannot be overemphasized.

Below is the complete `fdisk` session. The warning concerning the default device can be avoided if the device file is passed as an argument to `fdisk` (i.e., call "`fdisk /dev/hda`" rather than "`fdisk`" from the shell).

Listing 1.1 *The fdisk help menu.*

```
fdisk
Using /dev/hda as default device!

Command (m for help): m
Command action
   a   toggle a bootable flag
   b   edit bsd disklabel
   c   toggle the dos compatibility flag
   d   delete a partition
   l   list known partition types
   m   print this menu
   n   add a new partition
   o   create a new empty DOS partition table
   p   print the partition table
   q   quit without saving changes
   s   create a new empty Sun disklabel
   t   change a partition's system id
   u   change display/entry units
   v   verify the partition table
   w   write table to disk and exit
   x   extra functionality (experts only)
```

The help command used above displays all the options for `fdisk`. The first thing to do in such a situation is to examine the existing partition table on the drive:

```
Command (m for help): p

Disk /dev/hda: 128 heads, 63 sectors, 847 cylinders
Units = cylinders of 8064 * 512 bytes

   Device Boot    Start       End    Blocks   Id  System
/dev/hda1   *         1       520   2096608+   6  FAT16
```

DOS or Windows has been installed on this drive. A 2 gigabyte partition has been allocated for the DOS area. Linux will be installed on the remainder of the drive, in an extended partition.

The Boot column indicates the active partition. The LILO loader ignores which partition is marked active, so this information is irrelevant in a normal Linux installation. See Listing 1.2.

Listing 1.2 *Creating an extended partition.*

```
Command (m for help): n
Command action
   e   extended
   p   primary partition (1-4)
e
Partition number (1-4): 2
First cylinder (521-847): 521
Last cylinder or +size or +sizeM or +sizeK ([521]-847): 847

Command (m for help): p

Disk /dev/hda: 128 heads, 63 sectors, 847 cylinders
Units = cylinders of 8064 * 512 bytes

   Device Boot    Start       End    Blocks   Id  System
/dev/hda1   *         1       520   2096608+   6  FAT16
/dev/hda2           521       847   1318464    5  Extended
```

An extended partition has now been created over the remainder of the drive. It must now be populated with Linux partitions. See Listing 1.3.

Listing 1.3 *Creating the partition for the root file system.*

```
Command (m for help): n
Command action
   l   logical (5 or over)
   p   primary partition (1-4)
l
First cylinder (521-847): 521
Last cylinder or +size or +sizeM or +sizeK ([521]-847): +700M

Command (m for help): p

Disk /dev/hda: 128 heads, 63 sectors, 847 cylinders
Units = cylinders of 8064 * 512 bytes
```

```
   Device Boot    Start       End    Blocks   Id  System
/dev/hda1   *         1       520   2096608+   6  FAT16
/dev/hda2           521       847   1318464    5  Extended
/dev/hda5           521       698    717664+  83  Linux
```

Warning

The entire root file system must lie within the first 1024 cylinders, or LILO will have great difficulty in booting the Linux system. Please ensure that the ending cylinder of the root file system falls below 1024.

A 700 megabyte Linux partition has now been created. This partition will later be used as a root file system. Notice that the extended partitions are numbered starting with `/dev/hda5`.

Notice also that the last cylinder of a new partition can be specified as a size offset, rather than a specific ending cylinder. See Listing 1.4.

Listing 1.4 *Creating the partition for the /home filesystem.*

```
Command (m for help): n
Command action
   l   logical (5 or over)
   p   primary partition (1-4)
l
First cylinder (648-847): 699
Last cylinder or +size or +sizeM or +sizeK ([648]-847): 830

Command (m for help): p

Disk /dev/hda: 128 heads, 63 sectors, 847 cylinders
Units = cylinders of 8064 * 512 bytes

   Device Boot    Start       End    Blocks   Id  System
/dev/hda1   *         1       520   2096608+   6  FAT16
/dev/hda2           521       847   1318464    5  Extended
/dev/hda5           521       698    717664+  83  Linux
/dev/hda6           699       830    532192+  83  Linux
```

A new partition has been created that is slightly over 500 megabytes. In this case, it will be mounted on the `/home` directory. This file system will have better performance than any of the others, because it lies near the outer edge of the disk. See Listing 1.5 on page 10.

Listing 1.5 *Creating the swap partition.*

```
Command (m for help): n
Command action
   l   logical (5 or over)
   p   primary partition (1-4)
l
First cylinder (816-847): 831
Last cylinder or +size or +sizeM or +sizeK ([816]-847): 847

Command (m for help): p

Disk /dev/hda: 128 heads, 63 sectors, 847 cylinders
Units = cylinders of 8064 * 512 bytes

   Device Boot    Start       End    Blocks   Id  System
/dev/hda1   *         1       520   2096608+   6  FAT16
/dev/hda2           521       847   1318464    5  Extended
/dev/hda5           521       698    717664+  83  Linux
/dev/hda6           699       830    532192+  83  Linux
/dev/hda7           831       847     68512+  82  Linux
```

A final 64 megabyte partition, intended for use as swap space, has been created.

Note 128 megabytes is the largest that any single swap partition can be. If larger swap partitions are created, the extra space will go to waste.

The fact that 16 cylinders translates to approximately 64 megabytes can be verified by adding a +64M partition, recording the number of cylinders that it consumes, then deleting that partition. The size of the `/home` file system is then resolved by subtracting the cylinder size of the swap partition from the total remaining cylinders. However, before the swap partition can be initialized, it must be tagged for use as swap. See Listing 1.6.

Listing 1.6 *Tagging the swap partition.*

```
Command (m for help): t
Partition number (1-7): 7
Hex code (type L to list codes): L

 0  Empty           16  Hidden FAT16    61  SpeedStor       a6  OpenBSD
 1  FAT12           17  Hidden HPFS/NTF 63  GNU HURD or Sys a7  NeXTSTEP
 2  XENIX root      18  AST Windows swa 64  Novell Netware  b7  BSDI fs
```

```
 3  XENIX usr       24  NEC DOS         65  Novell Netware  b8  BSDI swap
 4  FAT16 <32M      3c  PartitionMagic  70  DiskSecure Mult c1  DRDOS/sec (FAT-
 5  Extended        40  Venix 80286     75  PC/IX           c4  DRDOS/sec (FAT-
 6  FAT16           41  PPC PReP Boot   80  Old Minix       c6  DRDOS/sec (FAT-
 7  HPFS/NTFS       42  SFS             81  Minix / old Lin c7  Syrinx
 8  AIX             4d  QNX4.x          82  Linux swap      db  CP/M / CTOS / .
 9  AIX bootable    4e  QNX4.x 2nd part 83  Linux           e1  DOS access
 a  OS/2 Boot Manag 4f  QNX4.x 3rd part 84  OS/2 hidden C:  e3  DOS R/O
 b  Win95 FAT32     50  OnTrack DM      85  Linux extended  e4  SpeedStor
 c  Win95 FAT32 (LB 51  OnTrack DM6 Aux 86  NTFS volume set eb  BeOS fs
 e  Win95 FAT16 (LB 52  CP/M            87  NTFS volume set f1  SpeedStor
 f  Win95 Ext'd (LB 53  OnTrack DM6 Aux 93  Amoeba          f4  SpeedStor
10  OPUS            54  OnTrackDM6      94  Amoeba BBT      f2  DOS secondary
11  Hidden FAT12    55  EZ-Drive        a0  IBM Thinkpad hi fe  LANstep
12  Compaq diagnost 56  Golden Bow      a5  BSD/386         ff  BBT
14  Hidden FAT16 <3 5c  Priam Edisk
Hex code (type L to list codes): 82
Changed system type of partition 7 to 82 (Linux swap)

Command (m for help): p

Disk /dev/hda: 128 heads, 63 sectors, 847 cylinders
Units = cylinders of 8064 * 512 bytes

   Device Boot    Start       End    Blocks   Id  System
/dev/hda1   *         1       520   2096608+   6  FAT16
/dev/hda2           521       847   1318464    5  Extended
/dev/hda5           521       698    717664+  83  Linux
/dev/hda6           699       830    532192+  83  Linux
/dev/hda7           831       847     68512+  82  Linux swap
```

The swap partition has been marked, and all that remains is to write the changes to the partition table using the following command:

```
Command (m for help): w
```

Pre-installation Concerns with X11

Generally speaking, in order to configure XWindows for a new video monitor, the horizontal and vertical scanning rates of the monitor must be known (assuming that the video card is supported).This information is usually in the manual that shipped with the monitor—a great argument for not throwing manuals away. The rates can also sometimes be obtained from the monitor manufacturer's website.

The horizontal rates are usually listed in KiloHertz (KHz), and the vertical rates are usually listed in Hertz (Hz). The rates may be specified as discrete values, or as a range of frequencies. A Mitsubishi Diamond Plus 72, for example, has horizontal frequencies of 30 to 86 KHz, and vertical frequencies of 50 to 130 Hz.

The `Xconfigurator` utility distributed with Red Hat Linux 6.0 contains the scanning rates for many monitors (see Appendix A for a complete listing). `Xconfigurator` is run as part of the install process, and can also be executed post-installation should additional configuration be necessary. If the monitor to be installed is in the list provided in Appendix A, installation should be simple. If not, call `Xconfigurator` after installation with special parameters.

If the horizontal and vertical scanning rates absolutely cannot be determined, choose either the "Generic Multisync" or the "Generic Monitor." Before making such a choice, however, pay attention to the following warning from XFree86:

Warning "It is VERY IMPORTANT that you do not specify a monitor type with a horizontal sync range that is beyond the capabilities of your monitor. If in doubt, choose a conservative setting."

The reason for this warning is that it is actually possible to physically damage some older monitors by driving them with scan rates that are beyond the design tolerances.

Warning Do not configure XFree86 to use scan rates that are higher than your monitor's specifications, or physical damage to the monitor could result.

The risk surfaces only if the **startx** command is used at the console, or if the system enters **init 5** and activates the `xdm` login console. There is no danger if neither of these commands are run. To completely remove any danger, delete the `/etc/X11/XF86Config` file, which prevents XWindows from starting at all (some server machines have no need for XWindows).

In the case of an unknown monitor, the **Xconfigurator** command can be run by the root user with the following arguments:

Xconfigurator --kickstart --hsync "30-86" --vsync "50-130"

This command writes an `/etc/X11/XF86Config` file for the previously mentioned Mitsubishi monitor. The **startx** command can then be run after installation.

For the utmost control over the configuration of XWindows, use the `xf86config` utility, rather than `Xconfigurator`. Because of its complexity, `xf86config` is not covered in this text.

Once XWindows has been properly configured, the Xserver can be started with various color bit depths with the following commands:

startx

This command starts XWindows with the default color bit depth. This is usually 256-color, 8 bits per pixel. `Xconfigurator` might choose a different default color depth, however.

startx -- -bpp 8

This command starts XWindows in 256-color mode, with 8 bits per pixel. This color depth is not very good, and most window managers will quickly exhaust the available colors.

startx -- -bpp 16

This command starts XWindows in 65,536-color mode, with 16 bits per pixel. This is the most popular color depth.

startx -- -bpp 24

This command starts XWindows in 16,777,216-color mode. This mode has much more precise color reproduction, but is much more processor-intensive.

Warnings for SCSI Systems

Nearly every Linux kernel has built-in support for IDE devices, including hard disks and CD-ROM drives. This is not so for SCSI devices.

Drivers for various brands of SCSI cards are stored as modules, which are loaded dynamically by the kernel as it boots. Unless arrangements are made for the module to be loaded, the entire SCSI system will be unavailable to a generic kernel. The Red Hat Linux installation disks and the kernel installed by this process use a special RAM disk to hold modules for SCSI cards. If the kernel or the RAM disk become corrupt, the bootdisk will be required. This is why it is *so* important to create boot images for Linux systems with SCSI devices (although it is a good idea for all systems in general).

Take the opportunity to make a boot floppy when it is presented in the initial installation. Alternately, create a boot floppy later by using the command **mkbootdisk**.

A small amount of effort at installation time can save great effort when a system won't boot. Make the boot floppy.

A Sample Installation

Before installation can begin, the required boot disk images must usually be written to blank floppies. This operation is accomplished through either a DOS or UNIX environment.

The layout of the boot images for Red Hat 6.0 has changed substantially from earlier releases. The following boot images are available on the CD-ROM included with this text:

boot.img
This image is used for all types of disk media installs (including CD-ROM).

bootnet.img
This image is used to install Red Hat Linux over a network connection. A variety of protocols are supported, including NFS, FTP, SMB, and HTTP.

pcmcia.img
This image is required when PCMCIA (PC-Card) devices play any role in the installation. Notebook computers often require this image.

However, if the BIOS of the PC supports the *El Torito* bootable CD format, the creation of boot floppies might not be necessary. Simply place the Red Hat CD in the drive, set the BIOS to boot from the CD (if applicable), and attempt to boot normally. If a LILO boot prompt appears, and PCMCIA services are not required, the creation of the boot floppies can be safely skipped. If it is necessary to create a set of boot floppies, the instructions for both DOS and UNIX follow:

UNIX

Under most UNIX environments, the images can be written with the **dd** command. The CD must be mounted as an active file system. Under Linux, if a `/cdrom` directory exists, one of the following mount commands will usually mount a CD:

mount /dev/scd0 /cdrom
mount /dev/hdc /cdrom
mount /dev/hdb /cdrom

Once the CD is mounted, the following **dd** commands will write the image to a floppy drive:

dd if=/cdrom/images/boot.img of=/dev/fd0 bs=1440k

(The boot.img file can also be downloaded from a number of FTP sites, if the CD is not available.)

DOS

Under DOS with CD-ROM support, place the CD in the drive. Open a DOS shell if a Windows variant is in use. Change the active drive to the CD (usually by entering "d:" and pressing enter), then enter the following commands:

cd dosutils
rawrite

When prompted, write the `\images\boot.img` file to the `A:` drive, or whatever other image is required for the local installation.
Once the images are in hand, boot from the boot floppy. Press "Return" to pass the LILO boot prompt.

As a note for the technically-minded, the boot floppy is in MS-DOS format. The `vmlinuz` file can be replaced with a specially-compiled kernel image as long as the new image fits in the free space available on the floppy. This is one way to build specific device support into the installation session, in the unlikely event that it is necessary.

Once the Linux kernel has booted (which may take some time), the welcome message shown in Figure 1.1 on page 16 is presented.

Welcome to Red Hat Linux
********************** Red Hat Linux ************************
* Welcome to Red Hat Linux!
* This installation process is outlined in detail in the
* Official Red Hat Linux Installation Guide available from
* Red Hat Software. If you have access to this manual, you
* should read the installation section before continuing.
* If you have purchased Official Red Hat Linux, be sure to
* register your purchase through our web site,
* http://www.redhat.com
* OK *
<Tab>/<Alt-Tab> between elements | <Space> selects | <F12> next screen

Figure 1.1 *Linux welcome message.*

Press "Enter"/"Return" to begin the installation. The language menu shown in Figure 1.2 is displayed. Select the desired language for the installation session, then press "Space" or "Enter"/"Return." Select the appropriate keyboard from the menu shown in Figure 1.3.

If PCMCIA devices are required for the installation (such as a CD-ROM controller, or a network card), have the PCMCIA disk ready and answer "Yes" to the menu shown in Figure 1.4 on page 18.

From the menu shown in Figure 1.5, select the Local CD-ROM by choosing "OK." Red Hat Linux can be installed without a CD by using other options (especially those contained in bootnet.img), but they are not covered in this text.

Ensure that the CD is in the drive, and proceed through the dialog shown in Figure 1.6 on page 19.

At this point, the *second stage install* begins. From the menu shown in Figure 1.7, select the "Install" option to configure a new system. The "Upgrade" option is very effective at bringing an older Red Hat Linux system up to date. The "Upgrade" option is very simple and straightforward and it is not covered in this text.

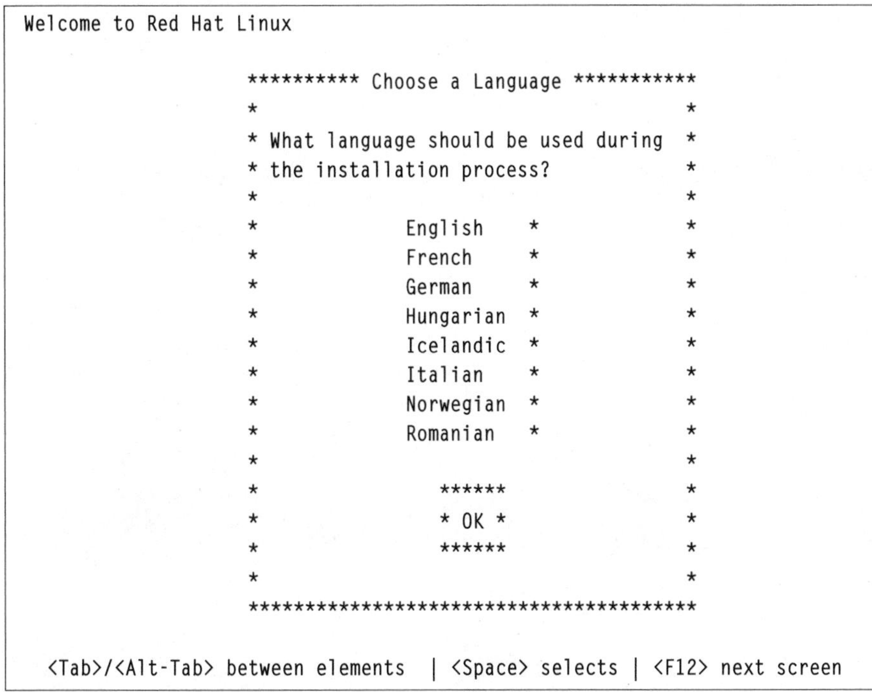

```
Welcome to Red Hat Linux

                    ********** Choose a Language ***********
                    *                                      *
                    * What language should be used during  *
                    * the installation process?            *
                    *                                      *
                    *             English    *             *
                    *             French     *             *
                    *             German     *             *
                    *             Hungarian  *             *
                    *             Icelandic  *             *
                    *             Italian    *             *
                    *             Norwegian  *             *
                    *             Romanian   *             *
                    *                                      *
                    *                ******                *
                    *                * OK *                *
                    *                ******                *
                    *                                      *
                    ****************************************

  <Tab>/<Alt-Tab> between elements  | <Space> selects | <F12> next screen
```

Figure 1.2 *Language menu.*

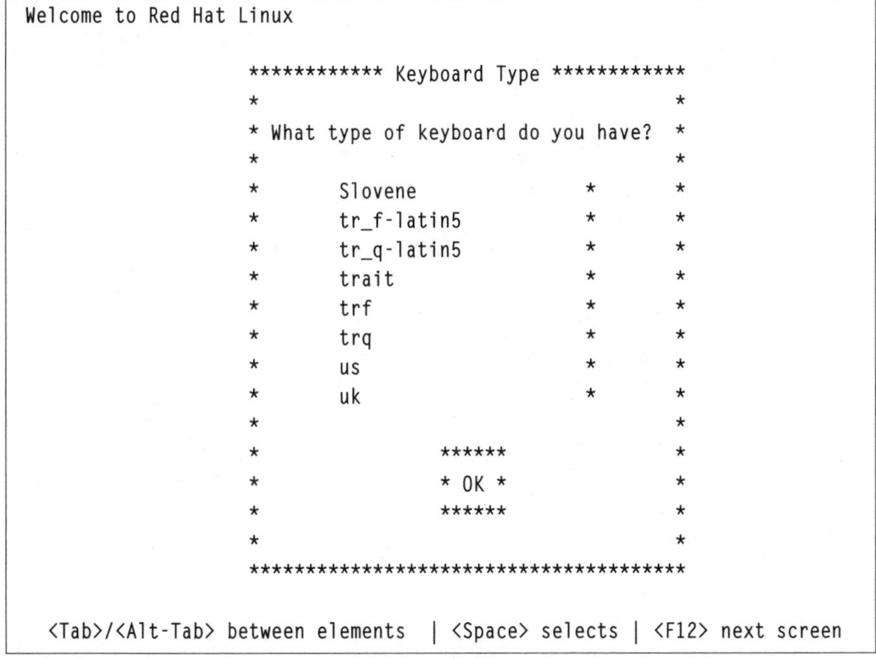

```
Welcome to Red Hat Linux

                    ************ Keyboard Type ************
                    *                                     *
                    * What type of keyboard do you have?  *
                    *                                     *
                    *       Slovene               *       *
                    *       tr_f-latin5           *       *
                    *       tr_q-latin5           *       *
                    *       trait                 *       *
                    *       trf                   *       *
                    *       trq                   *       *
                    *       us                    *       *
                    *       uk                    *       *
                    *                                     *
                    *                ******               *
                    *                * OK *               *
                    *                ******               *
                    *                                     *
                    ***************************************

  <Tab>/<Alt-Tab> between elements  | <Space> selects | <F12> next screen
```

Figure 1.3 *Keyboard selection menu.*

```
Welcome to Red Hat Linux

          ********************** PCMCIA Support **********************
          *                                                          *
          * Do you need to use PCMCIA devices during the install?    *
          * Answer no this question if only need PCMCIA support      *
          * after the install. You do not need install-time PCMCIA   *
          * support if you are installing Red Hat Linux on a laptop  *
          * with a built-in CDROM drive.                             *
          *                                                          *
          *      *******             ******            ********      *
          *      * Yes *             * No *            * Back *      *
          *      *******             ******            ********      *
          *                                                          *
          ************************************************************

  <Tab>/<Alt-Tab> between elements  | <Space> selects | <F12> next screen
```

Figure 1.4 *PCMCIA device selection menu.*

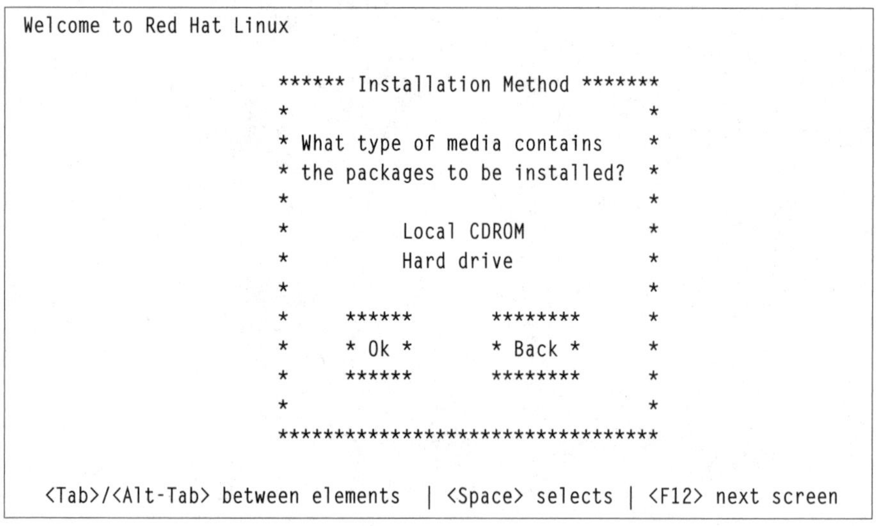

```
Welcome to Red Hat Linux

                       ****** Installation Method *******
                       *                                *
                       * What type of media contains    *
                       * the packages to be installed?  *
                       *                                *
                       *          Local CDROM           *
                       *          Hard drive            *
                       *                                *
                       *     ******       ********      *
                       *     * Ok *       * Back *      *
                       *     ******       ********      *
                       *                                *
                       **********************************

  <Tab>/<Alt-Tab> between elements  | <Space> selects | <F12> next screen
```

Figure 1.5 *Media selection menu.*

```
Welcome to Red Hat Linux

                        ************** Note **************
                        *                                *
                        * Insert your Red Hat CD into    *
                        * your CD drive now.             *
                        *                                *
                        *    ******        ********      *
                        *    * Ok *        * Back *      *
                        *    ******        ********      *
                        *                                *
                        **********************************

   <Tab>/<Alt-Tab> between elements   | <Space> selects | <F12> next screen
```

Figure 1.6 *Insert CD Note screen.*

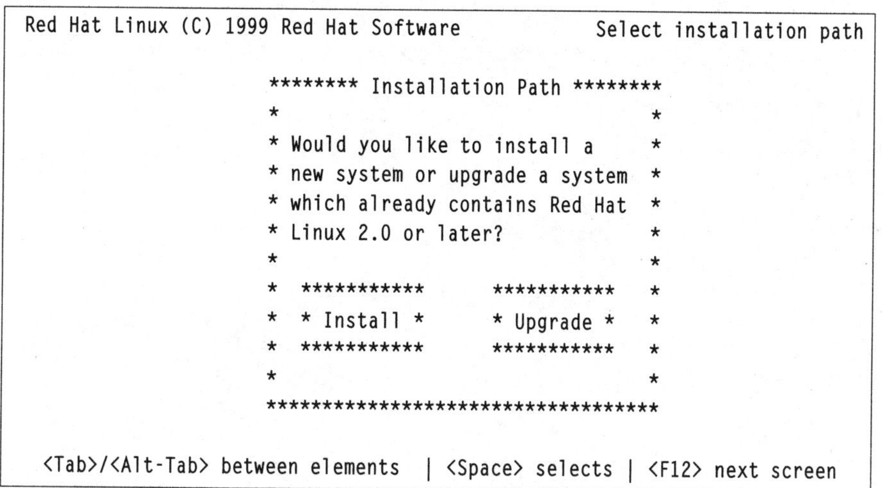

```
Red Hat Linux (C) 1999 Red Hat Software            Select installation path

                       ******** Installation Path ********
                       *                                 *
                       * Would you like to install a     *
                       * new system or upgrade a system  *
                       * which already contains Red Hat  *
                       * Linux 2.0 or later?             *
                       *                                 *
                       *  ***********      ***********   *
                       *  * Install *      * Upgrade *   *
                       *  ***********      ***********   *
                       *                                 *
                       ***********************************

   <Tab>/<Alt-Tab> between elements   | <Space> selects | <F12> next screen
```

Figure 1.7 *Installation Path menu.*

For the maximum flexibility during the installation process, choose the "Custom" option from the menu shown in Figure 1.8 on page 20. The other options automatically partition the drive and install a set of software applications appropriate for either a workstation or server Linux system. For our purposes, we assume the "Custom" option has been chosen.

If SCSI adapters are present, they must be probed and configured. In this example, we assume that only IDE devices are in use, but the SCSI adapter selection menu is shown in Figure 1.9 for reference.

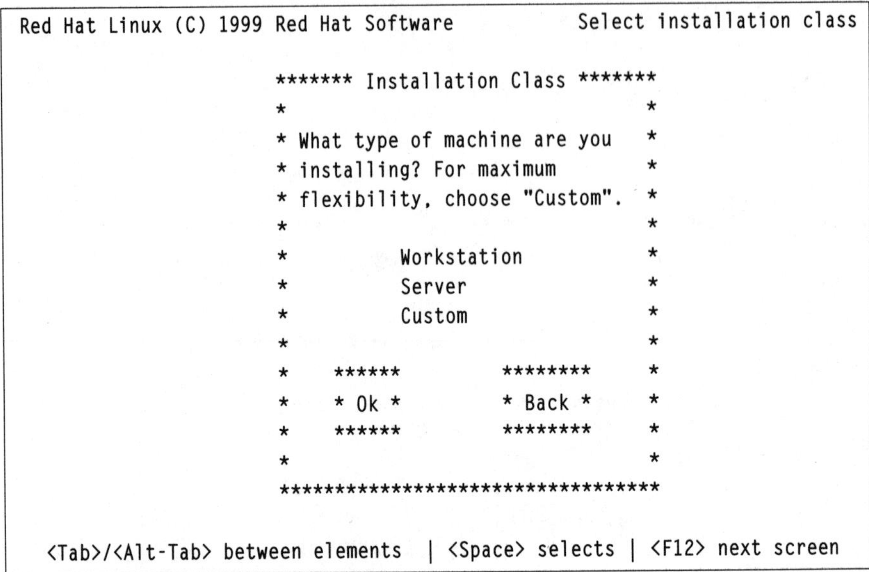

```
Red Hat Linux (C) 1999 Red Hat Software          Select installation class

                      ******* Installation Class *******
                      *                                *
                      * What type of machine are you   *
                      * installing? For maximum        *
                      * flexibility, choose "Custom".  *
                      *                                *
                      *          Workstation           *
                      *          Server                *
                      *          Custom                *
                      *                                *
                      *     ******         ********    *
                      *     * Ok *         * Back *    *
                      *     ******         ********    *
                      *                                *
                      **********************************

   <Tab>/<Alt-Tab> between elements   | <Space> selects | <F12> next screen
```

Figure 1.8 *Installation Class menu.*

```
Red Hat Linux (C) 1999 Red Hat Software                         Setup SCSI

                      ******* SCSI Configuration ********
                      *                                 *
                      * Do you have any SCSI adapters?  *
                      *                                 *
                      *  ******    *******   ********   *
                      *  * No *    * Yes *   * Back *   *
                      *  ******    *******   ********   *
                      *                                 *
                      *                                 *
                      ***********************************

   <Tab>/<Alt-Tab> between elements   | <Space> selects | <F12> next screen
```

Figure 1.9 *SCSI adapter selection menu.*

If a SCSI adapter is present in the system, its brand must be specified in the menu shown in Figure 1.10. At this point, disk partitioning can be performed.

If multiple hard drives are available on a system, a menu such as the one shown in Figure 1.11 is presented, allowing a target hard drive to be chosen.

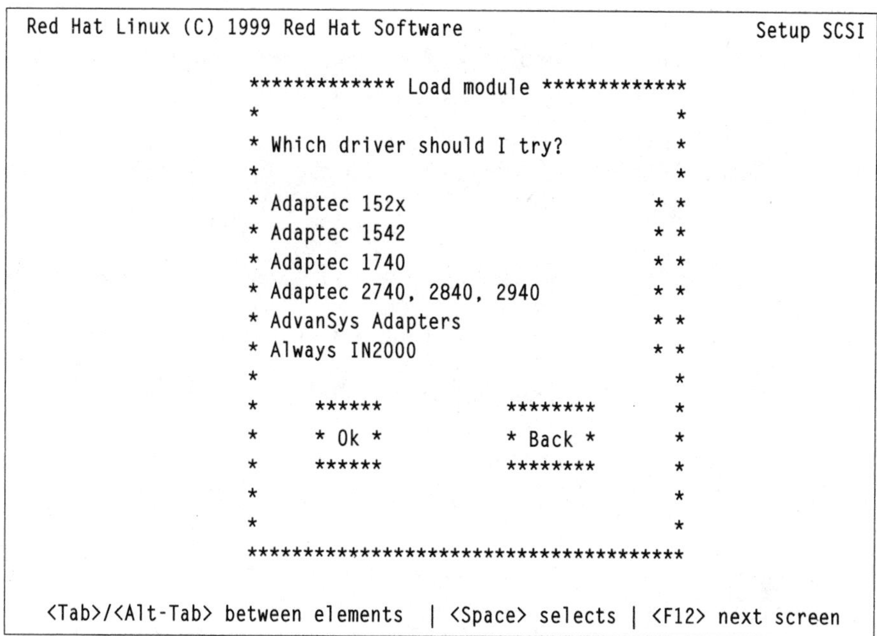

```
Red Hat Linux (C) 1999 Red Hat Software                         Setup SCSI

                    ************* Load module *************
                    *                                     *
                    * Which driver should I try?          *
                    *                                     *
                    * Adaptec 152x                      * *
                    * Adaptec 1542                      * *
                    * Adaptec 1740                      * *
                    * Adaptec 2740, 2840, 2940          * *
                    * AdvanSys Adapters                 * *
                    * Always IN2000                     * *
                    *                                     *
                    *     ******          ********        *
                    *     * Ok *          * Back *        *
                    *     ******          ********        *
                    *                                     *
                    *                                     *
                    ***************************************

  <Tab>/<Alt-Tab> between elements   | <Space> selects | <F12> next screen
```

Figure 1.10 *SCSI driver selection menu.*

```
Red Hat Linux (C) 1999 Red Hat Software                 Setup filesystems

        *********************** Partition Disks ***********************
        *                                                             *
        * To install Red Hat Linux, you must have at least one        *
        * partition of 150 MB dedicated to Linux. We suggest placing  *
        * that partition on one of the first two hard drives in your  *
        * system so you can boot into Linux with LILO.                *
        *                                                             *
        *    /dev/hda - Model FUJITSU MPA3035ATU - Model FUJITS       *
        *    /dev/hdb - Model WDC AC2120 - Model WDC AC2120           *
        *                                                             *
        *     ********            ********            ********        *
        *     * Done *            * Edit *            * Back *        *
        *     ********            ********            ********        *
        *                                                             *
        *                                                             *
        ***************************************************************

  <Tab>/<Alt-Tab> between elements   | <Space> selects | <F12> next screen
```

Figure 1.11 *Target hard drive menu.*

The disk partitions must be created before Red Hat Linux can be installed. A complete session with the `fdisk` utility was covered in a previous section of this chapter. From the menu shown in Figure 1.12, choose either `disk druid` or `fdisk`. `Disk druid` menus can be confusing but must be used in the next step to establish file system mount points.

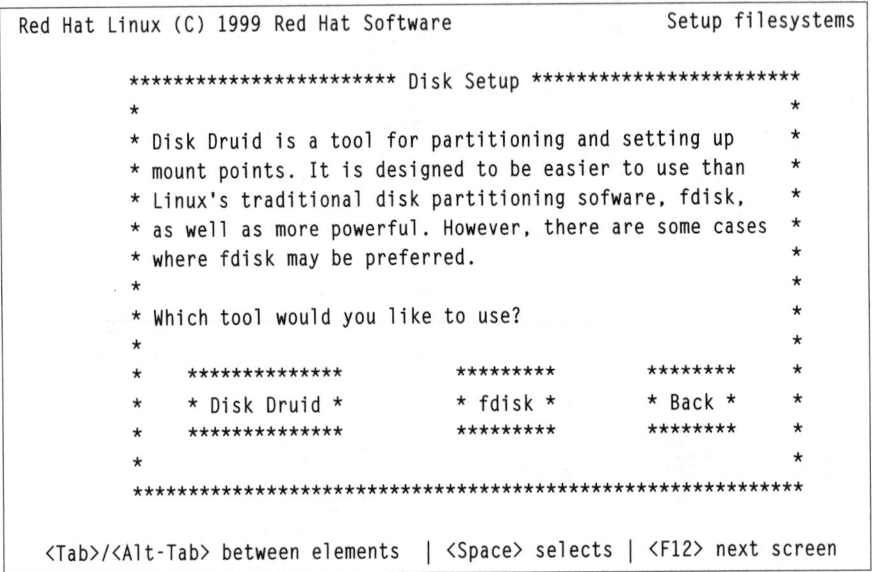

Red Hat Linux (C) 1999 Red Hat Software
Setup filesystems
Disk Setup
Disk Druid is a tool for partitioning and setting up mount points. It is designed to be easier to use than Linux's traditional disk partitioning sofware, fdisk, as well as more powerful. However, there are some cases where fdisk may be preferred.
Which tool would you like to use?
Disk Druid
fdisk
Back
<Tab>/<Alt-Tab> between elements | <Space> selects | <F12> next screen

Figure 1.12 *Disk Setup menu.*

After the fdisk session has completed, a mount point must be chosen for each file system. This is done by moving the highlight on the disk druid menu (see Figure 1.13) to a particular partition, using the "Tab" key to move to the "Edit" option, then selecting "Edit" and indicating a mount point. The root file system must be specified with a "/". The root file system must exist and other file system mount points are optional. DOS FAT partitions can also be mounted.

Warning The entire root file system must lie within the first 1024 cylinders, or LILO will have great difficulty in booting the Linux system. Please ensure that the ending cylinder of the root file system falls below 1024.

```
Red Hat Linux (C) 1999 Red Hat Software                         Setup filesystems
************************** Current Disk Partitions ***************************
*    Mount Point            Device     Requested   Actual        Type          *
*    /dos                    hda1        2047M     2047M     DOS 16-bit >=32  * *
*    /                       hda5         700M      700M     Linux native     * *
*    /home                   hda6         519M      519M     Linux native     * *
*                            hda7          66M       66M     Linux swap       * *
*                            hdb1         119M      119M     Linux native     * *
*                                                                             * *
*                                                                             * *
*                                                                             * *
* Drive Summaries                                                               *
*   Drive      Geom [C/H/S]      Total     Used     Free                        *
*    hda       [  847/128/63]     3335M    3334M       1M     [##########]     **
*    hdb       [  872/  8/35]      119M     119M       0M     [##########]     **
*                                                                              **
*                                                                              **
*                                                                               *
*     *******        ********        **********       ******       ********     *
*     * Add *        * Edit *        * Delete *       * Ok *       * Back *     *
*     *******        ********        **********       ******       ********     *
*                                                                               *
*********************************************************************************

    F1-Add    F2-Add NFS    F3-Edit    F4-Delete    F5-Reset    F12-Ok    v 1.00
```

Figure 1.13 *Partition modification menu.*

Once the layout of the file system is complete, the installation program prompts you to format a swap partition (see Figure 1.14 on page 24). It is strongly recommended that all areas be checked for bad blocks.

The installer will then format the swap partition (see Figure 1.15).

After the swap space has been formatted, the new partitions must also be formatted. On a new installation, all of the Linux partitions should be formatted with bad block checks, as shown in Figure 1.16 on page 25.

When the partition configuration is complete, a list of available components is presented:

- The C Compiler and Development Libraries are required for firewall tools, web development tools, Kernel builds, CD recording, and many other tasks. These packages should probably be installed. The C++ package is less frequently needed.

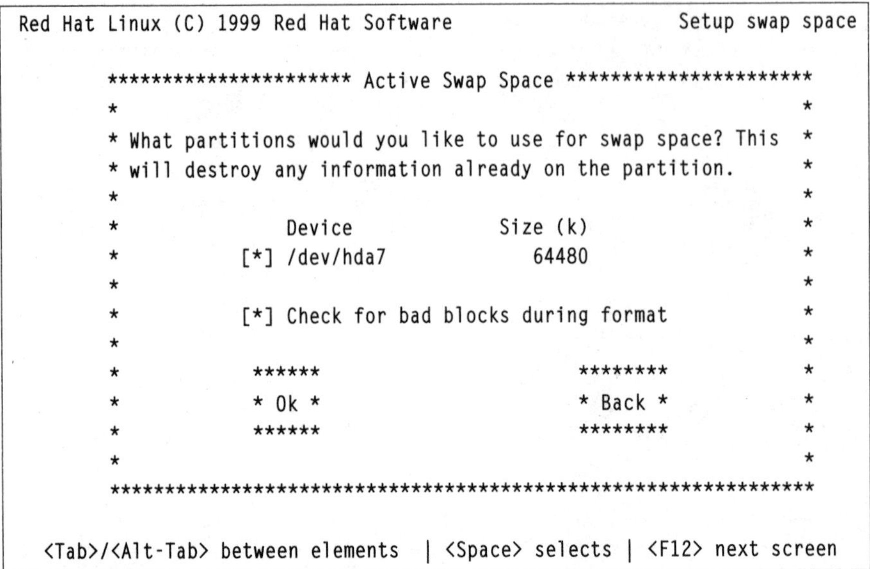

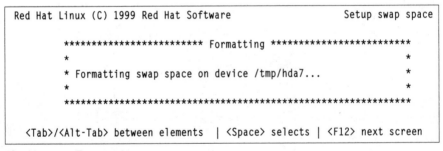

```
Red Hat Linux (C) 1999 Red Hat Software                    Setup swap space

      ********************* Active Swap Space *********************
      *                                                           *
      * What partitions would you like to use for swap space? This *
      * will destroy any information already on the partition.    *
      *                                                           *
      *             Device                Size (k)                *
      *         [*] /dev/hda7               64480                 *
      *                                                           *
      *         [*] Check for bad blocks during format            *
      *                                                           *
      *          ******                    ********               *
      *          * Ok *                    * Back *               *
      *          ******                    ********               *
      *                                                           *
      *************************************************************

  <Tab>/<Alt-Tab> between elements   | <Space> selects | <F12> next screen
```

Figure 1.14 *Swap partition format menu.*

```
Red Hat Linux (C) 1999 Red Hat Software                    Setup swap space

       ************************* Formatting ************************
       *                                                           *
       * Formatting swap space on device /tmp/hda7...              *
       *                                                           *
       *************************************************************

  <Tab>/<Alt-Tab> between elements   | <Space> selects | <F12> next screen
```

Figure 1.15 *Formatting status screen.*

- The electronic mail tools include `sendmail`, which should be installed if networked email is required.

A complete install with all packages requires large amounts of space. It is best to choose the installed subsystems carefully, because some can be a nuisance to shut down later.

A listing of all the packages associated with these subsystems can be found in the `/RedHat/base/comps` file on the CD-ROM included with this text.

When the package selection is completed, the partitions will be formatted and the packages will be installed. Scrolling through the form, you will have an opportunity to select and de-select various packages (see Figure 1.17).

```
 Red Hat Linux (C) 1999 Red Hat Software        Choose partitions to format

       ********************** Partitions To Format *********************
       *                                                               *
       * What partitions would you like to format? We strongly suggest *
       * formatting all of the system partitions, including /, /usr,   *
       * and /var. There is no need to format /home or /usr/local if   *
       * they have already been configured during a previous install.  *
       *                                                               *
       *       [*] /dev/hda5   /                                       *
       *       [*] /dev/hda6   /home                                   *
       *                                                               *
       *            [*] Check for bad blocks during format             *
       *                                                               *
       *             ******                   ********                 *
       *             * Ok *                   * Back *                 *
       *             ******                   ********                 *
       *                                                               *
       *****************************************************************

   <Tab>/<Alt-Tab> between elements   | <Space> selects | <F12> next screen
```

Figure 1.16 *Partition format menu.*

```
 Red Hat Linux (C) 1999 Red Hat Software         Choose packages to install

                   ********* Components to Install *********
                   *                                       *
                   * Choose components to install:         *
                   *                                       *
                   * [ ] Printer Support                 * *
                   * [*] X Window System                 * *
                   * [*] GNOME                           * *
                   * [ ] KDE                             * *
                   * [*] Mail/WWW/News Tools             * *
                   * [ ] DOS/Windows Connectivity        * *
                   * [*] File Managers                   * *
                   *                                       *
                   *    [ ] Select individual packages     *
                   *                                       *
                   *       ******          ********        *
                   *       * Ok *          * Back *        *
                   *       ******          ********        *
                   *                                       *
                   *****************************************

   <Tab>/<Alt-Tab> between elements   | <Space> selects | <F12> next screen
```

Figure 1.17 *Component installation menu.*

The final alert before installation begins advises of the location of the installation log (see Figure 1.18).

```
Red Hat Linux (C) 1999 Red Hat Software                         Install system

                 *************** Install log ***************
                 *                                         *
                 * A complete log of your installation     *
                 * will be in /tmp/install.log after       *
                 * rebooting your system. You may want to  *
                 * keep this file for later reference.     *
                 *                                         *
                 *      ******              ********       *
                 *      * Ok *              * Back *       *
                 *      ******              ********       *
                 *                                         *
                 *                                         *
                 *******************************************

  <Tab>/<Alt-Tab> between elements   | <Space> selects | <F12> next screen
```

Figure 1.18 *Installation log alert.*

The formatting of the partitions then begins. If a bad block search is also run, then the formatting could take a few minutes or more. The partitions are formatted with the second extended file system, which is the current native file system for Linux (see Figure 1.19). Preparation of an ext2 file system is rather quick if bad block checks are not performed.

```
Red Hat Linux (C) 1999 Red Hat Software                         Install system

        ************************** Running ***************************
        *                                                            *
        * Making ext2 filesystem on /dev/hda5...                     *
        *                                                            *
        **************************************************************

  <Tab>/<Alt-Tab> between elements   | <Space> selects | <F12> next screen
```

Figure 1.19 *ext2 creation status screen.*

An overlapping file search is then conducted (see Figure 1.20). A scan of the packages to be installed is performed, and any files common to two or more packages are identified and installed only once.

```
Red Hat Linux (C) 1999 Red Hat Software                        Install system

        ************************ Processing ************************
        *                                                          *
        * Finding overlapping files...                             *
        *                                                          *
        *                                                          *
        *                                                          *
        ************************************************************

   <Tab>/<Alt-Tab> between elements  | <Space> selects | <F12> next screen
```

Figure 1.20 *Overlapping file search status screen.*

The installation then begins; software and system files are loaded onto the disk. An informative message about each individual package is displayed as it is installed (see Figure 1.21). These packages are in a special format called *RPM* files, which facilitate installation and de-installation (if needed). RPMs are manipulated with a variety of methods explained in the following sections.

```
Red Hat Linux (C) 1999 Red Hat Software                        Install system

        ********************** Install Status **********************
        *                                                          *
        * Package:    filesystem-1.3.4-4                           *
        * Size    :   80k                                          *
        * Summary:    The basic directory layout for a Linux       *
        *             system.                                      *
        *                                                          *
        *                                                          *
        *                                                          *
        *              Packages       Bytes          Time          *
        * Total     :       358        438M       7:51.31          *
        * Completed :         1          0M       0:00.01          *
        * Remaining :       357        438M       7:51.30          *
        *                                                          *
        *                                                          *
        *                                                          *
        ************************************************************

   <Tab>/<Alt-Tab> between elements  | <Space> selects | <F12> next screen
```

Figure 1.21 *Install status screen.*

After the main package installation, the mouse is configured. Choose from the scrollable list (see Figure 1.22). If *three-button* emulation is selected, then pressing both buttons simultaneously within XWindows on a two-button mouse will simulate the press of the third (middle) button.

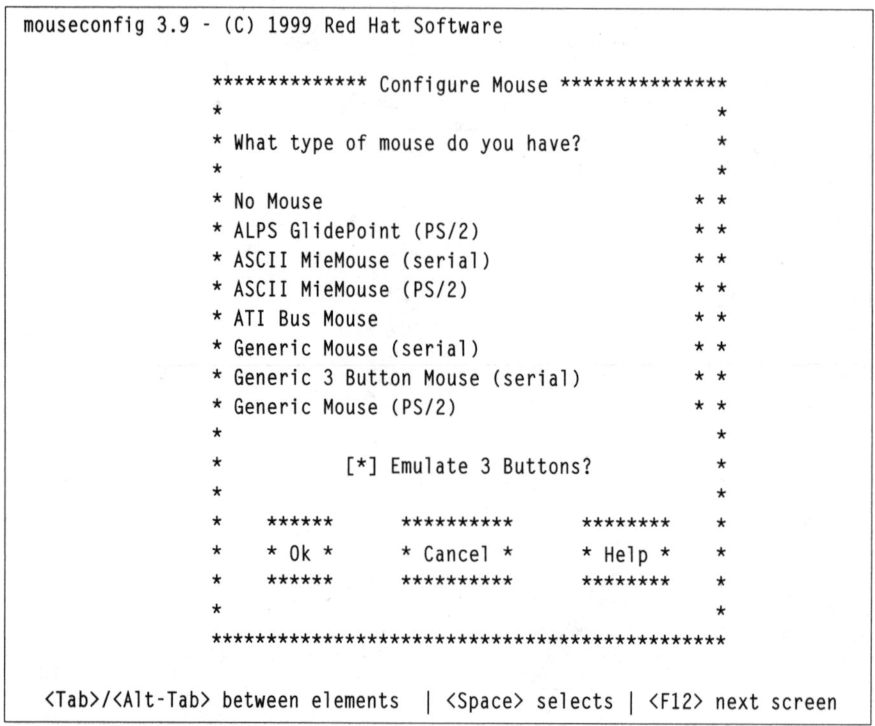

```
mouseconfig 3.9 - (C) 1999 Red Hat Software

                 ************** Configure Mouse ***************
                 *                                             *
                 * What type of mouse do you have?             *
                 *                                             *
                 * No Mouse                                  * *
                 * ALPS GlidePoint (PS/2)                    * *
                 * ASCII MieMouse (serial)                   * *
                 * ASCII MieMouse (PS/2)                     * *
                 * ATI Bus Mouse                             * *
                 * Generic Mouse (serial)                    * *
                 * Generic 3 Button Mouse (serial)           * *
                 * Generic Mouse (PS/2)                      * *
                 *                                             *
                 *          [*] Emulate 3 Buttons?             *
                 *                                             *
                 *    ******      **********      ********     *
                 *    * Ok *      * Cancel *      * Help *     *
                 *    ******      **********      ********     *
                 *                                             *
                 ***********************************************

  <Tab>/<Alt-Tab> between elements  | <Space> selects | <F12> next screen
```

Figure 1.22 *Mouse configuration menu.*

Network services (Ethernet or similar media) can then be configured, if desired (see Figure 1.23).

If network configuration is desired, the installer will attempt to probe the system for a network adapter. With a bit of luck, a successful message like the one shown in Figure 1.24 will appear.

Basic TCP/IP configuration will begin for the detected network card. The installer presents a list of methods for configuring these basic services (see Figure 1.25 on page 30). The "DHCP" and "BOOTP" options require servers configured to provide these protocols on the local network segment. For our purposes, we choose a static IP.

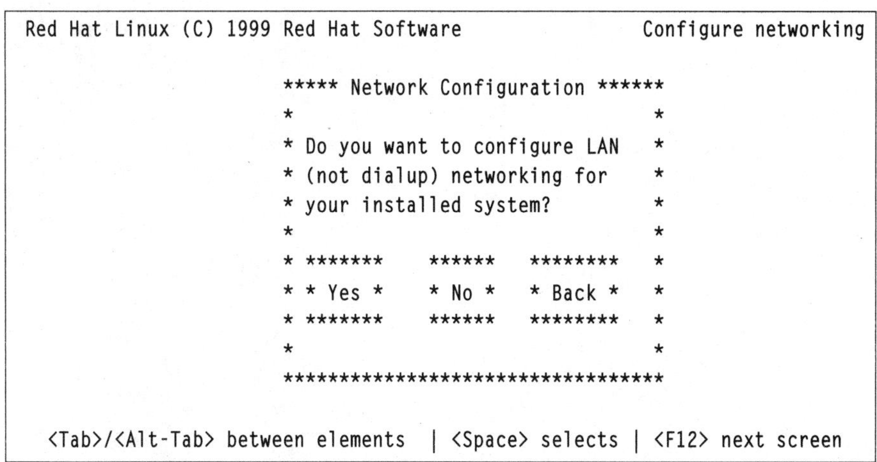

```
Red Hat Linux (C) 1999 Red Hat Software                Configure networking

                        ***** Network Configuration ******
                        *                                *
                        * Do you want to configure LAN   *
                        * (not dialup) networking for    *
                        * your installed system?         *
                        *                                *
                        * *******    ******   ********   *
                        * * Yes *    * No *   * Back *   *
                        * *******    ******   ********   *
                        *                                *
                        **********************************

  <Tab>/<Alt-Tab> between elements  | <Space> selects | <F12> next screen
```

Figure 1.23 *Network configuration menu.*

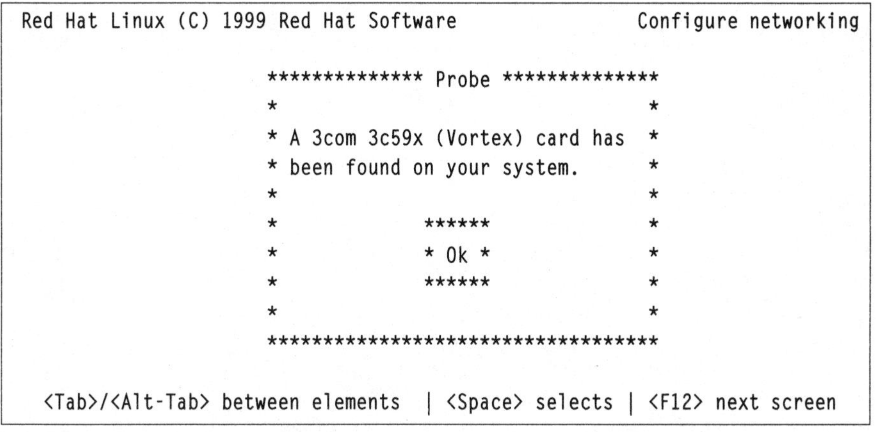

```
Red Hat Linux (C) 1999 Red Hat Software                Configure networking

                       ************** Probe **************
                       *                                 *
                       * A 3com 3c59x (Vortex) card has  *
                       * been found on your system.      *
                       *                                 *
                       *            ******               *
                       *            * Ok *               *
                       *            ******               *
                       *                                 *
                       ***********************************

  <Tab>/<Alt-Tab> between elements  | <Space> selects | <F12> next screen
```

Figure 1.24 *Probe message.*

Figure 1.26 on page 30 shows an example of a basic configuration for network services.

Warning

Network information, if entered incorrectly, can have harmful effects on network traffic. The configuration data should be obtained from a competent administrator, and it should be double-checked. Be cautious.

```
Red Hat Linux (C) 1999 Red Hat Software                 Configure networking

         ********************** Boot Protocol ***********************
         *                                                          *
         * How should the IP information be set? If your system     *
         * administrator gave you an IP address, choose static IP.  *
         *                                                          *
         *                   Static IP address                      *
         *                   BOOTP                                  *
         *                   DHCP                                   *
         *                                                          *
         *          ******                      ********            *
         *          * Ok *                      * Back *            *
         *          ******                      ********            *
         *                                                          *
         ************************************************************

   <Tab>/<Alt-Tab> between elements  | <Space> selects | <F12> next screen
```

Figure 1.25 *Boot protocol menu.*

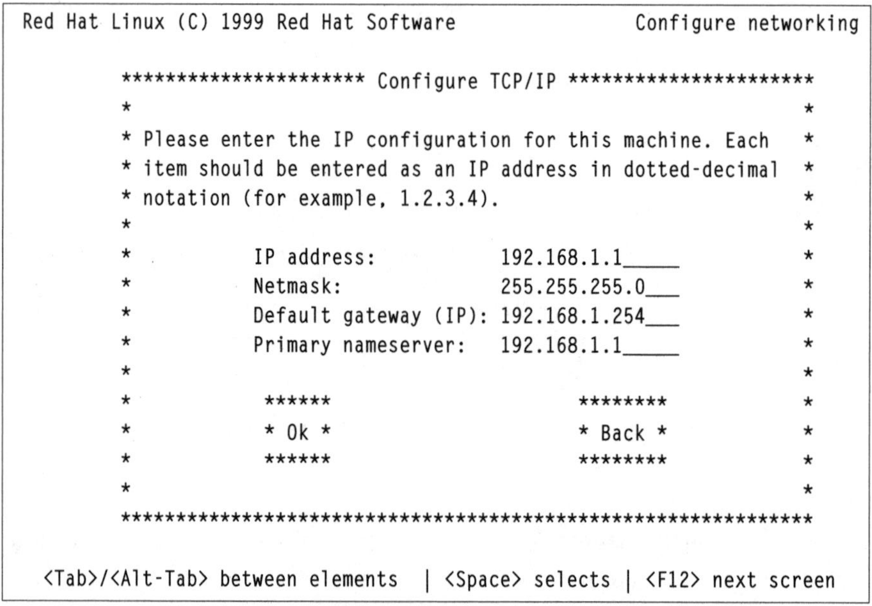

```
Red Hat Linux (C) 1999 Red Hat Software                 Configure networking

        ********************** Configure TCP/IP **********************
        *                                                            *
        * Please enter the IP configuration for this machine. Each   *
        * item should be entered as an IP address in dotted-decimal  *
        * notation (for example, 1.2.3.4).                           *
        *                                                            *
        *          IP address:            192.168.1.1_____           *
        *          Netmask:               255.255.255.0___           *
        *          Default gateway (IP): 192.168.1.254___            *
        *          Primary nameserver:    192.168.1.1_____           *
        *                                                            *
        *          ******                      ********              *
        *          * Ok *                      * Back *              *
        *          ******                      ********              *
        *                                                            *
        **************************************************************

   <Tab>/<Alt-Tab> between elements  | <Space> selects | <F12> next screen
```

Figure 1.26 *TCP/IP configuration menu.*

Additional information is required to completely configure TCP/IP networking (see Figure 1.27). This information is covered in greater detail in Chapter 2, "Configuring TCP/IP."

Next, the local time zone must be selected (see Figure 1.28). The PC clock is not normally set to GMT.

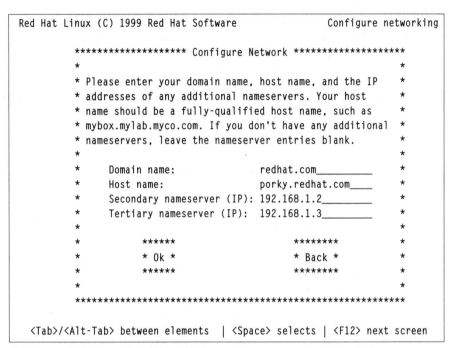

```
Red Hat Linux (C) 1999 Red Hat Software                Configure networking

        ******************** Configure Network ********************
        *                                                         *
        * Please enter your domain name, host name, and the IP    *
        * addresses of any additional nameservers. Your host      *
        * name should be a fully-qualified host name, such as     *
        * mybox.mylab.myco.com. If you don't have any additional  *
        * nameservers, leave the nameserver entries blank.        *
        *                                                         *
        *    Domain name:                redhat.com_________      *
        *    Host name:                  porky.redhat.com____     *
        *    Secondary nameserver (IP):  192.168.1.2________      *
        *    Tertiary nameserver (IP):   192.168.1.3________      *
        *                                                         *
        *         ******                     ********             *
        *         * Ok *                     * Back *             *
        *         ******                     ********             *
        *                                                         *
        ***********************************************************

   <Tab>/<Alt-Tab> between elements  | <Space> selects | <F12> next screen
```

Figure 1.27 *Network configuration menu.*

```
timeconfig 2.7 - (C) 1999 Red Hat Software

                   ******** Configure Timezones ********
                   *                                   *
                   * Format machine time is stored in: *
                   *                                   *
                   * [ ] Hardware clock set to GMT     *
                   *                                   *
                   *  US/Alaska                     *  *
                   *  US/Aleutian                   *  *
                   *  US/Arizona                    *  *
                   *  US/Central                    *  *
                   *  US/East-Indiana               *  *
                   *  US/Eastern                    *  *
                   *                                   *
                   *      ******        ********       *
                   *      * Ok *        * Back *       *
                   *      ******        ********       *
                   *                                   *
                   *************************************

   <Tab>/<Alt-Tab> between elements  |  <Space> selects |  <F12> next screen
```

Figure 1.28 *Timezone configuration menu.*

Next, the boot services menu is presented (see Figure 1.29). This menu allows various services to be configured to be started when the system boots. This menu can be brought up any time post-installation by entering the **ntsysv** command.

```
ntsysv 1.0.6 - (C) 1999 Red Hat Software

          ******************* Services *********************
          *                                                 *
          * What services should be automatically started? *
          *                                                 *
          *                [*] apmd        *                *
          *                [*] atd         *                *
          *                [*] crond       *                *
          *                [*] gpm         *                *
          *                [*] httpd       *                *
          *                [*] inet        *                *
          *                [*] keytable    *                *
          *                [*] linuxconf   *                *
          *                                                 *
          *          ******                ********         *
          *          * Ok *                * Back *         *
          *          ******                ********         *
          *                                                 *
          ***************************************************

Press <F1> for more information on a service.
```

Figure 1.29 *Boot services menu.*

A description of the available services is provided below.

`apmd`
: Advanced Power Management Daemon—controls system power consumption.

`atd`
: At Daemon—schedules one-time jobs to run at a future date.

`cron`
: Cron Daemon—schedules repetitive jobs.

`dhcpd`
: Dynamic Host Control Protocol Daemon—assigns IP addresses and associated information to other hosts on a local network.

The daemon will not start without a number of important control files in place. An entry for this daemon does not appear in the initial installation, but appears later with the `ntsysv` command if the DHCP subsystem is installed.

`gpm`
General Purpose Mouse—allows the use of the mouse to cut and paste text on the console (not XWindows).

`httpd`
Hyper-Text Transport Protocol Daemon—this daemon is the web server.

`inet`
Internet Superserver—this daemon launches many other Internet-related daemons, including `ftpd`, `telnetd`, `pop`, etc.

`keytable`
Keytable—this controls the keyboard map.

`linuxconf`
Linuxconf—Allows configuration data specified in the `linuxconf` utility to be loaded.

`lpd`
Line Printer Daemon—the printer spooler.

`named`
Name Server Daemon—the Berkeley Internet Name Server daemon. Installed as a caching-only server out-of-the-box.

`netfs`
NetFS—this utility mounts any remote NFS, SMB and NCP volumes specified in `/etc/fstab`.

`network`
Network—this script brings up networking devices.

`nfs`
Network File System Daemon—launches NFS daemon. It requires `portmap`.

`pcmcia`

Personal Computer Memory Card International Association—configures the PCMCIA cards usually found in laptop computers.

`portmap`

Portmap—launches the portmapper, which is required for ONC RPC services like NFS and NIS.

`postgresql`

Postmaster—this script launches the postmaster for the PostgreSQL database system. The postmaster will not launch unless a number of control files are in place.

`random`

Random Number Seed—maintains the status of the random number generator.

`routed`

Routing Daemon—this daemon maintains dynamic routes with RIP. This is not needed for static routes.

`rstatd`

Remote Status Daemon—allows performance measurement by remote machines. It requires `portmap`.

`rusersd`

Remote Users Daemon—allows user lookup by remote machines. It requires `portmap`.

`rwhod`

Remote Who Daemon—allows user lookup by remote machines.

`sendmail`

Sendmail—daemon which acts as an electronic Mail Transfer Agent (MTA).

`smb`

Samba—this script launches `smbd` and `nmbd`, which are typically used to share files and printers with Windows systems.

`snmpd`

Simple Network Management Protocol Daemon—this daemon is used to monitor and control networks.

`sound`

Sound—this script configures a known sound device. The `sndconfig` utility must be run successfully before the device will function.

`syslog`

System Logging Daemon—logs status messages in a variety of locations. The most important is `/var/log/messages`. Logs are controlled by the logfile rotation system.

`xfs`

X Font Server—serves fonts for XWindows. The XWindow system will not function without a font server.

`ypbind`

Network Information Service—allows machines to share the same `/etc/passwd`, `/etc/group`, `/etc/hosts` and other files. It requires `portmap`. More secure password sharing (i.e., sharing among hosts) can be implemented with `ssh`.

Printer selection is accomplished next (see Figure 1.30).

```
Red Hat Linux (C) 1999 Red Hat Software                       Configure printer

                  ************ Configure Printer ************
                  *                                         *
                  * Would you like to configure a printer?  *
                  *                                         *
                  *   *******      ******      ********     *
                  *   * Yes *      * No *      * Back *     *
                  *   *******      ******      ********     *
                  *                                         *
                  *******************************************

  <Tab>/<Alt-Tab> between elements  | <Space> selects | <F12> next screen
```

Figure 1.30 *Printer configuration menu.*

Printer driver support is not as strong in Red Hat Linux as it is in other operating systems. All the printer drivers are configured to emulate a Postscript printer (which is accomplished through the `ghostscript` utility). All print jobs requiring graphics output are run through an intermediate Postscript stage (even if the final printer dialog is performed with some other protocol, such as PCL). The configuration of the print system can be adjusted later by running the **printtool** command from within XWindows.

Remote printers can also be specified (see Figure 1.31). Only the setup of a local printer is documented in this text.

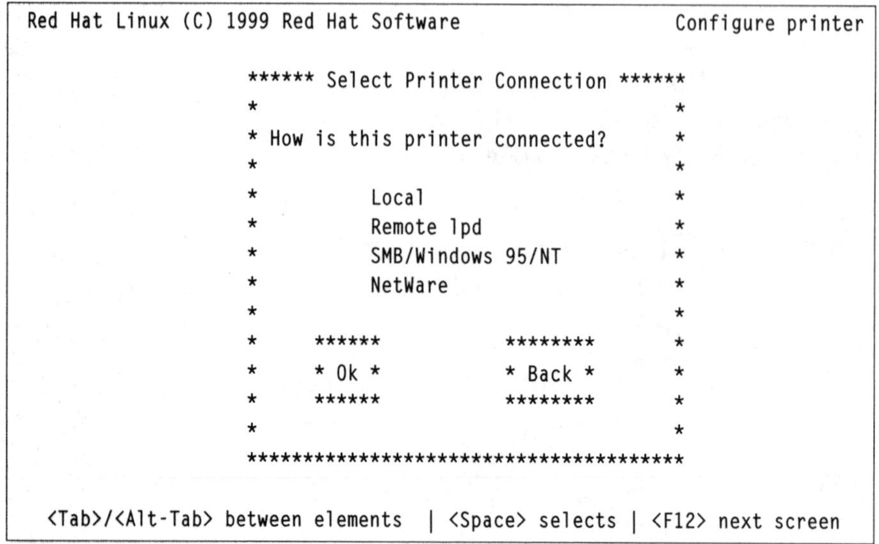

Figure 1.31 *Printer selection menu.*

The print queue is selected next (see Figure 1.32). The standard names are usually sufficient.

The detected ports are displayed next (see Figure 1.33).

The available printer drivers are displayed for selection, as in Figure 1.34 on page 38. If the exact model of the attached printer is not available in the list, try selecting a previous model number from the same manufacturer. If the attached printer is advertised to be compatible with another manufacturer's printer, select the equivalent model from the scrollable list.

The paper size for the new printer can then be selected, as in Figure 1.35. If your printer has any sort of resolution enhancement (through the resizing of pixels), the "Fix stair-stepping of text" option might be useful. Finally, a printer confirmation dialog is presented (see Figure 1.36 on page 39).

The root password must now be chosen (see Figure 1.37).

```
Red Hat Linux (C) 1999 Red Hat Software                   Configure printer

          ************** Standard Printer Options ***************
          *                                                     *
          * Every print queue (which print jobs are directed    *
          * to) needs a name (often lp) and a spool directory   *
          * associated with it. What name and directory should  *
          * be used for this queue?                             *
          *                                                     *
          *        Name of queue:   lp_________________         *
          *        Spool directory: /var/spool/lpd/lp___        *
          *                                                     *
          *         ******                  ********            *
          *         * Ok *                  * Back *            *
          *         ******                  ********            *
          *                                                     *
          *******************************************************

  <Tab>/<Alt-Tab> between elements  | <Space> selects | <F12> next screen
```

Figure 1.32 *Print queue selection menu.*

```
Red Hat Linux (C) 1999 Red Hat Software                   Configure printer

             ************* Local Printer Device **************
             *                                               *
             * What device is your printer connected to      *
             * (note that /dev/lp0 is equivalent to LPT1:)?  *
             *                                               *
             *         Printer Device: /dev/lp0_______       *
             *                                               *
             *   Auto-detected ports:                        *
             *                                               *
             *     /dev/lp0: Detected                        *
             *     /dev/lp1: Not Detected                    *
             *     /dev/lp2: Not Detected                    *
             *                                               *
             *         ******               ********         *
             *         * Ok *               * Back *         *
             *         ******               ********         *
             *                                               *
             *************************************************

  <Tab>/<Alt-Tab> between elements  | <Space> selects | <F12> next screen
```

Figure 1.33 *Port detection menu.*

```
Red Hat Linux (C) 1999 Red Hat Software                   Configure printer

          ****************** Configure Printer ******************
          *                                                     *
          * What type of printer do you have?                   *
          *                                                     *
          *   HP PaintJet                                   *   *
          *   HP PaintJet XL                                *   *
          *   HP PaintJet XL300 and DeskJet 1200C           *   *
          *   IBM 3853 JetPrinter                           *   *
          *   Imagen ImPress                                *   *
          *   Mitsubishi CP50                               *   *
          *   NEC P6/P6+/P60                                *   *
          *   NEC Prinwriter 2X (UP)                        *   *
          *   Okidata Microline 182                         *   *
          *   PostScript printer                            *   *
          *           ******                  ********          *
          *           * Ok *                  * Back *          *
          *           ******                  ********          *
          *                                                     *
          *******************************************************

<F1> will give you information on a particular printer type
```

Figure 1.34 *Printer driver selection menu.*

```
Red Hat Linux (C) 1999 Red Hat Software                   Configure printer

          ***************** PostScript printer *****************
          *                                                    *
          * You may now configure the paper size and resolution *
          * for this printer.                                  *
          *                                                    *
          *          Paper Size           Resolution           *
          *            letter              300x 300            *
          *            legal               600x 600            *
          *            ledger             1200x1200            *
          *            a3                                      *
          *            a4                                      *
          *          [ ] Fix stair-stepping of text?           *
          *                                                    *
          *          ******                ********            *
          *          * Ok *                * Back *            *
          *          ******                ********            *
          *                                                    *
          ******************************************************

<F1> will give you information on this printer driver.
```

Figure 1.35 *Printer confirmation screen.*

```
Red Hat Linux (C) 1999 Red Hat Software                    Configure printer

         *************** Verify Printer Configuration ***************
         *                                                          *
         * Please verify that this printer information is correct:  *
         *                                                          *
         *   Printer type:    LOCAL                                 *
         *   Queue:           lp                                    *
         *   Spool directory: /var/spool/lpd/lp                     *
         *   Printer device   /dev/lp0                              *
         *   Printer driver:  PostScript printer                    *
         *   Paper size:      letter                                *
         *   Resolution:      300x300                               *
         *   Bits per pixel:  Default                               *
         *                                                          *
         *          ******                      ********            *
         *          * Ok *                      * Back *            *
         *          ******                      ********            *
         *                                                          *
         ************************************************************

   <Tab>/<Alt-Tab> between elements   | <Space> selects | <F12> next screen
```

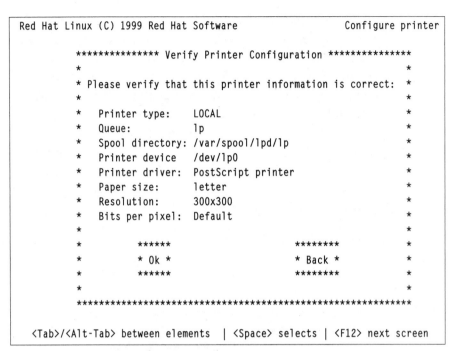

Figure 1.36 *Printer confirmation screen.*

```
Red Hat Linux (C) 1999 Red Hat Software                    Set root password

                *************** Root Password ****************
                *                                            *
                * Pick a root password. You must type it     *
                * twice to ensure you know what it is and    *
                * didn't make a mistake in typing. Remember  *
                * that the root password is a critical part *
                * of system security!                        *
                *                                            *
                * Password:           ________________________ *
                * Password (again):   ________________________ *
                *                                            *
                *        ******              ********        *
                *        * Ok *              * Back *        *
                *        ******              ********        *
                *                                            *
                **********************************************

   <Tab>/<Alt-Tab> between elements   | <Space> selects | <F12> next screen
```

Figure 1.37 *Root password selection menu.*

The password should not be obvious, especially if the machine is connected to the Internet. Mixtures of letters, numbers, and punctuation marks are best. The password must be entered twice, and the two entries must be identical. If you ever forget it, you can circumvent the root password by entering **linux single** at the LILO boot prompt. In single user mode, you can then remove the **encrypted** password from the file in which it is stored (`/etc/passwd` or `/etc/shadow`) and later reset it.

The format of the system password database can be specified with the dialog shown in Figure 1.38. For maximum compatibility with other UNIX installations, disable all the options.

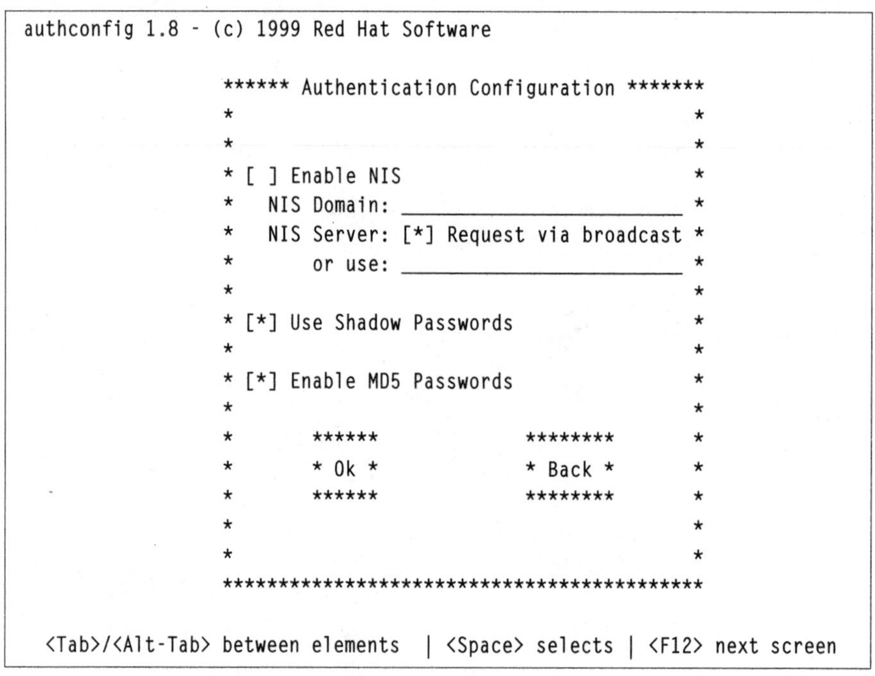

Figure 1.38 *Authentication configuration menu.*

It is highly recommended that a boot disk be created (see Figure 1.39), especially if the installation involves SCSI devices. Your boot disk then supports SCSI devices and is considerably more valuable should you need to use it.

Answer "Yes," and the bootdisk is created (see Figure 1.40).

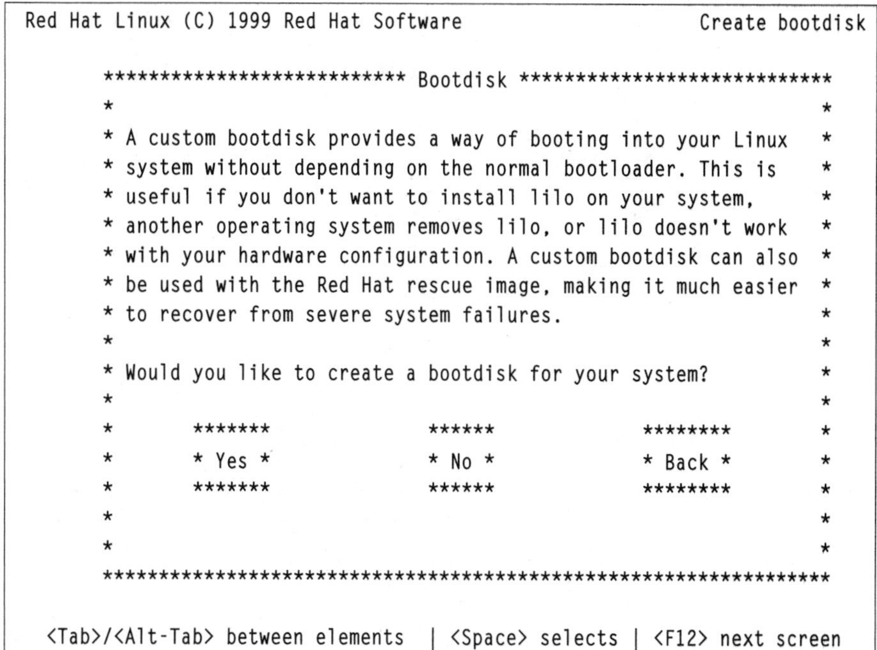

```
Red Hat Linux (C) 1999 Red Hat Software                    Create bootdisk

      ************************** Bootdisk ***************************
      *                                                              *
      * A custom bootdisk provides a way of booting into your Linux   *
      * system without depending on the normal bootloader. This is    *
      * useful if you don't want to install lilo on your system,      *
      * another operating system removes lilo, or lilo doesn't work   *
      * with your hardware configuration. A custom bootdisk can also  *
      * be used with the Red Hat rescue image, making it much easier  *
      * to recover from severe system failures.                       *
      *                                                              *
      * Would you like to create a bootdisk for your system?          *
      *                                                              *
      *       *******            ******             ********         *
      *       * Yes *            * No *             * Back *         *
      *       *******            ******             ********         *
      *                                                              *
      *                                                              *
      ****************************************************************

   <Tab>/<Alt-Tab> between elements  | <Space> selects | <F12> next screen
```

Figure 1.39 *Bootdisk menu.*

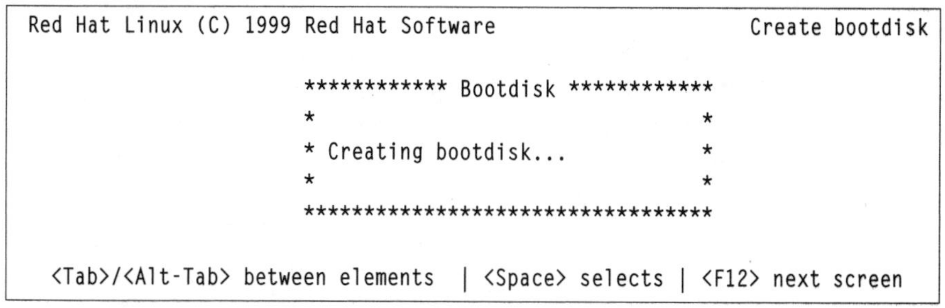

```
Red Hat Linux (C) 1999 Red Hat Software                    Create bootdisk

                      ************ Bootdisk ************
                      *                                *
                      * Creating bootdisk...           *
                      *                                *
                      **********************************

   <Tab>/<Alt-Tab> between elements  | <Space> selects | <F12> next screen
```

Figure 1.40 *Bootdisk status screen.*

LILO should normally be installed on the Master Boot Record of the primary hard drive. This configuration of LILO, however, does not co-exist well with Microsoft Windows NT. Figure 1.41 on page 42 shows LILO configured to be the system bootloader.

One need for special options (see Figure 1.42) is when the system has more than 64 megabytes of RAM. If this is the case, specify this option here. For example, if a machine with 128MB is installed, the parameter to pass is `mem=128M`.

```
Red Hat Linux (C) 1999 Red Hat Software                          Install bootloader

             **************** Lilo Installation *****************
             *                                                  *
             * Where do you want to install the bootloader?     *
             *                                                  *
             * /dev/hda           Master Boot Record            *
             * /dev/hda5          First sector of boot partition *
             *                                                  *
             *     ******         ********        ********      *
             *     * Ok *         * Skip *        * Back *      *
             *     ******         ********        ********      *
             *                                                  *
             *                                                  *
             ****************************************************

{{If LILO is the bootloader, say this clearly.  This is not obvious.}}
  <Tab>/<Alt-Tab> between elements   | <Space> selects | <F12> next screen
```

Figure 1.41 *LILO installation menu.*

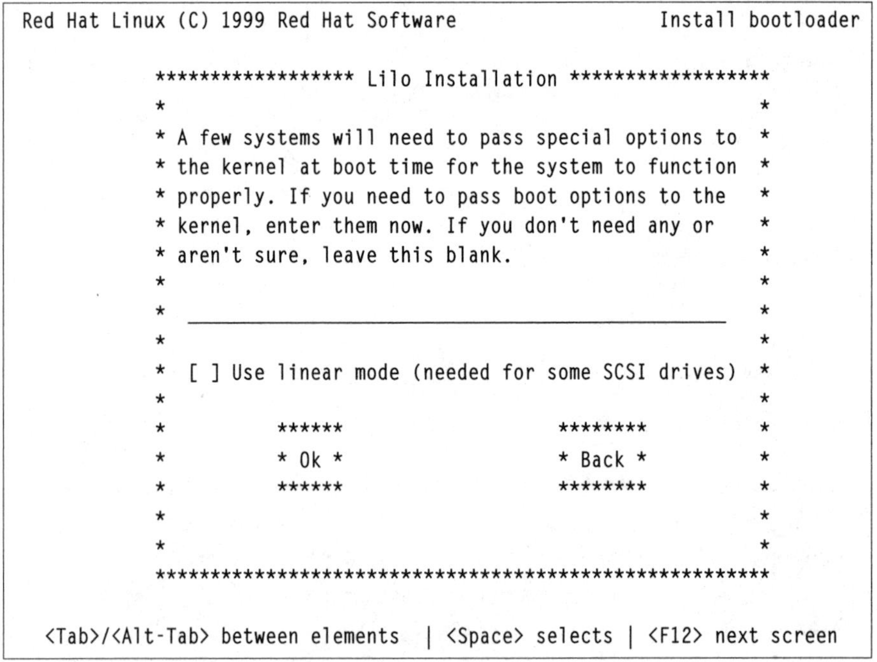

```
Red Hat Linux (C) 1999 Red Hat Software                          Install bootloader

            ***************** Lilo Installation *****************
            *                                                   *
            * A few systems will need to pass special options to *
            * the kernel at boot time for the system to function *
            * properly. If you need to pass boot options to the  *
            * kernel, enter them now. If you don't need any or   *
            * aren't sure, leave this blank.                     *
            *                                                   *
            *  ______________________________________________  *
            *                                                   *
            *  [ ] Use linear mode (needed for some SCSI drives) *
            *                                                   *
            *         ******                  ********          *
            *         * Ok *                  * Back *          *
            *         ******                  ********          *
            *                                                   *
            *                                                   *
            *****************************************************

  <Tab>/<Alt-Tab> between elements   | <Space> selects | <F12> next screen
```

Figure 1.42 *Special options menu.*

Other operating systems can also be booted by LILO, which presents them (along with Linux) as options at boot time. The installer presents a list of partitions (see Figure 1.43). If other operating systems are installed on these partitions, select them here. At system startup, the default boot partition is used if the user does not respond to the LILO prompt before the time-out period. Select the operating systems you wish to make available to LILO in the form shown here.

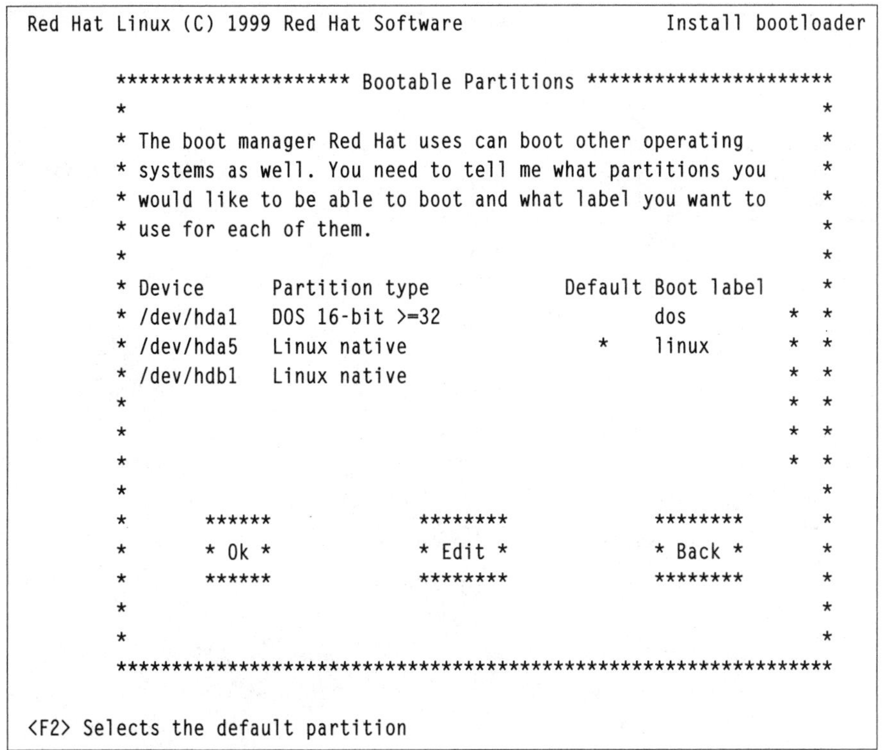

```
Red Hat Linux (C) 1999 Red Hat Software                  Install bootloader

        ******************** Bootable Partitions *********************
        *                                                            *
        * The boot manager Red Hat uses can boot other operating     *
        * systems as well. You need to tell me what partitions you   *
        * would like to be able to boot and what label you want to   *
        * use for each of them.                                      *
        *                                                            *
        * Device      Partition type            Default Boot label   *
        * /dev/hda1   DOS 16-bit >=32                   dos        * *
        * /dev/hda5   Linux native                 *    linux      * *
        * /dev/hdb1   Linux native                                 * *
        *                                                          * *
        *                                                          * *
        *                                                          * *
        *                                                            *
        *       ******             ********           ********       *
        *       * Ok *             * Edit *           * Back *       *
        *       ******             ********           ********       *
        *                                                            *
        *                                                            *
        **************************************************************

<F2> Selects the default partition
```

Figure 1.43 *Operation system selection menu.*

In the last stage, XWindows is configured. With luck, the system graphics adapter will be detected and an RPM with an appropriate Xserver installed (see Figure 1.44 on page 44). If not, you must choose from a scrollable list of adaptors or choose "Unlisted."

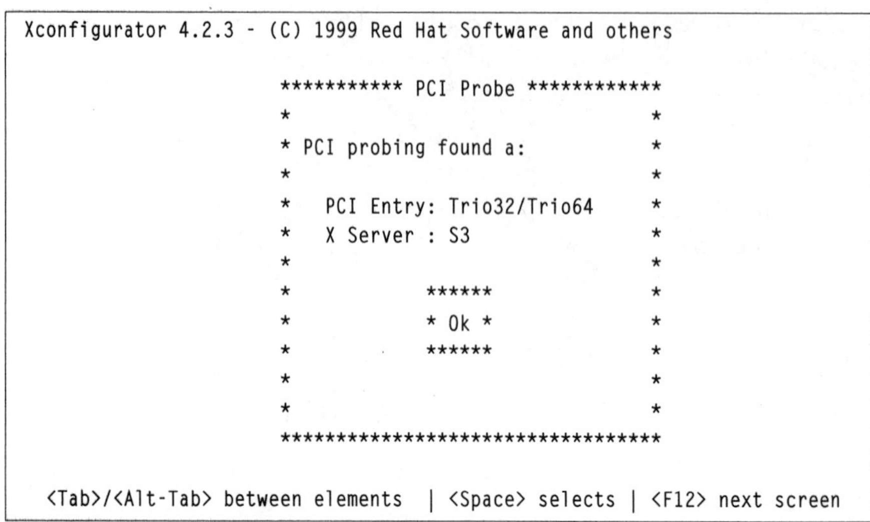

Figure 1.44 *Xserver selection menu.*

The next step is the selection of a monitor (see Figure 1.45). If your monitor is not in the list, then choose either *generic* or *generic multisync.*

A graphics probe is then launched to determine the best screen resolution (as shown in Figure 1.46). The best probed resolution—hopefully better than 640x480—is then presented (see Figure 1.47 on page 46).

The Xserver will be started (see Figure 1.48 on page 46). While it is active, the user is presented with an option to boot the system directly into XWindows. The Xserver is the last installation component. When it is fully installed, the installation is concluded (Figure 1.49 on page 47).

At this point, all the installation media (including the CD) should be removed and the system rebooted. With any luck, the computer will boot to a `login` prompt, and the root user can then login and begin to add new users (with the **useradd** command, or through a number of GUI utilities).

```
Xconfigurator 4.2.3 - (C) 1999 Red Hat Software and others

     *************************** Monitor Setup ****************************
     *                                                                    *
     * What type of monitor do you have? If you would rather specify the *
     * sync frequencies of your monitor, choose "Custom" from the list.  *
     *                                                                    *
     *         Mitsubishi Diamond Plus 100 (TFW1105)         *            *
     *         Mitsubishi Diamond Plus 70 (TF-7700P)         *            *
     *         Mitsubishi Diamond Plus 71 (TFV6708)          *            *
     *         Mitsubishi Diamond Plus 72 (TFV8705)          *            *
     *         Mitsubishi Diamond Pro 1000 (TFX1105)         *            *
     *         Mitsubishi Diamond Pro 1010 (TUX1107)         *            *
     *         Mitsubishi Diamond Pro 14 (FW6405)            *            *
     *                                                                    *
     *            ******                           ********               *
     *            * Ok *                           * Back *               *
     *            ******                           ********               *
     *                                                                    *
     *                                                                    *
     **********************************************************************

   <Tab>/<Alt-Tab> between elements   | <Space> selects | <F12> next screen
```

Figure 1.45 *Monitor selection menu.*

```
Xconfigurator 4.2.3 - (C) 1999 Red Hat Software and others

                    ********* Probing to begin **********
                    *                                  *
                    * Xconfigurator will now run the X *
                    * server you selected to probe     *
                    * various information about your   *
                    * video card. It is normal for the *
                    * screen to blink several times.   *
                    *                                  *
                    *              ******              *
                    *              * Ok *              *
                    *              ******              *
                    *                                  *
                    *                                  *
                    ************************************

   <Tab>/<Alt-Tab> between elements   | <Space> selects | <F12> next screen
```

Figure 1.46 *Graphics probe screen.*

```
Xconfigurator 4.2.3 - (C) 1999 Red Hat Software and others

      ********************** Probing finished **********************
      *                                                            *
      * Xconfigurator has sucessfully probed your video card. The  *
      * default video mode will be:                                *
      *                                                            *
      *    Color Depth: 16 bits per pixel                          *
      *    Resolution : 1024x768                                   *
      *                                                            *
      * Do you want to accept this setting, or select for yourself? *
      *                                                            *
      *   ***************      *****************      ********    *
      *   * Use Default *      * Let Me Choose *      * Back *    *
      *   ***************      *****************      ********    *
      *                                                            *
      **************************************************************

  <Tab>/<Alt-Tab> between elements  | <Space> selects | <F12> next screen
```

Figure 1.47 *Best resolution results.*

```
Xconfigurator 4.2.3 - (C) 1999 Red Hat Software and others

                    *********** Starting X ***********
                    *                                *
                    * Xconfigurator will now start X *
                    * to test your configuration.    *
                    *                                *
                    *    ******        ********      *
                    *    * Ok *        * Skip *      *
                    *    ******        ********      *
                    *                                *
                    **********************************

  <Tab>/<Alt-Tab> between elements  | <Space> selects | <F12> next screen
```

Figure 1.48 *Xserver start-up screen.*

It is also possible to enter **linux single** at the LILO prompt to boot the system into single user mode without a password. Linux will boot to a bash prompt (owned by root), and all of the file systems will be mounted, but no network services will be started.

```
Red Hat Linux (C) 1999 Red Hat Software
Complete

          ************************** Done **************************
          *                                                          *
          * Congratulations, installation is complete.               *
          *                                                          *
          * Remove the boot media and press return to reboot. For    *
          * information on fixes which are available for this        *
          * release of Red Hat Linux, consult the Errata available   *
          * from http://www.redhat.com.                              *
          *                                                          *
          * Information on configuring your system is available in   *
          * the post install chapter of the Official Red Hat Linux   *
          * User's Guide.                                            *
          *                                                          *
          *                          ******                          *
          *                          * Ok *                          *
          *                          ******                          *
          *                                                          *
          ************************************************************

   <Tab>/<Alt-Tab> between elements   | <Space> selects | <F12> next screen
```

Figure 1.49 *Final installation screen.*

"Cloning" a Running Red Hat System

If your Red Hat Linux system runs on only one hard drive, it is easy to clone it onto a second.

First, unmount all extraneous file systems (such as CD-ROMs, DOS FAT file systems, NFS connections, and anything else that is not directly related to the local installation).

Next, obtain a boot disk for the system. The disk created during the installation is appropriate. Another can be created with the `mkbootdisk` utility. On IDE systems, the Red Hat Linux boot floppy can be used as a boot disk by passing it the parameters "`linux single root=/dev/hdXX initrd=`" (substitute the partition of the root file system for "`XX`"), but this trick will not work if there are active file systems on SCSI devices.

Next, run the following commands as root:

```
cd /
ls | grep -v proc > /root/files
mkdir /drive
```

Edit the list of files in `/root/files` and remove any extra directories that should not be copied. The `/proc` directory should be explicitly omitted.

Next, shutdown the system and attach the new drive. Boot Linux and use the `fdisk` utility to create the partitions, then use `mke2fs -c` to create the file systems on the new drive, and `mkswap - c` to format the new swap partition. The new (i.e., copied) drive should probably have the same partition layout as the old drive (if not, then the new `/etc/fstab` must be modified).

Warning Be careful not to accidentally wipe out areas on the source drive when running these commands.

Take the system into single user mode by running the following command as root:

init 1

Mount the partitions on the new drive onto the `/drive` directory. Mount them with the same hierarchy with which the source drive is mounted. For example, if a file system on the source drive holds `/home`, then a file system on the target drive should be mounted as `/drive/home`.

To clone the drive, enter the following commands:

```
cd /
tar cf - `cat /root/files` | (cd /drive; tar xvpf -)
```

When the copy completes, make any necessary modifications to `/drive/etc/fstab` (none should be required unless the partition arrangement differs), then shut down the system. Remove the source drive and install the target drive as the boot drive (as the primary master on an IDE system, or as ID 0 on SCSI). Boot with the boot diskette.

Lastly, login to the new system as root and run the **lilo** command. Remove the boot diskette and reboot. The new drive should be functionally equivalent to the old one.

RPM Basics and Red Hat Errata

The Redhat Package Manager (RPM) is a powerful system that allows software installation and upgrades to be applied with a minimum of effort. It is a software distribution scheme that allows source code to be distributed in a pristine original format. But it also encompasses binary distributions, which allow for extremely rapid installation.

RPM has become so popular that several other Linux distributions have endorsed it as their preferred installation method. There are also utilities that convert packages between RPM and the competing Debian DEB package format.

All the RPM packages that make up Red Hat Linux 6.0 are contained in the `RedHat/RPMS` directory on the CD-ROM included with this text. For example, one of the packages that is included is the Samba distribution in the `samba-1.9.18p10-3.i386.rpm` file. The various extensions on the RPM file identify the processor architecture for which it was produced (alpha, sparc, or i386) or whether or not it is a source distribution (src).

It is assumed in this section (and most of this text) that the Intel 386 architecture is the target platform.

Following is a list of the more common ways that RPM is used:

rpm -Uvh package.i386.rpm

Causes RPM to either install or upgrade a package file.

rpm -e package

Removes the installed package from the system. Notice the lack of the `.386.rpm` extension.

rpm -q package

Queries installed packages. Release numbers can be omitted, so the command **rpm -q samba** might produce the result `samba-1.9.18p10-3`, if the package is installed.

rpm -qa

Generates a list of all installed packages on the system. It is sometimes useful to pipe the output to either `sort`, `grep`, or `more`.

rpm -ql package
Generates a list of all files that have been installed by a package.

rpm -qf file
Generates the name of the package that installed a particular file.

rpm -qpl package.i386.rpm
Generates a list of all files included in a package file.

rpm -qi package
Generates a detailed description of an installed package.

rpm -qpi package.i386.rpm
Generates a detailed description of a package file.

rpm2cpio package.src.rpm
Extracts individual files within a package. It is most useful with source RPMs. The most common usage is `rpm2cpio package.i386.rpm | cpio -i`, which extracts all included files in the current directory.

rpm --rebuild package.src.rpm
Unpacks and builds a binary RPM distribution file under `/usr/src/redhat`.

One of the most important post-installation uses of the RPM format is for security patches issued by Red Hat. Information about the patches can usually be found in the support areas of the Red Hat website, and the patches themselves are located at *ftp://ftp.redhat.com/redhat/updates/6.0/i386* (at the time that this text was composed). A partial copy of this updates directory is included on the CD-ROM (there are so many updates that they won't all fit on the distribution CD).

To give an example, a security vulnerability was found in the Netscape distribution that was included with Red Hat Linux 6.0. To quote the information at the Red Hat website:

> New netscape packages are available. While these are not specifically security updates, among the changes listed are "Fixes to improve security"; therefore it is recommended that users update to the new packages.

The patched Netscape distribution can be found in the `updates/netscape-common-4.6-1.i386.rpm` and `updates/netscape-communicator-4.6-1.i386.rpm` files on the CD-ROM included with this text. To install the updated Netscape distribution, enter the following commands as root (it might be necessary to add the `--nodeps` option to RPM to successfully install these updates):

```
rpm -Uvh netscape-common-4.6-1.i386.rpm
rpm -Uvh netscape-communicator-4.6-1.i386.rpm
```

Generally, this syntax for RPM is used to upgrade everything except the Linux kernel. Kernel updates are of sufficient complexity that it is preferable to download the true kernel source and build kernel images from them. This process is documented in Chapter 10, "Rebuilding the Linux Kernel." Also, be advised that the Linux kernel source itself is available as an RPM, but kernel source patches commonly will not run against these packaged versions because they do not contain all of the source files.

Also, Netscape installations (all versions) crash on Java pages in Red Hat Linux 6.0. To fix this problem, run the following command as root:

```
chkfontpath --add /usr/X11R6/lib/X11/fonts/75dpi
```

Setting the Time

It is quite a simple thing to set the clock in the BIOS on a PC. However, synchronizing clocks on a large network of PCs can be much more complex.

Red Hat Linux provides several utilities that set the system time based upon data received over the Internet. All must be run by root, as the root user is the only user allowed to modify the system time. The simplest invocation is as follows:

```
/usr/bin/rdate -s time.nist.gov; /usr/sbin/setclock
```

These commands first set Linux's time, then set the BIOS time. The two clocks are separate; Linux reads the BIOS time only at boot. This command can be automated by setting a `crontab`:

```
echo '0 3 * * * /usr/bin/rdate -s time.nist.gov;
/usr/sbin/setclock' > ~/crontab
crontab ~/crontab
```

The previous commands cause the date to be adjusted at 3 a.m. every day.

Note This command removes any previously existing `crontab` entries; see the `crontab` manual pages for details.

For those who are especially concerned with keeping accurate time, it is beneficial to load the Network Time Protocol RPM package using the following command:

```
rpm -Uvh xntp3-5.93-12.i386.rpm
```

Then, select a server from the list published at *http://www.eecis.udel.edu/~mills/ntp/servers.html* (be sure to select from the appropriate strata). One might choose the ntp host *tock.cs.unlv.edu*, for example, and issue the following command:

```
ntpdate tock.cs.unlv.edu
```

With the `xntp` package, it is also possible to run the `xntpd` daemon, which keeps the system time continuously updated. The configuration of `xntpd` is beyond the scope of this book.

Advice on Editors

Editing text files is a critical operation within UNIX, especially for an administrator. For serious UNIX aficionados, `vi` is the one true editor. It is practically guaranteed to be installable on any version of UNIX available.

However, `vi` itself is not free software, and it is generally not included with open-sourced versions of UNIX. Other versions of Linux include clones of `vi`, with esoteric names such as `vile`, `elvis`, or `nvi`.

Red Hat Linux uses `vim` which is short for "VI Improved," and improved it is. A wonderful tutorial for novice users is included in the `vim` package. Any user can start the tutorial by issuing the following commands:

```
cp /usr/doc/vim-common-5.3/tutor/tutor ~
vi ~/tutor
```

The behavior of the bash shell can be set to mimic `vi` if the root user issues the following commands:

```
mv /etc/inputrc /etc/inputrc.old
echo 'set editing-mode vi' > /etc/inputrc
```

All shells invoked after this point can use `vi`-style cursor movement commands (you must press the escape key, then "j" or "k" to cycle through commands, rather than using the arrows directly). This affects not only the shell, but also every application that uses the GNU Readline library (such as `gdb`, `psql`, `sqsh`, etc).

If all references to the `INPUTRC` environment variable are removed from `/etc/profile`, each user can set an `.inputrc` file in their home directory with their shell editing settings (which was the default behavior in previous versions of Red Hat Linux). Additional information on the format of these files is available in the `readline` manual pages.

However, for those unfortunate miscreants with the audacity to look elsewhere for their editing tools, there are a few alternatives.

For the truly uninitiated, there is the `pico` editor that is included with the `pine` mail client. In its favor, `pico` has a very handy justification tool and an easy spell checker. It is also almost trivially easy to learn. It is, however, sorely lacking in features and flexibility. When using `pico` to edit important system files, it is usually much safer to call it with the single argument `pico -w`, which disables its habit of wrapping long lines.

The basic XWindows installation also includes `xedit`, but it is not very powerful.

The apparent GNU-endorsed editing environment is `emacs`. `emacs` is extremely powerful, but it is also big—very big. It includes a LISP interpreter and has modes that run in character or XWindows.

There are many choices in editors, but care should be taken in the final selection. Availability and features will soon come to be much more important than ease of use.

02

Configuring TCP/IP

Since early days of UNIX, the Transmission Control Protocol/Internet Protocol (TCP/IP) has been thoroughly integrated into the heart of most versions of the operating system. Linux is no exception. In fact, the Linux TCP/IP stack has been redesigned several times. The current version boasts speed and reliability that rival any other implementation.

It is impossible to have a serious network based upon TCP/IP that is devoid of the influence of UNIX. If the network is connected in some way to the Internet, it relies upon the root name servers (which run UNIX). If the network uses the global SMTP mail system, chances are that UNIX is involved. If the network has access to the World Wide Web, one out of every two accessed web servers runs Apache on UNIX. While it may be possible to implement these protocols over other operating systems, UNIX was the origin, and UNIX remains the preferred implementation.

This chapter discusses TCP/IP and basic network services. The physical networking media (usually Ethernet) is addressed only tangentially. If it is configured correctly, this hardware should be detected automatically during installation. Information on cabling is available from many sources, and is mentioned only in passing.

Basic IP Configuration

This section will attempt to explain the three major components of a basic TCP/IP configuration: the IP address, the default gateway, and the DNS server.

If a host computer is being connected to a Class C IP network (i.e., a TCP/IP LAN allowing up to 254 host systems), and no connections are being made to external networks and/or the Internet, only a single configuration parameter is required (the IP address).

IP Address

Standard IP addresses are unsigned 32-bit integers, but they are normally represented as 4 unsigned bytes in decimal notation, separated by dots. For example, the IP address C0A80101 would normally be represented as 192.168.1.1. Every computer on a TCP/IP network (or internetwork) must have a unique IP address. In entering the IP address, you must also provide a *netmask* and *broadcast address,* as explained below.

If the computer is connected to a TCP/IP network where routing is required, a default gateway address will likely be necessary.

Default Gateway

This is the IP address of a router that is on the local network and connects to other networks or to the Internet. On a Class C

IP address, only the last byte of the router's IP address should be different from the IP addresses of any other hosts on the local networks. Be careful. Routers always have more than one IP address. Choose only the one on the local network.

If the computer is being connected to the Internet (or to another TCP/IP network where DNS is performed), one last basic parameter is required.

DNS Server

The Domain Name Server (DNS) is a computer that can translate Internet hostnames into IP addresses. At the time that this text was composed, for example, one of the IP addresses of *www.redhat.com* was 199.183.24.133. The DNS server provides this translation—it does so by sending queries to the distributed, fault-tolerant, domain name system.

In Class C IP networks, the *netmask* parameter is almost always 255.255.255.0. The network number is obtained by changing the last digit to a 0 in any IP address on the network (i.e., a *bitwise and* of the IP address and the netmask). The broadcast address, if required, is the network number with a 255 as the last byte (the broadcast address allows data to be sent to all hosts on the local network - pinging the broadcast address will generate replies from up to 254 other hosts).

For example, let us pretend that a small home network is being constructed, and this network will not (at least most of the time) be connected to the Internet. Good choices for the IP address, network mask, and broadcast are shown in Table 2.1.

Table 2.1 *Basic IP configuration.*

IP Address:	192.168.1.1
Netmask:	255.255.255.0
Broadcast:	192.168.1.255

If a second computer were added to this network, it could be given an IP address of 192.168.1.2, and so on until 192.168.1.254. All hosts on an IP network must share the same network number. If the Class C hosts 192.168.1.5 and 192.168.100.5 are connected directly without an intervening gateway, they will not be able to communicate because they do not share the same network number.

It might be a good idea to create an `/etc/hosts` file with pairs of IP addresses and hostnames. This would allow network connections to be made without the bother of remembering IP addresses. This function is subsumed by a DNS server in larger networks.

Please note that the Class C network number, 192.168.1.0, is an excellent choice for a home network (see Chapter 4, "Firewalls,"for more details).

Now, let us imagine that a neighbor also constructs a home network, and he uses the network number 192.168.2.0. If a network cable was run between the two homes, a router device could be installed that would carry traffic between the two networks. The router would require two IP addresses. Two common choices are 192.168.1.254 and 192.168.2.254. (Host number 254 is commonly assigned as a gateway, and host 1 is commonly assigned to the DNS server; these are values that Red Hat assumes during installation.) Linux can be a router if it is explicitly instructed to do so—this behavior is controlled by the `/etc/sysconfig/network` file in Red Hat Linux. This file also contains the IP address of the default gateway. Settings from this file are normally activated at boot time. Hosts on the first network could define their default gateway as 192.168.1.254, and any data not bound for hosts on the local network would automatically be sent to the remote. If more than two local networks were connected, the default route might no longer be used to direct traffic, and a more explicit routing table would be required.

Bearing all of this in mind, see Figure 2.1 and Figure 2.2, which are screenshots of the `netcfg` utility. You can use `netcfg` to edit network interface configurations once they are installed.

The `linuxconf` utility can also be used to add network devices. In Listing 2.1, a 3Com 509 Ethernet card is configured.

Listing 2.1 *Using* `linuxconf` *to configure an Ethernet interface.*

```
************ This host basic configuration *************
* You are allowed to control the parameters            *
* which are specific to this host and related          *
* to its main connection to the local network          *
*                                                      *
*                      *********************************
*                      ***********Adaptor 2*************
*                      *[X] Enabled                   **
*Config mode           *(o) Manual ( ) Dhcp ( ) Bootp **
*Primary name + domain *                              **
*Aliases (opt)         *                              **
*IP address            *192.168.1.1                   **
*Netmask (opt)         *255.255.255.0                ***
*Net device            *eth1                         ***
*Kernel module         *3c509                        ***
*I/O port (opt)        *                              **
*Irq (opt)             *                             ***
*                      ***********Adaptor 3*************
*                      *[ ] Enabled                   **
*                      *********************************
*       ********        ********        ******         *
*       *Accept*        *Cancel*        *Help*         *
*       ********        ********        ******         *
********************************************************
```

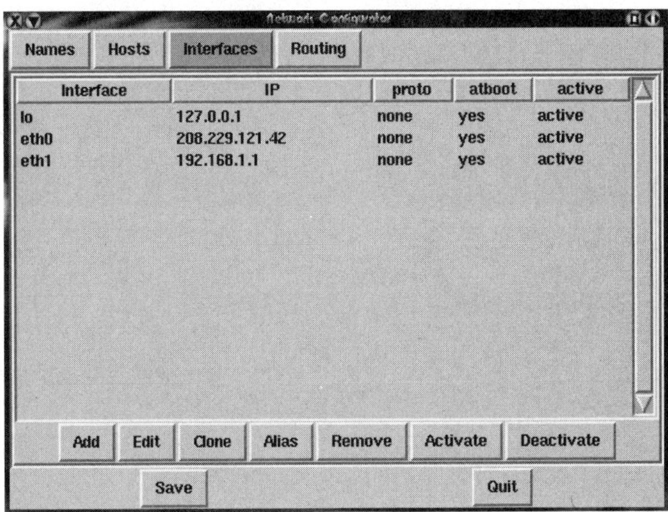

Figure 2.1 *The netcfg utility.*

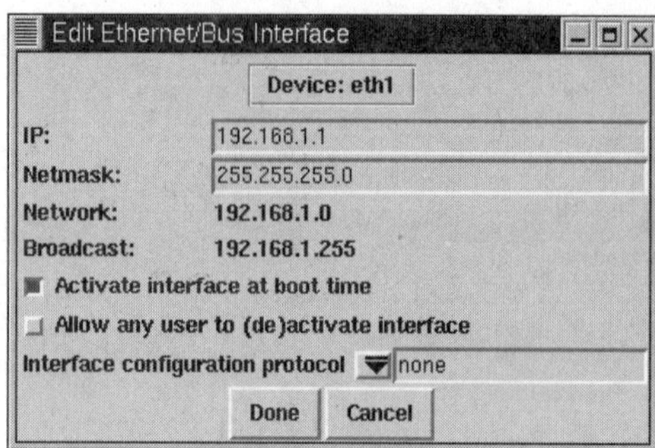

Figure 2.2 *Using* `netcfg` *to configure an interface.*

To accomplish the same operation from the command line, one could enter:

```
# modprobe 3c509.o
eth1: 3c509 at 0x300 tag 1, 10baseT port,
address  00 60 97 a6 b0 e5, IRQ 10.
3c509.c:1.16 (2.2) 2/3/98 becker@cesdis.gsfc.nasa.gov.
# ifconfig eth1 192.168.1.1 netmask 255.255.255.0 \
broadcast 192.168.1.255
eth1: Setting Rx mode to 1 addresses.
```

Adding the device with the command line, however, will not make entries for it in the system initialization scripts. When Linux is rebooted, the card definition will be lost. Cards defined for boot-time initialization leave entries in `/etc/conf.modules` and the `/etc/sysconfig/network-scripts` directories.

When adding a network device as shown above, a route to the network will automatically be added to the routing table, enabling access to the network, which is directly attached to the adapter. Access to additional networks (including the default route) must be added explicitly.

The only piece of information that is not immediately clear in the above shell commands is the **modprobe 3c509.o** command. This command loads a kernel module. This module is a driver for a 3Com509 network card. An experienced Linux administrator might be able to pick up a network card, find a Digital 21040 network chip on it (for example), and realize that a call to **modprobe tulip.o** would properly initialize the card. However, such knowledge normally escapes the novice. For more information about kernel module drivers for network cards, install the Linux kernel source and examine the `/usr/src/linux/Documentation/networking` directory. Some of these network driver modules (especially modules for ISA network adapters, such as the NE2000) require extensive information about the card before they will load and initialize properly. It is generally more convenient to have these cards detected at installation time, rather than adding them to the system later.

To reiterate, basic network configuration requires the three parameters of IP address, netmask, and broadcast address. The network address is determined automatically by a bitwise and of the IP address and the netmask.

The more expansive configuration options of gateway address and DNS server are addressed by the `/etc/sysconfig/network` script and `/etc/resolv.conf` files. These files are configured at install time, and, with luck, they should not require modification.

The final point of this section is a trick with *10BaseT* Ethernet cabling used between two computers, allowing a home network to be constructed very inexpensively. If 10BaseT twisted-pair Ethernet is being used, a hub is required to allow two or more computers to communicate. Two 10BaseT devices, however, can communicate without a hub if a special cable is constructed (or obtained from a manufacturer). This cable reverses the transmit and receive wire pairs from end to end. Table 2.2 is a RJ-45 wiring diagram (note that pins 4, 5, 7, and 8 are unused).

Table 2.2 *Wiring guide for a 10baseT crossover cable.*

Pair	Host Lead	Remote Lead
TX	1	3
	2	6
RX	3	1
	6	2

Such a *crossover* cable dramatically reduces the expense of connecting two 10BaseT devices, which is useful in cost-conscious installations. These crossover cables can also be used to connect multiple 10BaseT hubs, at the cost of consuming one port of each hub where they are used.

Subnets

This section discusses techniques for subnetting Class C IP addresses. Subnetting an IP network is a method that can be used to transform a single network into many. It is usually employed when multiple networks must be maintained, but multiple Class A, B, or C networks are not available.

Unless you have specific reasons for using subnets with a Class C network, it is probably a very bad idea. IP masquerading techniques, as discussed in Chapter 4, might be a much more convenient method for attaching multiple hosts to the Internet with a limited IP address space. It should also be noted that two IP addresses will be sacrificed for each subnet formed (one for the network number, and one for the broadcast address), and a third will be required for a router.

Despite these difficulties, let us pretend that a system administrator at a branch office of some company has been allocated the Class C IP network of 192.168.1. Let us further suppose that this single office opens up two additional satellite offices close by. The administrator is expected to network the additional offices using the Class C already in use (another Class C will not be granted).

A quick reminder of the powers of 2 might be in order (see Table 2.3).

Table 2.3 *The powers of 2.*

2^0	=	1
2^1	=	2
2^2	=	4
2^3	=	8
2^4	=	16
2^5	=	32
2^6	=	64
2^7	=	128

The regular Class C netmask used before the split is shown in Table 2.4, in both decimal and binary form:

Table 2.4 *A Class C netmask.*

255.	255.	255.	0
11111111.	11111111.	11111111.	00000000

The administrator decides to expand the netmask two bits beyond the Class C, as in Table 2.5.

Table 2.5 *A user-defined netmask.*

255.	255.	255.	192
11111111.	11111111.	11111111.	11000000

In the modified netmask, the final byte has the two leftmost (or most significant) bits set. A sequence of two bits can be arranged in four different ways (00, 01, 10, or 11). Expanding the netmask in this way, therefore, will create four new networks. Only three are needed, but the fourth must follow because networks can only be allocated in powers of two (unless Variable Length Subnet Masking is in use, which is beyond the scope of this text).

By expanding the subnet mask in this way, four networks have been created (see Table 2.6).

Table 2.6 *Results of subnetting a Class C network.*

Network	Netmask	Broadcast	Starting IP	Concluding IP
192.168.1.0	255.255.255.192	192.168.1.63	192.168.1.1	192.168.1.62
192.168.1.64	255.255.255.192	192.168.1.127	192.168.1.65	192.168.1.126
192.168.1.128	255.255.255.192	192.168.1.191	192.168.1.129	192.168.1.190
192.168.1.192	255.255.255.192	192.168.1.255	192.168.1.193	192.168.1.254

A router will be required to route traffic on each network, and the router will consume an IP address on each network. In total, twelve IP addresses will be consumed between the new network numbers, broadcast addresses, and the new gateways. Use this technique only when necessary.

DNS

The Domain Name System (DNS) is the engine that translates host names into IP addresses. It is a cornerstone of Internet design. No domain with connectivity to the Internet can afford to ignore it.

If a system with Red Hat Linux will *ever* be connected to the Internet in any way except through proxies, it should probably have at least a caching-only DNS server installed, and an `/etc/resolv.conf` that points to 127.0.0.1. Such a caching server will be loaded at installation time if `named` is selected from the package list in the `ntsysv` menu. This is especially true for PPP-modem users, or users of transient or limited bandwidth connections, as DNS traffic is reduced with an active caching server.

The DNS server and caching-only settings can be loaded at any time after installation by issuing the following commands from the RedHat/RPMs directory of the installation tree:

```
rpm -Uvh bind-8.2-6.i386.rpm
rpm -Uvh caching-nameserver-6.0-2.noarch.rpm
```

Installing the *Bind* package will automatically configure it to be launched at boot time through the `/etc/rc.d/init.d/named` startup script. If this isn't what is wanted, use the `ntsysv` utility to alter the boot status.

Please note that if Red Hat Linux is installed over a network (with either FTP, NFS, or SMB) and a name server is specified, that server will be used in preference to any name server running on the local host if the network settings were retained at the end of the installation. To specify the local host as the primary name server, make sure that the first `nameserver` directive in `/etc/resolv.conf` reads as follows:

```
nameserver 127.0.0.1
```

The IP address—127.0.0.1—is a special address, called the *loopback*, which always refers to the local host.

The `/etc/resolv.conf` file can also be removed to force the local nameserver to be used. If the local server fails, however, connectivity to the Internet will essentially be lost. It is preferable to list up to three nameserver entries; the local will fail over to the backup(s) should the primary server(s) cease responding.

Be cautious in setting the permissions on the `/etc/resolv.conf` file, as well. If a user does not have read permissions on this file, their DNS lookup will fail.

A name server is normally used in two ways:

- It is asked to provide information about hosts which it knows about first hand (over which it is *authoritative*).
- It is asked about hosts over which it is *not* authoritative, and it must query other (authoritative) nameservers to gain the information, which it then caches.

The caching-only settings for the nameserver above create a nameserver that is authoritative about *nothing,* and it must ask other nameservers about every host. Even if it is the administrator's intention to create an authoritative nameserver, the installation of the caching-only nameserver is recommended; a caching-only server is the skeleton of an authoritative server.

Files for Forward Lookups

Before DNS authority records can be created, a domain must be obtained from InterNIC. This can be accomplished through their website at *http://www.internic.net.* In order to register a domain, two authoritative nameservers for the requested domain must be available at the time of the registration.

The popular `whois` utility is now included in Red Hat Linux and can be used to query the InterNIC databases. (The utility was sorely lacking in past releases.) See Listing 2.2 on page 66.

Listing 2.2 *Using* `whois`.

```
# whois redhat.com
[rs.internic.net]

Registrant:
Red Hat Software (REDHAT-DOM)
   4201 Research Commons, Suite 100
   79 T.W. Alexander Dr.
   P.O. Box 13588
   Research Triangle Park, NC 27709
   US

   Domain Name: REDHAT.COM

   Administrative Contact, Technical Contact, Zone Contact:
      Network Operations Center  (NOC144-ORG)
noc@REDHAT.COM
      919-572-6500 x235Fax- 919-361-2711
Fax- - 919-361-2711
   Billing Contact:
      Accounts Payable  (AP1279-ORG)  accounts@REDHAT.COM
      (919) 572-6500
Fax- (919) 361-2711

   Record last updated on 23-Jul-97.
   Record created on 26-May-94.
   Database last updated on 16-Dec-98 03:49:10 EST.

   Domain servers in listed order:

   NS.REDHAT.COM          207.175.42.153
   SPEEDY.REDHAT.COM      199.183.24.251

The InterNIC Registration Services database contains ONLY
non-military and non-US Government Domains and contacts.
Other associated whois servers:
   American Registry for Internet Numbers - whois.arin.net
   European IP Address Allocations        - whois.ripe.net
   Asia Pacific IP Address Allocations    - whois.apnic.net
   US Military                            - whois.nic.mil
   US Government                          - whois.nic.gov
```

Let us say that we have obtained the domain *acme.com*, and it has been registered with the InterNIC. To configure the primary name server, we might save the text shown in Listing 2.3 in `/var/named/db.acme`.

Listing 2.3 *Forward lookups.*

```
@                IN SOA  acme.com.        root.acme.com. (
                         199901010        ; Serial
                         10800            ; Refresh
                         1800             ; Retry
                         3600000          ; Expire
                         86400 )          ; Minimum
                         IN      NS
dns1.other.com.
                         IN      NS
dns2.other2.com.
                         IN      MX       10       acme.com.

localhost                IN      A                 127.0.0.1

acme.com.                IN      A                 1.2.3.4
www                      IN      A                 1.2.3.4

mail                     IN      CNAME             acme.com.
ftp                      IN      CNAME             acme.com.
```

This file is probably the simplest format for a small domain registration. The IP address of *www.acme.com* and *acme.com* are both listed as 1.2.3.4. Additional hosts for the domain could be listed with more "IN A" records.

This file will essentially allow anyone on the Internet to connect to the hostname *www.acme.com,* which will be quietly resolved to 1.2.3.4. To see such a resolution in action, the UNIX **nslookup** command can be used:

nslookup www.acme.com

```
Server:  localhost
Address:  127.0.0.1

Name:    www.acme.com
Address:  1.2.3.4
```

Files for Reverse Lookups

In order to configure a file for reverse lookups, an Internet network number must be obtained. These network numbers are usually received through network service providers, who obtain them from the Internet Assigned Numbers Authority (IANA) at *http://www.iana.org.*

Assuming that the Internet Class C network 1.2.3 has been obtained, the file shown in Listing 2.4 would be placed in `/var/named/db.1.2.3.`

Listing 2.4 *Reverse lookups.*

```
@                  IN SOA  acme.com.    root.acme.com. (
                           199901010 ; Serial
                           10800     ; Refresh
                           1800      ; Retry
                           3600000   ; Expire
                           86400 )   ; Minimum
                           IN NS       dns1.other.com.
                           IN NS       dns2.other2.com.

4                          IN PTR acme.com.
```

The term *reverse lookup* means that the IP address can be looked up to obtain the hostname:

nslookup 1.2.3.4

```
Server:  localhost
Address: 127.0.0.1

Name:    www.acme.com
Address: 1.2.3.4
```

If a domain does not define a reverse lookup for an IP address (which is bad practice if the address is in use), the registered owner of the IP can be determined with `whois`, as shown in Listing 2.5.

Listing 2.5 *Using* `whois` *with the ARIN server.*

whois 199.183.24.253@whois.arin.net

```
[whois.arin.net]
NETCOM On-Line Communication Services, Inc. (NETBLK-
NETCOMCBLK-3)                  NETBLK-NETCOMCBLK-3
                               199.182.0.0 - 199.183.255.255
Red Hat Software (NET-REDHAT) REDHAT  199.183.24.0
```

To single out one record, look it up with "!xxx", where xxx is the handle, shown in parenthesis following the name, which comes first.

The ARIN Registration Services Host contains *only* Internet Network Information: networks, ASN's, and related POC's. Please use the `whois` server at *rs.internic.net* for domain-related information and *nic.mil* for NIPRNET information.

Configuring /etc/named.conf

Once the master files have been created, the primary nameserver must be instructed to use them. This is done by modifying `/etc/named.conf`. The modified file for this case is shown in Listing 2.6.

Listing 2.6 *The* `named` *configuration file.*

```
options {
        directory "/var/named";
};

// no longer a caching only nameserver config

zone "." {
        type hint;
        file "named.ca";
};

zone "0.0.127.in-addr.arpa" {
        type master;
        file "named.local";
};

zone "acme.com" {
        type master;
        file "db.acme";
};

zone "3.2.1.in-addr.arpa" {
        type master;
        file "db.1.2.3";
};
```

After the file has been placed, the primary nameserver should be restarted with the following command:

/etc/rc.d/init.d/named restart

The secondary server can be configured by instructing it to replicate the new domains from the primary server. This means that the data files can be maintained in only one place, easing administration work load. However, when the files are changed on the primary, the serial number near the top must be increased so that the replication will be invoked (the serial numbers are compared). This is generally done by using the current date for the serial number.

The secondary must be told the IP address of the primary in the `named.conf` file. Assuming that the IP address of the primary is 5.6.7.8, the proper form of the `named.conf` file on the secondary is shown in Listing 2.7.

Listing 2.7 *The* `named` *configuration file for the secondary server.*

```
options {
        directory "/var/named";
};

zone "." {
        type hint;
        file "named.ca";
};

zone "0.0.127.in-addr.arpa" {
        type master;
        file "named.local";
};

zone "acme.com" {
        type slave;
        file "db.acme";
        masters {
                5.6.7.8;
        };
};

zone "3.2.1.in-addr.arpa" {
        type slave;
        file "db.1.2.3";
        masters {
                5.6.7.8;
        };
};
```

When the secondary name server is restarted, it will automatically transfer the domain information from the primary and build the `db.acme` and `db.1.2.3` files in `/var/named` (they will look nothing like the original files on the primary).

The file `/var/named/named.ca` (which exists on both the primary and the secondary) must be reloaded from time to time. Instructions for doing so are in the file itself. This must even be done for caching-only nameservers. The file should be checked for changes once every six months. If the computer is regularly upgraded with new versions of Red Hat Linux, the upgrade of `named.ca` will be performed automatically.

Round-Robin DNS and *Clustering*

The version of `named` distributed with Red Hat Linux supports a simple method of server load balancing. Several hosts can be given the same name. When this is done, `named` will automatically cycle through the entire list of IP addresses when asked to resolve the name, answering each query with a different IP.

Obviously, this method of load distribution will not be even across all servers. If a firewall's DNS query resolves to a certain host, it may direct thousands of clients there for the period that it is allowed to cache the results of the lookup.

This rotation is configured in the forward lookup files. If records such as the following were entered into `/var/named/db.acme`,

```
www                    IN     A            1.2.3.4
                       IN     A            1.2.3.5
                       IN     A            1.2.3.6
                       IN     A            1.2.3.7
                       IN     A            1.2.3.8
```

the first lookup on *www.acme.com* would be 1.2.3.4, the second would be 1.2.3.5, the third would be 1.2.3.6, and so on.

IP Alias and Virtual Hosting

IP Alias is a mechanism where a single Ethernet interface can respond to multiple IP addresses. This has many applications, including the virtual hosting of websites and fault-tolerant network services design.

Let us imagine that the `eth0` device has been configured with the standard Class C network address of 192.168.1.1. The interface could be also configured to respond to 192.168.1.2 with the following sequence of commands (issued by root):

```
/sbin/ifconfig eth0:0 192.168.1.2
/sbin/route add -host 192.168.1.2 dev eth0:0
```

Any normal network services which run on the first interface (i.e., Telnet, FTP, etc.) will run on the second. Some services pay particular attention to IP Alias settings, and will modify their behavior for each interface if configured to do so (e.g., Apache). Additional interfaces can be created by following the sequence

```
/sbin/ifconfig eth0:1 192.168.1.3
/sbin/route add -host 192.168.1.3 dev eth0:1
```

A computer could provide backup network services for another by issuing ping packets at regular intervals. If the remote host does not respond, the first computer could automatically execute an IP Alias for the inoperative host's network address. This provides a rudimentary form of fault tolerance.

DHCP

The Dynamic Host Configuration Protocol (DHCP) is a method of allocating IP addresses and other relevant parameters for TCP/IP from a centralized repository, rather than recording the information statically on each host. A DHCP server should be a computer that is operational and attached to its network continuously—it must be available whenever clients request its services. If a network has more than a few hosts, and it has a Linux system that is in continual operation, it should have a DHCP server to ease network administration.The server portion of the protocol is implemented by the `dhcpd` daemon. This server protocol is compatible with the DHCP implementations used by other operating systems (e.g., the variants of Microsoft Windows). The Linux client portion is controlled by `dhcpcd` or `pump`. It is automatically configured if DHCP is selected for the TCP/IP configuration at installation time. It can be implemented after installation via `netcfg`.

The DHCP server is not automatically installed when a Red Hat Linux system is prepared. It can be installed by running the following commands as *root* from the `RedHat/RPMs` directory of the CD included with this text:

```
rpm -Uvh dhcp-2.0b1pl6-6.i386.rpm
touch /etc/dhcpd.leases
```

Installing the package will automatically configure it to be launched at boot time through the `/etc/rc.d/init.d/dhcpd` startup script. If this is not what you want, use the `ntsysv` utility to alter the boot status.

There is a Linux-specific issue in the configuration of the DHCP server. A routing command must be run to allow traffic to be sent to the 255.255.255.255 IP address. This issue is documented in the file `/usr/doc/dhcp-2.0b1pl6/README`. The exact command is:

/sbin/route add -host 255.255.255.255 dev eth0

This command must be run every time the system is restarted, so it should be placed in one of the boot scripts. A good location for it is in the startup section of the `/etc/rc.d/init.d/dhcpd` file. Listing 2.8 shows a fragment of a startup script from a running system, which introduces another important DHCP issue and some related points.

Listing 2.8 *A modified version of the dhcp startup script.*

```
# See how we were called.
case "$1" in
  start)
        # Start daemons.
        echo -n "Starting dhcpd: "
        /sbin/route add -host 255.255.255.255 dev eth1
        daemon /usr/sbin/dhcpd eth1

        /sbin/ipchains -P forward DENY
        /sbin/ipchains -F
        /sbin/ipchains -A forward -j MASQ \
         -s 192.168.1.0/24 -d 0.0.0.0/0
        /sbin/modprobe ip_masq_ftp
        echo
        touch /var/lock/subsys/dhcpd
        ;;
```

Notice that the route command in the above script routes not to `eth0`, but to the `eth1` network device. Note further that `eth1` has been passed as an argument to the `dhcpd` command line. In a system with multiple network devices, `dhcpd` must be told which device to use.

The calls to `ipchains` and `modprobe` are not directly related to DHCP. They configure the local system as a masquerading router.

A synthetic network with a 192.168.1 network number will have all outgoing packets rewritten with the local IP address that forwards to the default gateway. This technique is extremely useful in the conservation of valuable Internet IP addresses, and is discussed at some length in Chapter 4, "Firewalls."

If an advanced development kernel is utilized, it might be necessary to issue the following command (although it is not necessary with the kernel distributed with Red Hat Linux 6.0):

echo 1 > /proc/sys/net/ipv4/ip_bootp_agent

The last step in bringing a Linux DHCP server online is writing an `/etc/dhcpd.conf` file. Listing 2.9 shows an example.

Listing 2.9 *An example* `dhcpd.conf`.

```
subnet 192.168.1.0 netmask 255.255.255.0 {
        range 192.168.1.128 192.168.1.254;
        default-lease-time 600; max-lease-time 7200;
        option subnet-mask 255.255.255.0;
        option broadcast-address 192.168.1.255;
        option routers 192.168.1.1;
        option domain-name-servers 192.168.1.1;
        option domain-name "fake.com";
}
```

This configuration is designed for a 192.168.1 network. Each directive is described below:

`range 192.168.1.128 192.168.1.254;`

This command sets the range of IP addresses which the server may hand out to clients. The addresses that will be dispensed here are from 128 to 254.

`default-lease-time 600; max-lease-time 7200;`

This directive controls how long clients may keep the IP addresses that the DHCP server allocates to them. The time is specified in seconds.

`option subnet-mask 255.255.255.0;`

The actual subnet mask that is passed to the clients is stated here.

`option broadcast-address 192.168.1.255;`

The broadcast address that is passed to the clients is stated here.

`option routers 192.168.1.1;`

The address of the router that is passed to the clients is stated here. Notice that this is the address of the DHCP server, which is also serving as a router.

`option domain-name-servers 192.168.1.1;`

The address of the DNS server that is passed to the clients is stated here. Notice that this is the address of the DHCP server, which is also serving as a Domain Name Server (DNS). It must either be configured as a DNS server that is authoritative for some domain, or as a caching-only name server.

`option domain-name "fake.com";`

The actual text of the domain name that is passed to the clients is stated here.

To start the DHCP server, either reboot the system, or run the following command as root:

/etc/rc.d/init.d/dhcpd start

Many additional configuration parameters are available. Specifically, individual computers can be granted specific settings by the DHCP server based upon the Media Access Controller (MAC) address of the network card within them (the MAC address is a truly unique identifier that vendors of Ethernet devices embed into their products).

For additional information on the operation of DHCP services, check the online manual pages for `dhcpd`, `dhcpd.conf`, and `dhcpcd`. When debugging the behavior of `dhcpd`, examine `/var/log/messages` because all DHCP activity is logged there.

NFS/NIS

The Network File System (NFS) is a protocol designed by Sun Microsystems that allows entire file systems or individual directories to be easily shared with remote computers.If you have purchased any books on basic NFS operation for Linux, throw them away. NFS is extremely easy to configure and use. The NFS server is configured through the `/etc/exports` file. The simplest (and least secure) configuration simply lists directories that may be shared with other servers:

```
/home
/usr/local/bin
/var
```

The Red Hat Linux NFS server is started by calling the `portmap` and `nfs` scripts in `/etc/rc.d/init.d`. These can be configured to run at boot time, or they can be launched with the following commands:

/etc/rc.d/init.d/portmap start
/etc/rc.d/init.d/nfs start

If the server is already active and the `/etc/exports` file has been changed, the server can be instructed to reread the file with the command of the form:

exportfs –rv

Once the server has been initialized, a client can use the exported directories (called *volumes* when used over NFS) with a simple mount command:

mount nfs.remotehost.com:/path/to/exported/directory /mnt

An IP address can be used instead of a hostname. Several other options can be passed that influence performance (particularly `rsize=8192,wsize=8192`). Check the `mount` man page for more information.

If a hostname is used, rather than an IP address, the system must be able to change the name of the remote NFS server into an IP address. Since DNS failures can prevent this change from taking place, it is always advisable to place entries in `/etc/hosts` for NFS servers whose file systems are mounted at boot time. It might also be profitable to examine `/etc/nsswitch.conf` and `/etc/fstab`, for additional flexibility in boot time mounts.

Once the mount command has been executed, the local host will see the remote file system within the local directory tree, and manipulate the files natively. File locking can be a problem; if there is great contention over a file, it is best not to place it within an NFS volume.

Please note that mounting an NFS file system over the Internet is not wise. NFS generally uses UDP packets, which are best suited to local networks; UDP packets over the Internet can be discarded easily, forcing retransmissions and reduced performance. FTP is much more appropriate for Internet usage, and scp with compression is even better (scp is discussed in Chapter 4,"Firewalls.").

Please also note that the root user is usually restricted in accessing remote file systems through a mechanism called *root squash*. The root will usually work as user *nobody* on the volume. Every other user is completely vulnerable to whatever the remote administrator may do, so do not export an NFS volume to a system that you do not trust (or at least export it as read-only, which is discussed shortly).

As previously mentioned, /etc/exports can be made much more secure. Examine the following:

```
/home             remotehost.com
/usr/local/bin    anotherhost.com(ro)
/var              thelasthost.com(no_root_squash)
```

This file allows only remotehost.com to access /home via NFS, and root squash is in effect. The /usr/local/bin directory is set for read-only access from anotherhost.com, and the /var directory has been completely shared with thelasthost.com; root may work natively on this last remote host with full access to the exported volume.

NIS presents a different issue entirely. The Network Information System (NIS) is a framework that allows several important files to be shared between UNIX hosts (namely /etc/passwd, /etc/group, and /etc/hosts, among others). Unfortunately, NIS has a reputation of being rather insecure. It also can be cumbersome to use, because the local /etc/passwd file is no longer the authoritative source of local account information.

Several alternatives to NIS exist, including NIS+, the DCE registry, and Hesiod Bind. They are all extremely difficult to configure and use.

A much simpler and better solution would be to use scp to copy these files from an arbitrarily-allocated master server to the slave servers whenever the files change. The programs that change these files (such as chfn, chsh, passwd, and chgrp) should be disabled on the slave servers.

03

PPP

Modem communication under Linux is powerful, but complex. Modems can be run as either standard terminal devices, or as network links that are directly maintained by the kernel. One way to approach network communications under Linux is with the Point to Point Protocol (PPP). PPP can be used to provide support for TCP/IP (the protocol associated with the Internet) and IPX (used by Novell Netware).

The approach to PPP taken in this chapter will be one that is compatible with the methods used in Microsoft Windows. The approach used by Windows is not particularly secure, but it is ubiquitous.

Client PPP

Establishing a PPP client connection under Linux is rather simple. The Control Panel application that runs under XWindows can be used to establish PPP connections. The shell scripting approach outlined below, however, is much more flexible. It can be used in non-X environments, and it does not require root access. For completeness, the method utilizing the control panel is addressed later. Regardless of the method used to establish PPP, `/etc/resolv.conf` must be configured to allow Internet host names to be resolved. A Linux system can rely upon a remote DNS server for these functions, or it can run a caching-only server itself.

The Scripting Approach

To connect to a remote PPP server, the three files—`/bin/network`, `/bin/network.chat` and `/etc/ppp/pap-secrets`—should be placed on the local Linux system. The content of these files is shown below.

The /bin/network file

```
#!/bin/sh

exec /usr/sbin/pppd -detach lock modem crtscts \
  defaultroute user USERNAME /dev/ttyS1 57600 \
  connect "/usr/sbin/chat -f /bin/network.chat"
```

The /bin/network.chat file

```
'ABORT' 'BUSY'
'ABORT' 'ERROR'
'ABORT' 'NO CARRIER'
'ABORT' 'NO DIALTONE'
'ABORT' 'Invalid Login'
'ABORT' 'Login incorrect'
''
'ATZ'
'OK'
'ATDT 1234567'
'CONNECT'
''
```

The /etc/ppp/pap-secrets file

```
# Secrets for authentication using PAP
# client server secret IP addresses
USERNAME     ""                  PASSWORD
```

The changes you must make to configure them for your site are as follows:

1. The correct serial port for the modem must be set in `/bin/network` (i.e., replace `/dev/ttyS1`).
2. Replace `1234567` with your ISP's telephone number in the `/bin/network.chat` script.
3. Replace the `USERNAME` and `PASSWORD` in the `/etc/ppp/pap-secrets` and `/bin/network` files with the PPP account name and password on the dial-up server.
4. Optionally, place the line `ogin:--ogin: ''` at the end of the `/bin/network.chat` file. This causes the local Linux system to expect the remote server to issue a login: message before the PPP session commences. If such a message is not received, a carriage return is sent in an effort to prod the remote server to supply it.
5. Run the command **chmod 755 /bin/network** to enable the network script to be executed from the shell.
6. Optionally, run the command **chmod u+s /usr/sbin/pppd** and change the permissions of the serial port device in the `/dev` directory to mode `666` (read and write access for everyone). This allows all users on the system to bring the PPP link up or down. The root user might also create a *ppp group* to permit only trusted users to administer the interface.

The `demand` option to `pppd` is quite useful in establishing on-demand PPP connections. It allows for the link to be initiated only in the event of outbound network traffic, and has options for the termination of a PPP connection that is idle for a certain amount of time, and the reestablishment of the connection if traffic is generated on an inactive link. Finally, with Red Hat Linux 6.0, the shipped kernel contains a driver for this option of `pppd`. (The option has been available but nonfunctional since a patch for version 5.0.) Following is a modified version of `/bin/network` that uses the demand-dialing approach:

```
#!/bin/sh

exec /usr/sbin/pppd demand idle 300 192.168.1.2:192.168.1.1\
   -detach lock modem crtscts \
   defaultroute user USERNAME /dev/ttyS1 57600 \
   connect "/usr/sbin/chat -f /bin/network.chat"
```

The above script has the `demand` option, which will bring the link down after a period of inactivity. This period is defined by the argument to the `idle` parameter. This parameter is given in seconds and is set to 5 minutes (300 seconds) in this case.

The main limitation to the `demand` parameter is that the IP address assigned to the device must be known before the connection is made. The manual page for `pppd` indicates that dynamically assigned IP addresses can be handled in a demand-dialing arrangement, but tests run by the author of this book did not confirm this assertion. If the IP address assigned by the remote PPP server cannot be held constant, the `diald` demand-dialing daemon should be investigated, because it is much more flexible in such an arrangement.

More information on attaching Linux to an ISP is available in the ISP-Hookup-HOWTO at *ftp://sunsite.unc.edu/pub/Linux/docs/HOWTO/ISP-Hookup-HOWTO*.

From the Control Panel

To use the graphical PPP controls, XWindows must be running correctly. From within X, open a terminal window and enter the command **control-panel** to launch it.

Before the control panel can launch a PPP session, a symbolic link must be set from `/dev/modem` to the actual serial port device. This can be done manually from a shell, or it can be accomplished through the control panel itself. To do so, click the Modem Configuration icon (Figure 3.1).

Select the serial port device for the modem from the list (Figure 3.2), and click "OK."

Figure 3.1 *The modem configuration icon.*

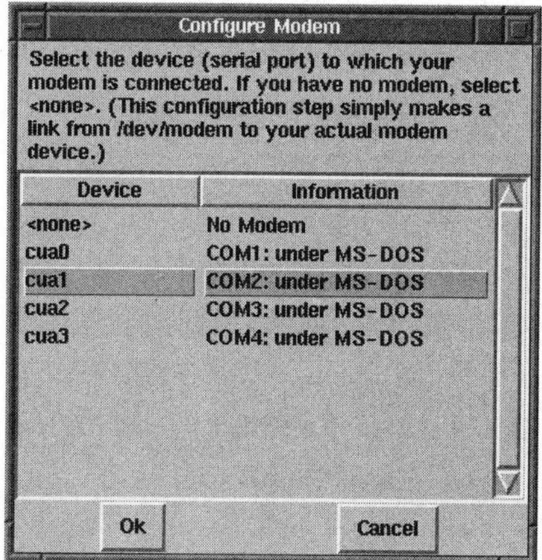

Figure 3.2 *Modem configuration.*

From the control panel, click the Network Configuration icon (Figure 3.3).

Figure 3.3 *The network configuration icon.*

The Network Configuration dialog will be presented. Press the Interfaces button, and a window like the one shown in Figure 3.4 on page 84 will be displayed.

Choose the Add option, and a menu of possible interface types will be displayed (Figure 3.5).

Ensure that PPP is selected, and click "OK." A dialog to create the PPP interface will follow (Figure 3.6). Replace the relevant sections with settings for your own ISP.

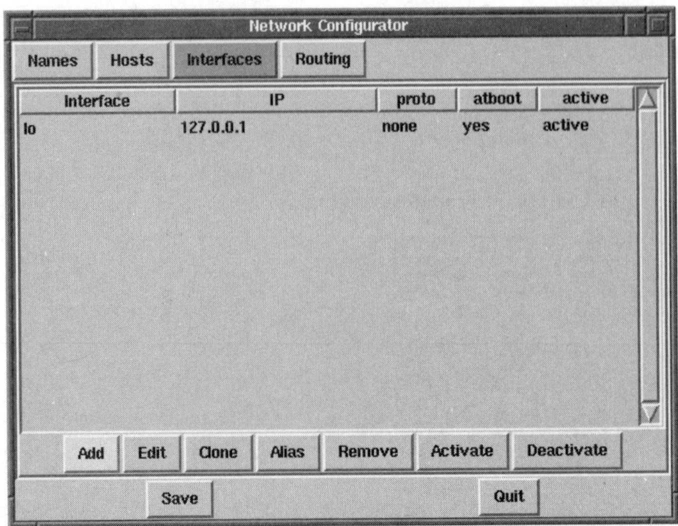

Figure 3.4 *Network configuration.*

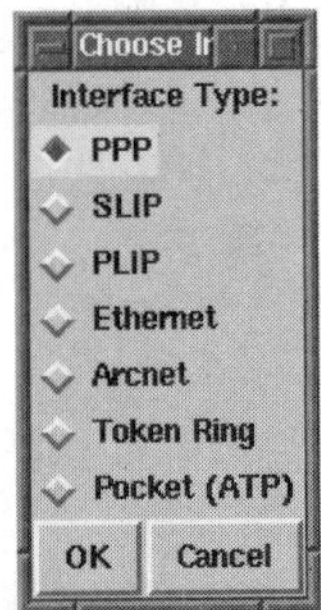

Figure 3.5 *Interface types.*

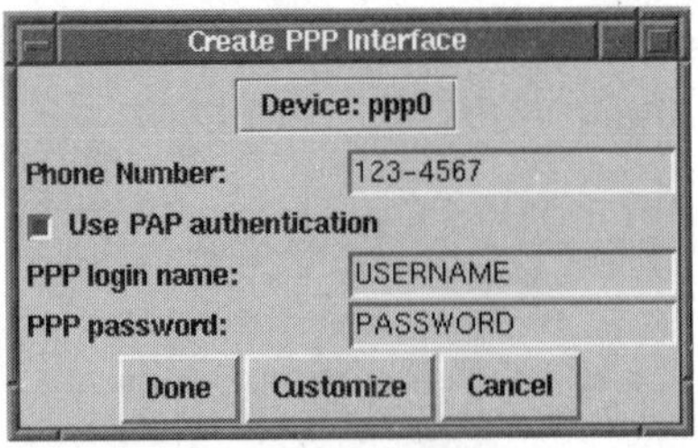

Figure 3.6 *PPP interface creation.*

Click "Done" when the settings are correct. A confirmation dialog box (Figure 3.7) will appear.

Figure 3.7 *PPP interface confirmation.*

After the settings are saved, the PPP device will be added in the Network Configuration dialog (Figure 3.8). Highlight it and click "Activate."

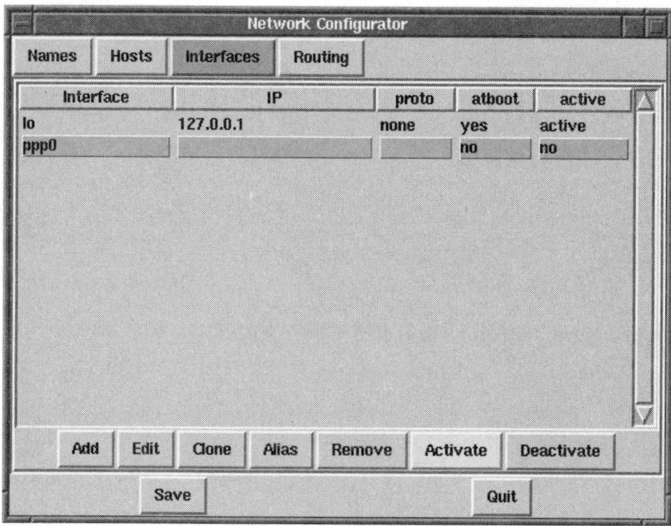

Figure 3.8 *PPP interface activation.*

If all is correct, the modem should go off-hook and begin dialing. A similar control interface for client PPP exists in the `linux-conf` utility, but it is not discussed here.

Name Resolution

On the Internet, there is no way to reach a host without its IP address. Regardless of the structure of a host name (such as `host.foo.com`), the host is unreachable unless the hostname can be converted into an IP address (such as 1.2.3.4, or any other real Internet address). This conversion does not happen by magic, but is caused by Internet DNS servers (as is discussed in the DNS administration section later in this chapter). A few name-IP translations can be entered into the `/etc/hosts` file, but such a lookup table becomes impractical for large numbers of hosts.

For a Linux system behind a PPP connection, there are two options for accomplishing DNS name resolution: Either rely upon a remote DNS server on the far side of the PPP link or run a local DNS server. There are advantages and drawbacks to each approach.

If a remote DNS server is used, configuration of the local Linux host is very simple. Traffic will be generated, however, for each hostname lookup, which will consume a small portion of the PPP connection bandwidth.If a local DNS server is configured and used, host name lookups are cached by the local DNS server. There is no further bandwidth consumption of the PPP connection after the first lookup of a remote host (until the caching period set by the remote authoritative DNS server expires). However, a caching-only name server running at boot time with no network access to the Internet can confuse some daemon processes (notably the Postgres SQL server, the Apache web server, and Sendmail). Also, the initial configuration of the name server is cumbersome.

To configure a Linux system to use remote DNS servers, the IP addresses of the servers will be required. Up to three servers can be used. These addresses can be obtained from the remote ISP or system administrator. Please note that Linux will not accept DNS servers passed in the negotiation phase of the PPP connection. (MSDNS is rejected for security reasons.)

When the addresses of the remote servers have been obtained, the `/etc/resolv.conf` should be configured as follows:

```
search isp.net
nameserver 1.2.3.4
nameserver 5.6.7.8
nameserver 9.10.11.12
```

Replace the `isp.net` entry above with the domain name of your ISP or upstream authority. The secondary and tertiary nameserver entries may be omitted, but at least one operational server must be entered. Be sure to replace the dummied entries above with the correct IP addresses.

If a local caching-only server is preferred, the server must be loaded and configured. The DNS server and caching-only settings can be loaded at any time after installation by issuing the following commands from the RedHat/RPMS directory of the installation tree:

rpm -Uvh bind-8.2-6.i386.rpm
rpm -Uvh caching-nameserver-6.0-2.noarch.rpm

Installing the Bind package will automatically configure it to be launched at boot time through the `/etc/rc.d/init.d/named` startup script. If this is not what you want, use the `ntsysv` utility to alter the boot status. The name server can also be manually started and stopped with this script.

Once the server is loaded, Linux must be instructed to use it. To specify the local host as the primary name server, make sure that the first `nameserver` directive in `/etc/resolv.conf` reads as follows:

```
nameserver 127.0.0.1
```

If the file does not exist, create it with permissions of `644`. The address 127.0.0.1 is the universal lookback address. Enter it as shown.

Server PPP

The Linux `pppd` daemon has flexible configuration options and it can communicate with a variety of IP protocol stacks. However, `pppd` has few options for controlling a modem. It does not send modem initialization strings and it does not answer ringing telephone lines.

The various `getty` implementations are usually responsible for controlling terminal hardware, including establishing modem sessions. `mingetty` is used on Red Hat Linux to control VGA console logins, but it has no options for manipulating a serial port. Some common `getty` implementations include `mgetty`, `agetty`, and `uugetty`. However, most of these know nothing about PPP network sessions.

Two software components will solve these problems: `mgetty` and `pppd`. `mgetty` can be used to control the serial lines and answer the modems. `mgetty` uses the `exec()` system call to spawn `pppd` if it detects the start of a PPP session (which is a unique feature of the `mgetty` implementation). `pppd` then authenticates the user (using either the system password database, or its own database of valid users), and then starts a network connection if access is granted.

Configuring mgetty

`mgetty` is not installed by default in Red Hat Linux. It must be explicitly loaded after installation has completed. This can be done by issuing the following command from the `RedHat/RPMS` directory of a Red Hat Linux installation tree (which is on the CD-ROM included with this text):

rpm -Uvh mgetty-1.1.14-8.i386.rpm

The above command will install the `mgetty` binary and associated configuration and documentation files. For the most common PPP server configuration, modify the file `/etc/mgetty+sendfax/mgetty.config` so that the top two lines read:

```
speed 115200
modem-type data
rings 1
```

If you want to enable fax transmissions with `mgetty`, you might want to use different options in this file. If so, consult the documentation at *http://www.leo.org/~doering/mgetty/mgetty_toc.html* for further information. (Additional RPM components are required.)

You should also modify the file `/etc/mgetty+sendfax/login.config` so that it contains the line:

/AutoPPP/ -   a_ppp   /usr/sbin/pppd 115200

There will be another commented `AutoPPP` line that passes many more options to `pppd`. It is more convenient to configure these switches in `/etc/ppp/options` (so `ps aux` listings remain uncluttered), so these options are removed here.

When `mgetty` is running, it places log files in `/var/log`. You may want to either clean them out manually from time to time, or put the log files on automatic rotation (i.e., removing the older files).

Options in /etc/ppp

After you have installed `mgetty`, run the following command to configure your `/etc/ppp/pap-secrets` file to allow PAM logins:

echo '* * "" *' >> /etc/ppp/pap-secrets

At this point, IP addresses must be assigned to each of the modem lines that will be providing PPP services. These IP addresses will be recorded in the `/etc/ppp/options*` files.

Your `/etc/ppp/options` file contains control parameters for all `pppd` sessions that run on your system. It should contain the following information:

```
auth
login
modem
crtscts
lock
proxyarp
ms-dns x.x.x.x
ms-dns y.y.y.y
```

All of these options are discussed in the `pppd` man page, but below is a quick synopsis:

auth
Force the remote PPP system to authenticate.

login
Authenticate against the system password database (`/etc/password`, `/etc/shadow` or whatever else PAM is configured to use), and record the session in the `wtmp` file.

proxyarp
Configure the Ethernet card to respond to ARP requests for the IP address of the remote PPP system.

ms-dns x.x.x.x
Pass the IP address of a DNS server to the client. This works for Windows clients only. You should have no more than two of these entries in the options file. This option won't work unless your `pppd` was compiled with `-DUSE_MS_DNS`, but it makes the configuration of the client *much* easier.

Each serial device that will support dialup PPP must have a unique options file. If you plan to attach a modem to `/dev/ttyS1` (DOS COM1:), the file `/etc/ppp/options.ttyS1` will contain parameters specific to that modem. For example, a PPP server at IP address 1.2.3.1 might allocate 1.2.3.4 as the IP address for the PPP dialup. This configuration would require the file `/etc/ppp/options.ttyS1` to contain the single line:

```
1.2.3.1:1.2.3.4
```

The first parameter above is the IP address of the dialup server. The second parameter is the IP assigned for that line. Each serial line must have a different IP address.

We should note that the address 1.2.3.4 is not really a Class C Internet address (it is a Class A address). We are using it in the context of a Class C to make the meaning clear. To emphasize, *neither the network 1.2.3 nor any derivative of it should ever be used on the Internet.*

The `proxyarp` option listed above deserves greater attention. If `proxyarp` is excluded, the serial devices will be able to transmit network data to the server, but they will not be able to communicate with any other machine. (The `proxyarp` option configures the Ethernet devices to answer ARP requests for the PPP IP addresses.) Specific dial-up lines that are intended for local access only might require that the `proxyarp` parameter be moved out of `/etc/ppp/options` and into the device-specific options files for the lines that will receive total network access.

In addition to `proxyarp`, one other step is required to allow the PPP device to exchange data with the LAN device: forwarding of packets across the networking interfaces must be enabled. To accomplish this, a modification must be made to the `/etc/sysconfig/network` file. If forwarding is disabled (which is the default), a line in the file reads:

```
FORWARD_IPV4=false
```

To enable forwarding, change the line to:

```
FORWARD_IPV4=true
```

The instructions in this file are executed at boot time only. To enable forwarding without rebooting the system, enter the command:

echo 1 > /proc/sys/net/ipv4/ip_forward

If no IP addresses are available to allocate for serial devices, consider using bogus IP addresses in the 192.168.x.x range, and use proxy software, such as the free TIS FireWall ToolKit discussed in Chapter 4. Normally, `proxyarp` cannot be used in such a situation. Information on IP Masquerade (discussed in the firewall section of this chapter) might also be helpful.

Adding mgetty to /etc/inittab

Each serial line will be controlled by an entry in `/etc/inittab`. An entry for `ttyS1` might look like:

```
S1:345:respawn:/sbin/mgetty ttyS1
```

Similar lines must be added describing each serial device on the system that is participating in the `mgetty/pppd` arrangement.

After the changes to `/etc/inittab` are complete, the Linux system must be rebooted, or the shell command **init q** must be entered while logged in as root. Lights on any external modems will flash.

Inactive modems can be reinitialized at any time by entering the command **killall mgetty**. (Be cautious of this command on non-Red Hat systems.)

Additional Logging Information

Most system services send activity messages to the `syslog` daemon. The `syslog` daemon records most of this information in `/var/log/messages`. Mail system log data goes to `/var/log/maillog`. Other logging locations can be found by examining `/etc/syslog.conf`.

It is relatively simple to copy this logging information to an inactive virtual console so that it can be examined in real time. To do so, enter the following command:

echo '*.* /dev/tty9' >> /etc/syslog.conf

Then reboot the system or send a HUP signal to the `syslog` daemon (i.e., **kill –HUP <pid>**).

If the CTRL-ALT-F9 keys are pressed simultaneously, virtual console number nine should come into view. It should contain the complete output of the `syslog` daemon. Any PPP activity should be immediately logged to this screen, as well as activity from other major system services (such as DHCP, the mail transport utilities, DNS, etc.).

To return to the login on virtual console number one, press CTRL-ALT-F1. To return to the XWindows session (if one is running), press CTRL-ALT-F7.

04

Firewalls

One extremely common use for Linux systems is the defense of critical computer networks and data. The power of the TCP/IP protocol is its openness and ubiquity. Unfortunately, these advantages can become great drawbacks when a computer network is attacked by a hostile intruder.

When a computer is configured in such a way that its primary function is the defense of a TCP/IP network, it is commonly called an Internet *firewall,* or sometimes a *bastion host.* There are two main firewall designs commonly in use on Linux. One is the *proxy* approach, where access to external resources can only be obtained by contacting a specific host that acts as an intermediary (or proxy). The other method involves the use of the Linux kernel as a *filtering router.* In this second approach, the kernel will simply forward, modify, or discard network data based upon a set of rules defined by the administrator.

It is far easier to maintain internal hosts where Linux is used as a filtering router. The use of a proxy can complicate the configuration of internal hosts enormously. The two techniques can be mingled to some extent, but proxies will always introduce additional layers of complexity.

This chapter assumes that one or more networking interfaces are properly configured and that routes to these interfaces are defined. A proxy firewall might be designed to use a single network interface in conjunction with blocking routers, but a firewall relying upon IP forwarding or masquerading will require at least two network interfaces. Information on network configuration can be found elsewhere in this text.

While a safe and efficient Linux firewall can be configured on a modest computer (an 80386-based system could conceivably be used), a high-utilization environment might benefit from more powerful hardware. In such a case, ISA-based network cards should be eschewed, as well as any cards based upon an NE2000 chipset. Currently, two very popular PCI Ethernet designs are the Tulip chipset (i.e., the 21040 and 21140 Ethernet chipsets designed by Digital Equipment Corporation), and the 3Com 905 series. Some cards based upon the 21140 Tulip design are very inexpensive and implement 100BaseT fast Ethernet. Either design is usually easy to configure, which is why they are mentioned here.

Dynamic Host Configuration Protocol (DHCP) can also play an extremely productive role in a protected network. DHCP should be omitted from a firewall design only for sound reasons, because the benefits it extends in centralized administration can dramatically reduce the complexity of a network. See "DHCP" on page 72 for more information.

Several UNIX security issues also have great bearing upon proper firewall design. You should pay close attention to the `inetd`—Internet *super server* daemon. Its configuration file, `/etc/inetd.conf`, should be examined carefully, and services that are not required should be removed. In particular, the `shell` and `login` services should be eliminated unless their presence is absolutely necessary. Serious consideration should also be given to the removal of `telnet` and `ftp` services, especially if `ssh` will be used. All other services should be studied and, if possible, removed.

Fictitious IP Addresses

It is occasionally necessary to *make up* IP addresses for positions on internal networks—especially as real Internet IP addresses become more difficult to obtain. Should this practice be necessary, the *synthetic* addresses should be selected from those shown in Table 4.1.

Table 4.1 *Private IP address ranges.*

Class	Network
A	10.0.0.0
B	172.16.0.0 through 172.31.0.0
C	192.168.0.0 through 192.168.255.0

These addresses are reserved for private use. They will not be routed over the Internet.

Kernel IP Forward and Masquerade Rules

Before a routing firewall can be configured on a Linux system, the kernel must be instructed to forward packets (i.e., on behalf of other systems) across the network interfaces. One way to accomplish this is with the `netcfg` command, run under XWindows. The option to enable forwarding is shown in Figure 4.1 on page 96.

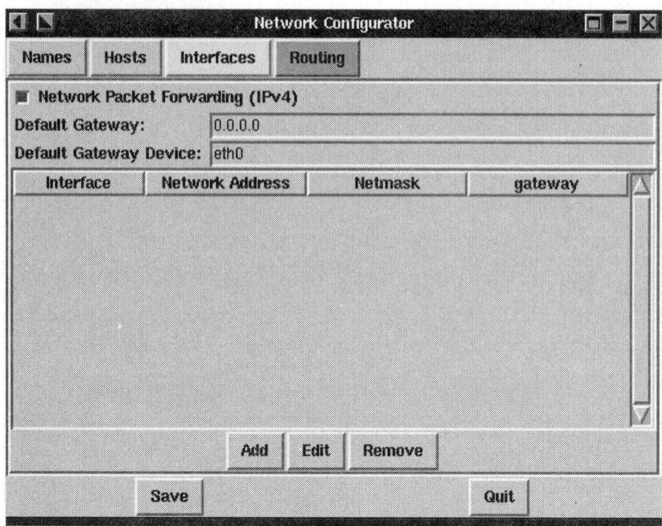

Figure 4.1 *The network configuration utility.*

This option does not take effect until the system is rebooted. While it may seem complex, it involves modifying only a single line in the `/etc/sysconfig/network` file. After the option is set, there will be an entry of the form:

```
FORWARD_IPV4=true
```

If an entry of *false* is present, it can be manually changed to *true* without the inconvenience of starting XWindows. However, the `/etc/sysconfig/network` file merely runs the following command, which enables forwarding across the network interfaces in the kernel, at boot time:

echo 1 > /proc/sys/net/ipv4/ip_forward

This command can be run at any time to enable packet forwarding. Conversely, if a "0" is echoed onto the file, packet forwarding will be disabled immediately.

A similar option to enable packet forwarding is available in the `linuxconf` utility.

Setting this option will transform Linux into a simple router. However, the normal (and safest) way to configure a firewall is to deny all packet forwarding by default, then allow only explicit types of routes to pass. The `ipchains` administration utility is used to make such changes. To change the default routing behavior to deny routing, for example, enter the command (if the ipchains RPM is installed):

ipchains -P forward DENY

Older Linux kernels use a different utility called `ipfwadm` to administer the kernel firewall resources. This utility was replaced with `ipchains` in the Linux 2.2 kernel because of several design deficiencies. Red Hat Linux 6.0 comes with a wrapper script called `ipfwadm-wrapper` which allows the older syntax to be used, as shown here:

ipfwadm-wrapper -F -p deny

Use the `ipfwadm-wrapper` script if the firewall controls must remain compatible with a system running an older version of the Linux kernel (such as Red Hat Linux 5.2 or below). However, `ipchains` and `ipfwadm-wrapper` cannot be mixed; use one or the other.

The following command can be used to flush all routing rules that might remain in the kernel, ensuring that all network traffic returns to the default behavior (which is to deny forwarding):

ipchains –F

The syntax to flush routing rules for `ipfwadm` is slightly different (the forwarding, input, output and accounting rules must be flushed separately):

ipfwadm-wrapper -F -f
ipfwadm-wrapper -I -f
ipfwadm-wrapper -O -f
ipfwadm-wrapper -A -f

At this point, individual acceptable routes can be added to the kernel. For example, the following command allows all hosts to access a web server on the host 1.2.3.4:

ipchains -A forward -s 0.0.0.0/0 -p TCP -d 1.2.3.4/32 http -j ACCEPT -b

A description of options to the previous command is in order:

`-A forward`

This option specifies that a rule should be added to the *forward* chain. There are three predefined chains: *input, output,* and *forward.* Additional chains can be created, but the procedure is not documented in this text.

`-s 0.0.0.0/0`

The `-s` option denotes a packet source. The network address of `0.0.0.0/0` is a special nomenclature indicating that the packet can have an origin of any IP address. If the `-s` option is omitted, `0.0.0.0/0` will be assumed.

`-p TCP`

Packets using the TCP protocol, and only those packets, will be passed. User Datagram Protocol (UDP) or Internet Control Message Protocol (ICMP) packets will be rejected.

`-d 1.2.3.4/32`

The `-d` option indicates a destination. The `1.2.3.4/32` is a fully-qualified Internet address (i.e., it represents a single host). A complete network can be specified for either source or destination by indicating the number of bits in the netmask. For example, a `1.2.3.0/24` would allow web traffic over the entire 1.2.3 Class C network. We should note that the address 1.2.3.4 is not really a Class C Internet address (it is really a Class A address). We are using it in the context of a Class C to make the meaning clear. To emphasize, neither the network 1.2.3 nor any derivative of it should ever be used on the Internet.

`http`

This is the name of a protocol from `/etc/services`. The numerical port number may also be used.

`-j ACCEPT`

The argument to the `-j` parameter is the desired target action for packets matching the previous parameters. In this case, the packet is accepted for forwarding. The allowable target actions are: `ACCEPT`, `DENY`, `MASQ`, `REDIRECT`, `REJECT`, and `RETURN`. `DENY` and `REJECT` are similar, but `REJECT` generates an ICMP destination unreachable message, while `DENY` discards the packet with no further action. `MASQ` allows one computer to masquerade as another. `REDIRECT` allows packets destined for a remote machine to be received locally (which can be useful for transparent proxies). `RETURN` indicates that the default chain policy should be used for this rule.

`-b`

The `-b` parameter indicates that the rule is bi-directional. This will allow packets to pass to and from either host. This behavior can also be achieved by adding the rule twice, reversing the source and destination for the second rule. The `-b` option in truth really inserts two rules. If an `ipchains -L` is issued to list the contents of the chains, rules for both forward and reverse will be observed.

The `ipfwadm` syntax is slightly different:

ipfwadm -F -a accept -P tcp -S 0.0.0.0/0 -D 1.2.3.4/32 http -b -o

The options used in this command are explained below.

`-F`

This argument indicates that the command will affect the forwarding rules (as opposed to input, output, or accounting rules).

`-S 0.0.0.0/0`

The `-S` option denotes a packet source. The network address of `0.0.0.0/0` is a special nomenclature indicating that the packet can have any origin.

`-D 1.2.3.4/32`

The `-D` option indicates a destination. The `1.2.3.4/32` is a fully-qualified Internet address. A complete network can be specified for either source or destination by indicating the number of bits in the netmask. For example, a `1.2.3.0/24` would allow web traffic over the entire 1.2.3 Class C network.

`http`

This is the name of a protocol from `/etc/services`. The numerical port number may also be used.

`-b`

This argument indicates that the traffic is bi-directional, and the reverse of the rule is also allowed.

`-o`

Logging of matching packets to `/var/log/messages` is activated by this option.

A list of rules similar to the ones above can be entered into the Linux kernel. This list is parsed from the top down. If two contradictory commands are entered, or if a packet matches several rules, the rule entered first will determine the packet's fate. Using commands of this form, holes can be *punched* through the bastion host, opening paths for desired services, but blocking potentially threatening traffic.

If the network on either side of this firewall is connected to the Internet, hosts on *both* sides must have valid Internet IP addresses. There is a method, however, to use synthetic network addresses on the side of the network not directly connected to the Internet. This has the valuable side-effect of conserving Internet IP addresses—only a single such *real* address will be required. The technique is called *IP masquerading,* and an example follows:

```
ipchains -P forward DENY
ipchains -F
ipchains -A forward -j MASQ -s 192.168.1.0/24 -d 0.0.0.0/0
```

The `ipfwadm` syntax follows:

```
ipfwadm-wrapper -F -p deny
ipfwadm-wrapper -F -f
ipfwadm-wrapper -I -f
ipfwadm-wrapper -O -f
ipfwadm-wrapper -A -f
ipfwadm-wrapper -F -a m -S 192.168.1.0/24 -D 0.0.0.0/0
```

Masquerading specifically requires that routing be disabled by default. This is accomplished by the first command in the list above. The last call to `ipchains` (or `ipfwadm`) establishes a masquerading rule.

In this case, it is assumed that one of the network interfaces has an address on the 192.168.1 Class C network. Hosts on this network should be configured to use the *masquerade server* network interface IP address as their default gateway.

Packets traveling through a masquerading route are usually rewritten so that their source network addresses are the same as the IP address of the network interface that lies on the default route of the masquerade server (the source port is also changed). The kernel will keep track of all masqueraded connections. When a remote server replies to the masquerade server, the kernel rewrites the return packet with the original (synthetic) IP address and port number, then forwards the packet onto the internal network. External hosts think the firewall is initiating all traffic, but internal hosts never know the difference.

Masquerade works for most protocols, but not all. FTP (in active mode) specifically ceases to function when it runs behind such a network. Masquerade servers for some of these protocols, however, are available as kernel modules. The following commands load all the additional available masquerade protocols:

```
depmod -a
modprobe ip_masq_autofw
modprobe ip_masq_cuseeme
modprobe ip_masq_ftp
modprobe ip_masq_irc
modprobe ip_masq_mfw
modprobe ip_masq_portfw
modprobe ip_masq_quake
modprobe ip_masq_raudio
modprobe ip_masq_user
modprobe ip_masq_vdolive
```

Obviously, only the masquerade modules that are required should be loaded. The others should be omitted. Loading additional kernel modules makes the kernel larger, and can open avenues for attack.

If a network application ceases to function when placed behind a masquerade server, it is probably creating a server on some port. If the server is on a random port (and not a well-defined port), the odds are slim that the application will work easily with masquerade. The use of proxies to access servers on synthetic networks is discussed in the next section.

Masquerade rules can co-exist with other forward rules. They can also apply to real Internet IP addresses. In the example below, all external hosts are allowed to access web and email services on the 1.2.3 network, but all other traffic originating from hosts in 1.2.3 is masqueraded:

```
ipchains -P forward DENY
ipchains -F
ipchains -A forward -s 0.0.0.0/0 -p TCP -d 1.2.3.0/24 http -j ACCEPT -b
ipchains -A forward -s 0.0.0.0/0 -p TCP -d 1.2.3.0/24 smtp -j ACCEPT -b
ipchains -A forward -j MASQ -s 1.2.3.0/24 -d 0.0.0.0/0
```

The `ipfwadm` version follows:

```
ipfwadm -F -p deny
ipfwadm -F -f
ipfwadm -I -f
ipfwadm -O -f
ipfwadm -A -f
ipfwadm -F -a accept -P tcp -S 0.0.0.0/0 -D 1.2.3.0/24 http -b
ipfwadm -F -a accept -P tcp -S 0.0.0.0/0 -D 1.2.3.0/24 smtp -b
ipfwadm -F -a m -S 1.2.3.0/24 -D 0.0.0.0/0
```

This will open only the HTTP and SMTP ports on the servers residing within the internal network; all other ports will be blocked. Connections on these ports will use the real IP addresses of the internal hosts. Any other outgoing communication from the internal network will be masqueraded.

Please note that the order of the last three commands is important. The sequence could be restated in the following manner:

```
ipchains -A forward -j MASQ -s 1.2.3.0/24 -d 0.0.0.0/0
ipchains -A forward -s 0.0.0.0/0 -p TCP -d 1.2.3.0/24 http -j ACCEPT -b
ipchains -A forward -s 0.0.0.0/0 -p TCP -d 1.2.3.0/24 smtp -j ACCEPT -b
```

Or, with the older syntax:

```
ipfwadm -F -a m -S 1.2.3.0/24 -D 0.0.0.0/0
ipfwadm -F -a accept -P tcp -S 0.0.0.0/0 -D 1.2.3.0/24 http -b
ipfwadm -F -a accept -P tcp -S 0.0.0.0/0 -D 1.2.3.0/24 smtp -b
```

This sequence, however, would never allow web or email traffic to get through. The rules are parsed top-down, so the connection would always be masqueraded.

It might also be important to prevent *IP spoofing* (i.e., when a host misrepresents its IP address to gain access to something which is normally denied). If so, there is a simple configuration directive for the kernel that enables *Source Address Verification.* To set up source address verification, and prevent spoofing, place the shell script fragment found in Listing 4.1 in a startup file that is executed after the networking devices are brought up.

Listing 4.1 *Source address verification script.*

```
# This is the best method: turn on Source Address
# Verification and get spoof protection on all
# current and future interfaces.

if [ -e /proc/sys/net/ipv4/conf/all/rp_filter ]; then
  echo -n "Setting up IP spoofing protection..."
   for f in /proc/sys/net/ipv4/conf/*/rp_filter; do
      echo 1 > $f
   done
   echo "done."
else
   echo PROBLEMS SETTING UP IP SPOOFING PROTECTION. BE WORRIED.
   echo "CONTROL-D will exit from this shell and continue system startup."
   echo
   # Start a single user shell on the console
   /sbin/sulogin $CONSOLE
fi
```

As a general rule, only machines running as servers should be given real Internet IP addresses; hosts that are mainly used as clients should be masqueraded if the client applications will allow it.

A complete example of a simple masquerade integrated with a DHCP configuration is presented in the "DHCP" section on page 72.

Extensive information on Linux firewall design is available in the IPCHAINS-HOWTO directory (which can be found on the CD-ROM included with this text, or at *ftp://tsx-11.mit.edu/pub/linux/docs/HOWTO*).

As a final point, it should be stressed that masquerading is not a security feature alone. Masquerading can be used in situations where a single IP address must be used to provide Internet service for several hosts. For example, it is commonly used with dialup PPP connections.

tcpd

Red Hat Linux 6.0 includes a simple utility for controlling access to services by host or by network address: `tcpd`. It provides a simple, but powerful, mechanism for selectively applying access restrictions.

The two main configuration files for `tcpd` are the `/etc/hosts.deny` and `/etc/hosts.allow` files. The only place where the `tcpd` program is invoked is in the `/etc/inetd.conf` file (`tcpd` should never be called from the command line).

If some Linux host has an `/etc/hosts.deny` file of the following form:

```
in.telnetd: ALL except 1.2.3.4
```

then Telnet access will be disabled on this Linux host from all sites except the 1.2.3.4 host. Similar entries will disable FTP and the Berkeley r-utilities:

```
in.ftpd: ALL except 1.2.3.4
in.rshd: ALL except 1.2.3.4
in.rlogind: ALL except 1.2.3.4
```

As another option, *all* available protocols controlled by `tcpd` can be disabled with an entry of the following form:

```
ALL: ALL EXCEPT 1.2.3.0/255.255.255.0, \
  5.6.7. \
  .allowed.com \
  .permitted.org
```

Note the addresses specified in the above entry. A network address with a full netmask can be specified, or a matching domain name can be used (which will require reverse lookups). Additional information on the `/etc/hosts.deny` file and its syntax can be obtained by entering the command **man 5 hosts_access** at a shell prompt.

A complete denial of access to all local services is the safest choice in the design of a firewall. Should this not be practical, a `tcpd` configuration such as the one above should deny access to all but a few hosts.

Obviously, this utility does not control traffic that is routed between the network interfaces on a firewall in its normal configuration; `tcpd` protects only local services. It is mentioned here only to further ensure the security of the bastion host.

Determining exactly what `tcpd` controls is quite simple. For example, the `telnet` configuration entry in `/etc/inetd.conf` is of the following form:

```
telnet stream  tcp  nowait  root  /usr/sbin/tcpd  in.telnetd
```

Any service entry in `/etc/identd.conf` containing a reference to `tcpd` (similar to the one above) will be controlled by `tcpd`. Please note that there are a number of such services that are not controlled by `inetd`, including SMTP, httpd, Postgres, and many others.

The TIS Firewall Toolkit

The FireWall ToolKit (FWTK) from Trusted Information Systems (TIS) is a free package containing a set of small programs that can be used for a variety of network functions, including firewall design.

If two hosts communicate across a *routing* firewall, it should not be necessary for either host to be aware of the mechanics of the connection. They generate packets for one another that are checked (and perhaps slightly modified) by the firewall, but the hosts would be otherwise oblivious to the presence of the bastion host.

A *proxy* firewall, on the other hand, normally requires that at least one of the pair of hosts be aware of the firewall's location and the methods used to access it.

The FWTK includes small programs that implement proxies for several types of services within the TCP/IP suite, including FTP, Telnet, HTTP (web), SMTP, Berkeley rlogin, and X. There is also a generic proxy which is extremely useful as a part of firewall design and UNIX administration in general.

Unfortunately, the TIS FWTK is not included with Red Hat Linux. While it is open source, its licensing agreement is somewhat more restrictive than the GNU Public License (GPL); certain types of commercial use are restricted. The FWTK can be obtained from *http://www.fwtk.org,* but do not download the product unless you can abide by the license.

Network Associates (who recently acquired Trusted Information Systems) also sells a commercial firewall called Gauntlet. Gauntlet is very powerful; it contains all the proxy features of the FWTK—the same packet masquerading features as the Linux kernel—plus a number of advanced features and a graphical administration interface. It is not difficult to migrate from the FWTK to Gauntlet. However, Gauntlet does not as yet run on Red Hat Linux, so a change in platform would be required.

The latest version of the FWTK (at the time this text was prepared) is `fwtk2.1.tar.Z`. By default, the proxy applications and a control file are installed in `/usr/local/etc` (the directory will be created if it does not exist).

There is a problem with the `crypt()` library function when building the FWTK on Red Hat Linux. Run the following commands as root to overcome this problem and then compile and install the package:

```
tar xvzf fwtk2.1.tar.gz
cd fwtk
sed 's/^AUXLIB=.*/AUXLIB= -lcrypt/
  s/^COPT=.*/COPT= -O2 $(DEFINES) -I\/usr\/include\/db1/
  s/^LDFL=.*/LDFL= -s -static/' Makefile.config.linux > Makefile.config
make
make install
```

Please note that the above commands enable optimization and stripping (and disable debugging) of the toolkit components in addition to setting the usage of the `crypt` library. This is not the default build environment for the kit. Review `Makefile.config.linux` for additional build configuration details.

These are some of the files that will be installed in `/usr/local/etc`:

`netperm-table`
: This is the master configuration file for the toolkit.

`ftp-gw`
: This is the FTP proxy.

`http-gw`
: This is the HTTP (web) proxy. It can be configured to block Java and JavaScript, should it be necessary. It can also route web requests to multiple hosts, depending upon the form of the URL.

`netacl`
: This is a utility similar to `tcpd`. It is somewhat more flexible in that it can execute different programs depending upon the origin of the network connection.

`plug-gw`
: This is the generic proxy. It can allow connections to and from arbitrary TCP ports.

`rlogin-gw`
: This is the Berkeley rlogin proxy.

`tn-gw`
: This is the telnet proxy.

`x-gw`
: This is the proxy for XWindows applications. It will only be built if the XWindows development libraries and include files were installed.

Each proxy application available with the FWTK can be configured to restrict the set of hosts that are allowed to access the proxy, the possible destinations that might be requested, or both. While the behavior of the proxies is configured with `netperm-table`, their invocation is *usually* controlled through `/etc/inetd.conf`. Below is an entry in this file that would configure the telnet proxy:

```
telnet stream tcp nowait.1024 root /usr/local/etc/netacl tn-gw
```

A particular point of interest is the parameter to `nowait` in the line above. `inetd` is configured by default to allow 40 invocations of any particular service over a 60-second period. Should this limit be exceeded, the service will be shut down for a time (`inetd` will cease forking it), and a note of the fact will be made to `/var/log/messages`. The above `1024` parameter to `nowait` increases this limit. This parameter is extremely important on busy firewalls.

Continuing the example configuration of a telnet proxy, the following lines in `netperm-table` will allow use of the proxy:

```
netacl-tn-gw:  permit-hosts * -exec /usr/local/etc/tn-gw
tn-gw:         permit-hosts * -passok -xok
```

Please note that this new configuration will not be activated until `inetd` has been refreshed. This can be accomplished by either rebooting the system or sending the HUP signal to the daemon. Conversely, there is no need to refresh `inetd` or any other process when the `netperm-table` file changes. This is because the proxies are re-spawned each time they are invoked. They scan `netperm-table` at that time. `inetd`, on the other hand, only reads its configuration file when it is started up or sent a HUP.

The `netperm-table` itself has limitations. The maximum line length allowed in this file varies, depending upon the operating system, but usually it is 1,024 characters. Also, no method is provided for continuing lines (e.g., a "\" to continue on the next line). Strict observance of these rules will allow your netperm-table to be easily ported.

Once inetd has been refreshed, attempts to telnet to the bastion host will be greeted with the following prompt:

```
tn-gw->
```

There are only a few options available at the proxy prompt. The most useful option opens a connection to another host:

```
tn-gw-> connect another.host.com
Trying 1.2.3.4 port 23...
Connected to another.host.com.
login:
```

This firewall configuration is not very secure, as it permits anyone to initiate connections anywhere. Restricting access, however, is straightforward:

```
netacl-tn-gw: permit-hosts 1.2.3.* 192.168.1.* -exec /usr/local/etc/tn-gw
tn-gw: permit-hosts 1.2.3.* 192.168.1.* -passok -xok -dest { 1.2.3.4
*.remotehost.com }
```

While it may appear redundant to list the allowed hosts twice (once for netacl, and once for tn-gw), it is safer to do so in case netacl is removed from /etc/inetd.conf at some later date. netacl in this case is somewhat superfluous. It can be configured, however, to run multiple server binaries on a connection based on the remote IP address—so its use is suggested. Note also that line breaks, such as the one appearing for tn-gw, are not allowed, but is used here for clarity.

Note that it is possible to allow Telnet connections into the bastion host, *but it is extremely inadvisable to do so*. If shell connections into the firewall are required, they should be done with an encrypted protocol such as ssh and careful access control.

Finally, make sure that the proxy can bridge the firewall in both directions. It should allow general connections out of the protected network(s) but, at the same time, allow restricted access inside.

The FTP proxy is somewhat similar in operation to tn-gw, though it is not normally configured with netacl. Following is a line that might be used in /etc/inetd.conf to configure it:

```
ftp stream tcp nowait.1024  root usr/local/etc/ftp-gw ftp-gw
```

A corresponding entry in `netperm-table` to permit maximum access would be:

```
ftp-gw: permit-hosts *
```

For a more restricted level of access, the entry might be:

```
ftp-gw: permit-hosts 1.2.3.* 192.168.1.* -dest { 1.2.3.4 *.remotehost.com }
```

While the FTP proxy is rather simple to configure, it can be frighteningly confusing to use. Consider the FTP session in Listing 4.2 that passes through the proxy.

Listing 4.2 *A session with the FTP proxy.*

```
$ ftp bastion
Connected to bastion.
220 bastion FTP proxy (Version V2.1) ready.
Name (bastion:root): ftp@ftp.redhat.com
331-(----GATEWAY CONNECTED TO ftp.redhat.com----)
331-(220 ProFTPD 1.2.0prel Server (ProFTPD) [gonzales.redhat.com])
331 Anonymous login ok, send your complete e-mail address as password.
Password:
230-            Red Hat Software -- FTP Site

        For the following sites, use the appropriate server:

        Red Hat Linux Updates    - ftp://updates.redhat.com
        Red Hat Rawhide          - ftp://rawhide.redhat.com

        Red Hat Contrib Net      - ftp://developer.redhat.com
        For Incoming RHCN RPMS   - ftp://in-rhcn.redhat.com

        User Contributed RPMS    - ftp://contrib.redhat.com
        To Upload Incoming RPMS  - ftp://incoming.redhat.com
230 Anonymous access granted, restrictions apply.
Remote system type is UNIX.
Using binary mode to transfer files.
ftp ls -l
200 PORT command successful.
150 Opening ASCII mode data connection for file list.
total 0
-rw-r--r--   1 root     root          4050 Nov 18 16:30 MIRRORS.html
drwxr-xr-x   3 root     root          1024 Nov 15 04:03 XBF
drwxr-xr-x   3 root     root          1024 Nov 15 04:03 XFCom
drwxr-xr-x  10 dledford dledford      1024 Dec  8 11:46 aic
drwxr-xr-x  31 root     root          1024 Dec  1 10:06 home
drwxr-xr-x   6 jbj      jbj           1024 Nov 14 04:03 large-fd
```

```
-rw-r--r--    1 root     root        2951395 Dec  9 04:07 ls-lR
-rw-r--r--    1 root     root         421475 Dec  9 04:07 ls-lR.gz
lrwxrwxrwx    1 root     root              1 Oct 21 10:53 pub - .
drwxr-xr-x   10 root     root           1024 Nov 14 04:05 redhat
drwxr-xr-x    7 root     root           1024 Nov 14 04:13 sound
drwx--x--x    2 root     root           1024 Nov 14 04:13 sybase
226 Transfer complete.
ftp get MIRRORS.html
local: MIRRORS.html remote: MIRRORS.html
200 PORT command successful.
150 Opening BINARY mode data connection for MIRRORS.html (4050 bytes).
226 Transfer complete.
4050 bytes received in 1.24 secs (3.2 Kbytes/sec)
ftp quit
221 Goodbye.
```

After a connection is established to the proxy, the login name is specified as `user@remotehost`. The proxy then initiates an FTP session with the remote server. Though this step as shown above may seem straightforward, this manipulation of the hostname/username can be extremely difficult on complex GUI FTP clients. It is also possible to pass through multiple `ftp-gw` servers, but the semantics in such a case are torturous.

The HTTP proxy has many features that make it especially powerful. Following is a line from `/etc/inetd.conf` which will allow it to run:

```
http stream tcp nowait.1024 root /usr/local/etc/http-gw http-gw
```

A netperm-table entry to allow access might be:

```
http-gw:  permit-hosts *
```

The web browser must still be configured to use the proxy. Figure 4.2 shows the relevant dialog boxes from Netscape Communicator that configure use of the proxy.

In the proxy configuration dialog box shown in Figure 4.3, insert the hostname or the IP address of the proxy. `http-gw` can also be used as the FTP and Gopher proxy. (Do not attempt to use `ftp-gw` here.)

The proxy can restrict the active content that it delivers to the browser as in the example shown here:

```
http-gw:  permit-hosts * -nojava -nojavascript -noactivex
```

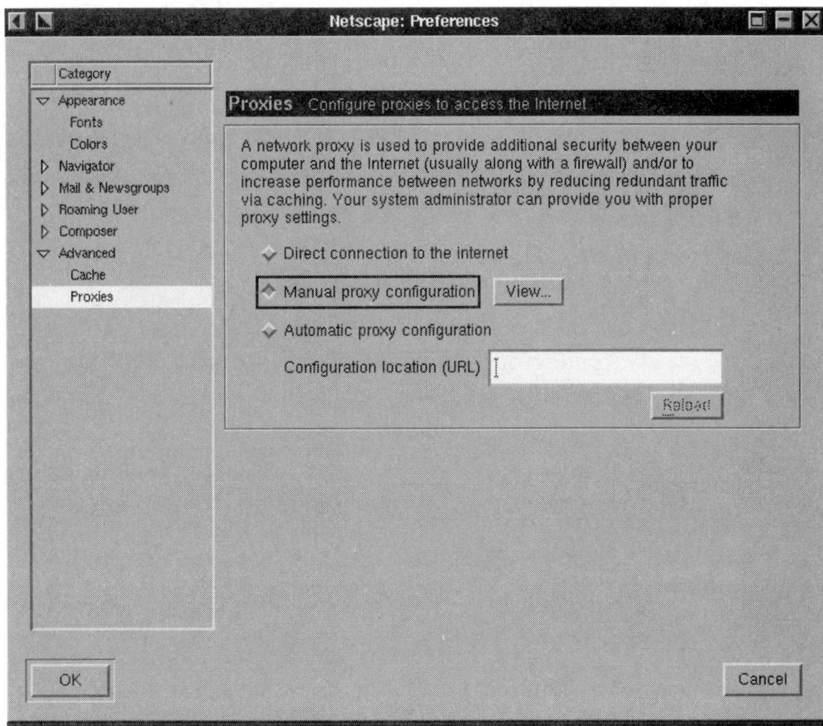

Figure 4.2 *Netscape proxy preferences.*

Figure 4.3 *Netscape proxy configuration.*

The HTTP proxy also can direct to various servers depending on the form of the URL:

```
http-gw: forward /Home* -protocol http -tohost www.tis.com
http-gw: forward /pub/* -protocol ftp -tohost ftp.uu.net
```

Perhaps the most flexible proxy is `plug-gw`. It allows the redirection of arbitrary TCP ports, and has great potential use beyond that of a firewall. For example:

```
pop-3 stream tcp nowait.1024 root /usr/local/etc/plug-gw plug-gw pop-3
```

The above line from `/etc/inetd.conf` directs the POP mail port to be served by `plug-gw`.

```
plug-gw: port pop-3 * -plug-to mail.remotehost.com -port 110
```

This configuration directive will automatically establish a connection to a remote POP port when a connection on the local POP port is initiated.

Note that the service name (pop-3) and the port number (110) are used interchangeably in the directives above (the service names are defined in `/etc/services`). The only place where the name *must* be used is in the service definition in `/etc/inetd.conf`. The final `-port 110` above is also optional, as `plug-gw` will, by default, redirect to the same numerical port from which it originated.

Note also that either the service name or number must be passed as an argument to `plug-gw` in `/etc/inetd.conf`. The plug proxy will not work without this argument.

There are a few other important proxies that are not covered here (Berkeley `rlogin`, `x-gw`, and `smap`), but their configuration is either similar enough to the previously discussed proxies to be trivial, or their configuration is complex enough to be beyond the scope of this text.

These proxies can also be configured as stand-alone applications, running outside of `inetd`. This configuration is not covered here.

The use of a proxy firewall (over a routing solution) has both advantages and drawbacks. A great advantage is the increased ability to filter both the data and the origin/destination. A tremendous drawback is the responsibility placed upon those behind the firewall to understand the architecture of the proxy.

Do not imagine, however, that proxy firewall components cannot coexist with route filtering. In fact, proxies are an ideal method for accessing network services within a masqueraded network (which would otherwise be inaccessible to the Internet at large). A well-balanced firewall will combine all of these techniques while preserving security concerns for the good of the network.

SSH

The SSH protocol and the suite of programs that implement it provide secure, encrypted network communication channels between hosts on a TCP/IP network. The primary focus of SSH is UNIX, but versions for Microsoft Windows, VMS, and OS/2 are also available.

Because SSH uses strong encryption technology, its distribution in many countries is complicated by legal restrictions. For example, its use is altogether forbidden in France, Russia, Iraq, and Pakistan and, once SSH has been brought into the United States, it cannot then leave the country in any form. Do not be overzealous to make use of this application. Understand and obey your nation's laws governing encryption before you even consider installing it.

The Internet web page for SSH is *http://www.ssh.fi.* (the company is based in Finland). Copies of SSH are available there, both for download and for purchase.

Please note that the later versions of SSH (2.0 and above) are free only for non-commercial use. If you intend to use it in any way that is connected with profit, you must pay a licensing fee.

There can be some confusion regarding different versions of SSH. A major rewrite of the software has recently occurred, and the current release of SSH at the time this text was prepared was 2.0.11. Many installations of SSH1, however, are still in use (even though there are bugs and security risks in the older versions). What is more problematic is that SSH1 clients will not work with SSH2 servers, so the major version numbers of the client and server SSH versions must match. If you must use SSH1, use the 1.2.26 release, and apply the kerberos security patches if you intend to use kerberos.

Part of the encryption technology behind SSH is *public key cryptography* (which is also used in SSL and PGP). It is not so important to understand the mechanics of SSH, so it will only be summarized. When most people think of conventional cryptography, they imagine a single key that can be used to unlock or decipher a message. Public key cryptography relies upon not one but a pair of keys—one a public key and the other a private key. When either key is used to encrypt a message, *only the other key* will be able to decrypt it. The public key is usually given out freely to others; the private key is kept secret. When two people exchange messages, they first exchange public keys. The person sending the message encrypts it with *both* their private key and the other's public. This technique allows secure encryption to take place without exchanging the data that unlocks the encryption; a design that used only a single password could never accomplish this. SSH is actually quite careful with these sets of keys, and a section of the host/server key is actually destroyed and rebuilt once an hour to ensure that if the server equipment is seized, the keys cannot be obtained. There are several other encryption technologies that may be included with SSH, including IDEA, Triple DES, and RSA, but these technologies are mostly transparent to the user.

SSH will also transparently forward communications from remote graphical XWindow clients over the secure connection (it will automatically configure `xauth` and the `DISPLAY` environment variable). Simply run XWindows applications on the remote server, and they will appear on the local display—usually no more configuration is required than that. This is a powerful convenience for users of XWindows.

SSH is not made available in an RPM format from the main distribution site. Only the C source code is available in a tar, gzip format. Assuming release 1.2.26 of SSH has been obtained, the commands shown in Listing 4.3 can be run by root to compile and install it on Red Hat Linux 6.0.

Listing 4.3 *Building SSH.*

```
# The below call to sed could also be written as:
# sed '/^#.*UTMPX/s/^/\/\//' config.h  config.h.new
#
tar xvzf ssh-1.2.26.tar.gz
cd ssh-1.2.26
```

```
LDFLAGS="-s" CFLAGS="-O2" ./configure
sed '556d' config.h > config.h.new
mv -f config.h.new config.h
make
make install
```

This will install most everything in `/usr/local/bin`, but will put `sshd` (the server daemon) in `/usr/local/sbin` if SSH1 is being installed. At this point, the `sshd` daemon should be started. The path to `ssh` and/or `sshd` may not be in the shell search path; add the path to `/etc/profile` if this is troubling. If SSH services should be started at boot, add the commands to the system `rc` files (at least `/etc/rc.d/rc.local`).

Install the SSH software on another host that can be used as a client. If a machine will only be an SSH client, it is not necessary to run `sshd`. One might simply copy the `ssh` and `scp` binaries from the server to the client. Then, as root, enter the command:

```
ssh remotehost.com
```

where *remotehost.com* is the fully qualified host name of a host running an SSH server. SSH will prompt for the remote root password, then a UNIX shell will be opened.

SSH uses command line arguments that are similar to the Berkeley r-utilities, and actually encompasses the function of both `rsh` and `rlogin`. For example, to log in as a user other than the one originating the connection, use the syntax:

```
ssh -l luser remotehost.com
```

Replace `luser` with any valid login id on the remote host. SSH will prompt for the remote password, then open a shell. It is possible to use SSH to run a single command on a remote host, rather than opening an interactive connection. For example, enter the following:

```
ssh -l luser remotehost.com "df; ps aux"
```

The remote computer will issue a disk free space report, then generate a process list (which will run correctly only on systems that use the BSD semantics for `ps`, such as Linux), and then close the connection.

Data can be piped into and out of ssh, even if password prompting occurs. Consider the following two commands:

```
cd /home/httpd/html; tar cf - * | \
  ssh remotehost.com "cd /home/httpd/html; tar xvf -"

ssh remotehost.com "cd /usr/local/bin; tar cf - *" | \
  (cd /usr/local/bin; tar xvf -)
```

These two commands launch tar processes on the local and remote servers that exchange data through an ssh connection. The first copies the contents of the local /home/httpd/html directory to the same location on the remote server, the second copies the remote /usr/local/bin directory onto the local server.

The two previous examples are perhaps the most convenient method available to cleanly move an entire directory hierarchy between two UNIX systems. These methods should be studied and practiced.

Of course, much simpler examples of ssh piping can be used:

```
ssh remotehost.com "cat /etc/passwd" | grep luser
```

This command will print luser's password file entry from the remote host.

Files can be transferred over encrypted connections between hosts using the **scp** command, with semantics similar to Berkeley rcp. Unfortunately, the full path to the remote files must be known before the transfer can take place. For example:

```
scp /local/file.txt remotehost.com:/long/paths/make/this/hard.txt
```

The file can be copied as another user by prepending the user's login and the "@" symbol to the host name:

```
scp /local/file.txt luser@remotehost.com:/long/paths/make/this/hard.txt
```

Of course, the transfer can go the other direction:

```
scp luser@remotehost.com:/long/paths/make/this/hard.txt /local/file.txt
```

A few final points concerning this brief introduction to scp should be made. Transfers can be conducted that do not involve files on the local system at all. More than one source file can be specified if the target is a directory (just like cp). Wildcards cannot be used on remote files, as the remote file system is not available to the shell for expansion (in other words, the command **scp remote:/root/* /root** simply will not work). If the `-p` option is supplied to `scp`, it will attempt to preserve modification times, access times, and modes on the copy. (This will fail if the destination is a DOS FAT file system, for example.) The `-r` option can be applied to recursively copy an entire directory structure, but it won't preserve soft links—use the previous `tar/ssh` examples to obtain a more *high-fidelity* copy. Currently, a *secure FTP* utility is available in later versions of SSH that use `scp` and `ssh` together to browse a directory structure over an `scp` connection. Such a utility, however, is not included with the UNIX SSH 1.2.26 distribution. Please also note that, unlike `telnet` and `rlogin`, `ssh` and `scp` allow `root` to login remotely.

The `/etc/sshd_config` and `/etc/ssh_config` files control the behavior of the server and client respectively. A few useful options deserve description.

In the `/etc/sshd_config` file

AllowHosts *.permitted.org 1.2.3.* 1.?.2.3
This option will permit `ssh` connections only from the specified hosts (wildcards are permitted).

AllowGroups groupname1 groupname2
This permits connections only from those users that are registered members of the specified groups (in the `/etc/group` file).

DenyHosts *.goaway-spammer.com 5.6.7.* 8.?.9.10
This option explicitly denies `ssh` connections from the specified hosts (wildcards are permitted).

DenyGroups groupname1 groupname2
This explicitly denies connections from those users that are registered members of the specified groups (in the `/etc/group` file).

In the `/etc/ssh_config` file

Compression yes
This will cause the data exchanged between the SSH client and server to be compressed. This will actually slow down transfers

on fast networks. Use only in limited bandwidth situations where every byte counts. Compression can also be enabled by passing the `-C` parameter to `ssh`.

CompressionLevel 6

The compression level can be set between 1 and 9 (which is similar to the `gzip` utility). 1 is fast, but the data is not compressed very well; 9 is very slow but the data is much more thoroughly compressed. The default is 6.

The `-g` and `-L` options to `ssh` can be particularly useful to firewall design. These options allow TCP ports to be forwarded to the remote server over a secure connection. The following command will allow encrypted `telnet` connections on port 2300 while the remote shell session is active (this behavior is rather similar to `plug-gw` from the TIS FWTK):

```
ssh -L 2300:remotehost.com:23 -g remotehost.com
```

If a user telnets to port 2300 on the local host, this connection is encrypted, sent to the remote, then forwarded to the destination port specified on the command line (23).

The one last issue for SSH is how to force it to not ask for a password. With the Berkeley r-utilities, a properly configured `.rhosts` file could allow password-free connections. SSH can use `.rhosts`, but this usage is disabled by default. A safer way to support password-free logins is with public key cryptography. Setting this up is easy.

First, run the following command as root on the local host to generate a key pair. Accept all the defaults, but *do not enter a passphrase.* Just press enter instead (this does open up a security risk, which will be discussed in a moment).

```
ssh-keygen
```

Next, copy the public key to the remote server using one or the other of the following two commands. Use this syntax to copy it:

```
scp ~/.ssh/identity.pub remotehost.com:/root/.ssh/authorized_keys
```

Alternately, use this syntax to append the key to a remote `authorized_keys` file:

```
ssh remotehost.com "cat >> ~/.ssh/authorized_keys" < ~/.ssh/identity.pub
```

The next `ssh` login should not require a password (`scp` should be open as well):

ssh remotehost.com

Password-free connections should not be tolerated unless they are absolutely required—because, they obviously circumvent an important UNIX security safeguard. Scripting invoked through `crontabs` might be a good excuse. In any case, try to do the work with a login that has few privileges. Keep root away from the automatic (i.e., password-free) logins if at all possible.

Please note that, in this example, if the local host is damaged or destroyed by an attacker, the remote host could very likely go down with it. In this case, the price of convenience is risk.

Conclusion

It is not wise for an Internet firewall administrator to consider his *secure* network unimpregnable. A determined attacker sees firewall security features as mere obstacles, not insurmountable obstructions. Only with true vigilance can hostile attacks be repelled.

An administrator should review each of the following system components:

- The function of each service entry in `/etc/inetd.conf`, and why the service cannot be disabled.
- Any running daemons reported by `ps aux` (although this can be forged by a rogue kernel).
- Permitted route origins and destinations, with documentation.
- All unencrypted communication channels passing through the firewall, and why they do not compose a security risk.
- The installation status of the Red Hat Errata packages that have been issued for the platform.

Also, neither the C compiler nor the Linux kernel source should be allowed to remain on an active firewall (in fact, no development tools, nor any other non-related packages—such as games, XWindows, etc.—should be installed).

In a perfect world bounded by courtesy, such bothersome security precautions would be unnecessary. Unintentional abuse would be corrected. Malevolence would be unthinkable. Such is, unfortunately, not the world in which we live. So, a word to the wise: good fences make good neighbors.

05

Basic Web Services

The Apache web server is by far the most popular web server platform in use on the Internet today. It has been ported to a plethora of operating systems. Unlike any other competing commercial web server, it is entirely open source. Because of the openness of the design, many powerful modules have been developed that extend Apache functionality enormously.

Apache is a major centerpiece of Red Hat Linux 6.0. The web server, however, is configured very differently from a standard Apache installation. This difference is so profound that some have begun to describe it as part of the "Red Hat Way."

Basic Apache Configuration

If Apache is compiled from source, it will usually install to the directory `/usr/local/etc/httpd`. This directory does not even exist in a fresh Red Hat Linux installation.

Following is a brief description of various Apache files and directories under Red Hat Linux:

/etc/httpd/conf

This directory contains the three critical Apache configuration files:

`httpd.conf`
: Main web server configuration

`access.conf`
: Access restrictions and security

`srm.conf`
: MIME and file associations

/var/log/httpd

The following web server logs reside here:

`access_log`
: Records all connections to the web server.

`error_log`
: Reports problems encountered by a running server (CGI, `.htaccess` misconfigurations, etc.).

The log rotation system renames and deletes these files at regular intervals.

Other directories & files

`/etc/mime.types`
: Apache uses this file to associate content types with filename extensions.

/etc/rc.d/init.d/httpd
: This script should be used to start and stop the web server. It should be called with an argument of `start` or `stop`. (A message to this effect will be generated if the script is executed without an argument.)

/usr/sbin/httpd
: This is the location of binaries for the web server. This directory also contains several web server support utilities (such as `htpasswd`, discussed later in this chapter).

/home/httpd/html
: This is the default *document root* directory. Files and directories placed under this directory will be visible to the web. The `index.html` file contained within this directory is seen by default when a web browser attaches to the Apache server.

/home/httpd/cgi-bin
: Files containing program code to support the web site can be executed from this directory. Programs that run from this location must conform to the CGI specification, but can be written in almost any language, including compiled C/C++ code, Java, Perl, PHP, `BASH`, `awk`, or any other compiled language or interpreter. These scripts will be executed by the `nobody` userid, so permissions issues are usually a concern. CGI programs implemented without care are a grave security risk.

/home/luser/public_html
: Each user on the system can have their own space on the web server by creating a `public_html` directory immediately off their home, and modifying their home directory permissions to allow directory scanning privileges. For example, the local user `luser` could create a personal web space with the following commands:

```
cd ~
chmod o+x ~
mkdir public_html
echo '<b>Sample HTML file</b>' > public_html/index.html
```

The contents of the file created in this directory can be accessed through the web server with a URL of the form *http://127.0.0.1/~luser/index.html.* (Substitute a fully-qualified domain name for `localhost`, if one is applicable.)

Virtual Hosts with and without IP Aliases

Virtual Hosts with IP Aliases

Assuming that a Linux system's `eth0` Ethernet interface has been configured with IP address 1.2.3.3, the following commands will configure `eth0` to respond to 1.2.3.4 as well (which is central to establishing a virtual host):

```
/sbin/ifconfig eth0:1 1.2.3.4
/sbin/route add -host 1.2.3.4 dev eth0:1
```

Obviously, no other machine on the network should be using the IP address 1.2.3.4. If you're unsure, do not guess—check with the administrator.

These commands should be added to the system boot scripts. Be certain that they execute after the main **ifconfig** command(s) (a good place might be `/etc/rc.d/init.d/network`).

A sequence of virtual interfaces can begin with `eth0:1` and continue with `eth0:2`, `eth0:3`, `eth0:4`... Individual IP addresses are then associated with each virtual interface. This allows a number of virtual IP addresses on one network interface—up to 255.

Once the additional IP addresses have been added to the interface, DNS entries should be added with address records that point to the new entries (discussed in Chapter 2, "Configuring TCP/IP").

The web server must then be configured to serve a different document root to each unique IP address.

This behavior can be initiated with the Red Hat Linux Apache server by adding a set of lines like those shown in Listing 5.1—one for each interface—to the end of `/etc/httpd/conf/httpd.conf`:

Listing 5.1 *Virtual Host.*

```
<VirtualHost 1.2.3.4>
ServerAdmin webmaster@luser.com
DocumentRoot /home/luser/public_html
ServerName www.luser.com
ErrorLog logs/luser-error_log
TransferLog logs/luser-access_log
RefererLog logs/luser-referer_log
AgentLog logs/luser-agent_log
</VirtualHost>
```

Several of the lines above must be changed to reflect the configuration of your web site. The directory used as the document root, the server name, and the names of the log files should be customized.

The Apache documentation suggests that the argument to the `VirtualHost` directive be an IP address, not a host name. If DNS should be unavailable for some reason when Apache is started, and the `VirtualHost` directives cannot be resolved, they will be ignored. Specifying an IP address avoids this potential problem.

A full discussion of virtual hosting under Linux is available in the IP-Alias-HOWTO. This file can be found in a HOWTO RPM distribution on the accompanying CD or from any of the online Linux documentation resources (such as *http://www.linuxhq.com*).

Name-based Virtual Hosts

The `HTTP/1.1` protocol supports a mechanism where the web server can obtain the name that the browser used to access the site. Apache can be configured to serve multiple web sites based upon this retrieved name, even when the DNS resolution of the sites all point to the same IP address.

The Apache configuration for such an arrangement is only slightly different from IP alias (the only difference is the "NameVirtualHost" directive). See Listing 5.2 on page 125.

Listing 5.2 *Name Virtual Host.*

```
NameVirtualHost 1.2.3.4

<VirtualHost 1.2.3.4>
ServerAdmin webmaster@luser.com
DocumentRoot /home/luser/public_html
ServerName www.luser.com
ErrorLog logs/luser-error_log
TransferLog logs/luser-access_log
RefererLog logs/luser-referer_log
AgentLog logs/luser-agent_log
</VirtualHost>
```

There is also a `ServerPath` directive that can be used to compensate for older browsers that are not compliant with `HTTP/1.1` (such as MS Explorer 2, which is shipped with Windows NT 4). The `ServerPath` directive takes a directory as an argument. This directory is relative to the document root. When files within this directory are requested, they are assumed to belong to this host.

Virtual Hosts with JavaScript

The best method for establishing virtual hosts is to configure the server network card with multiple network addresses, because this technique will work with all browsers. There is, however, an alternative method that can be used with JavaScript-enabled browsers.

Let us imagine that the server network card is configured with a single IP address, and that the names *www.company-a.com* and *www.company-b.com* both resolve to this same IP address. Let us further imagine that there is an `index.html` file in the document root of the web server, and that this document root must be used to serve different pages for the different companies.

The JavaScript `location` variable contains the URL used to access the current page. In addition, if `location` is modified, the browser will immediately load the new URL contained within the variable.

The JavaScript to exploit this feature for virtual hosts could be as simple as:

```
<script language="JavaScript">
<!--
if (location=="http://www.company-b.com/")
        location="http://www.company-a.com/company-b/"
//-->
</script>
```

With this approach, the *browser*, not the server, makes the decision as to which page to load.

JavaScript will clean up the `location` variable to some extent, insuring that it contains the *http://* and a trailing slash.This method is quite handy for webmasters who do not have full administrative control of their machine. It is much easier to apply a change to one file than perform extensive reconfiguration of the network interfaces.

The greatest drawback to this approach is that non-JavaScript-aware browsers (such as Lynx) will not execute the script and load the new page, nor will JavaScript-aware browsers (Netscape 2 and later versions, Internet Explorer 3 and later) if JavaScript has been disabled by the user.

There are also some other problems with this approach:

- To some degree, the browser will render the HTML of the main page before the location is changed to the alternate page. To minimize this effect, place the JavaScript near the beginning of the `<HEAD>` tag.
- The history list will contain the original URL, not the redirected location.
- If the user presses the browser's *Back* button, the original URL will be reloaded, which will immediately redirect. This essentially disables the use of the *Back* button.

The JavaScript `replace()` method offers enhanced flexibility. After the `replace()` method is executed, the user cannot navigate to the previous URL by pressing the *Back* button. Unfortunately, `replace()` is not supported in any of the Netscape Navigator 2 releases, so version tests must be performed. Listing 5.3 shows an example using `replace()`.

Listing 5.3 *Virtual Host with Javascript.*

```
<script language="JavaScript">
<!--
var js_ok = false;
if (navigator.appName.substring(0,9) == "Microsoft" &&
        parseInt(navigator.appVersion) >= 4 )
        js_ok = true;
if (navigator.appName.substring(0.8) == "Netscape" &&
        parseInt(navigator.appVersion) >= 3 )
        js_ok = true;

   if (location=="http://www.company-b.com/")
        if (js_ok == true)
             replace("http://www.company-a.com/company-b/")
        else
             location="http://www.company-a.com/company-b/"
//-->
</script>
```

Static Password Protection

Applying password protection to a web page is a relatively easy process. This simple form of web security requires the creation/ modification of only a few files on the web server.

This basic security feature is configured through the use of an `.htaccess` file. The settings in this configuration file apply to all HTML files that lie in its directory and subdirectories.

It is important to understand the limits of this type of protection. It is not very secure. In fact, it can be easily be abused. Do not trust an `.htaccess` file to protect critical data.

Web pages protected by an `.htaccess` file must be readable by the `userid` of the web server—usually userid `nobody`, group `nobody`. Unless the author of the web pages has configured the web server and the pages to share his own group (which cannot be done without the aid of the superuser—assuming that the server runs at the standard port), the pages must also have world-readable permissions to be visible to the web server. If such permissions are set, then any other user on the system with shell access can read the pages, regardless of the presence of an `.htaccess` file. Furthermore, CGI applications (specifically PHP, discussed in a later chapter) have access to this world-readable data. For the standard Red Hat web server configuration, if the web server process itself can read the data, anyone on the system can read it. If this discussion seems unclear, simply realize data served by the web daemon is not secure unless there are no other users on a system.

Also, it should be remembered that all standard HTTP data will pass over the intervening network in clear text. Unless Secure Sockets Layer (SSL) is configured (which is beyond the scope of this text), there is no encryption. This data can be intercepted by a packet sniffer (such as `sniffit`), or siphoned from a proxy cache.

Bearing these warnings in mind, a cursory discussion of this method of access control will follow.

The default Apache configuration in Red Hat Linux 6.0 does not allow `.htaccess` files to be used. To enable the use of these files for authentication, a change must be made to `/etc/httpd/conf/access.conf`. The change must be applied to a line in the `<Directory /home/httpd/html>` section in the file that begins with the words "`AllowOverride`" and ends with a series of options. At the very least, the line you are looking for should contain the following:

```
AllowOverride AuthConfig Limit
```

Rather than the above permissions (AuthConfig, Limit), the keyword `All` can be used to enable extensive control with `.htaccess`. Do not enable the extra features activated by the `All` setting unless this functionality is actually required.

The `AllowOverride` statement occurs three times in the default `/etc/httpd/conf/access.conf` file: once for global options, once for executing programs from /cgi-bin, and once for all pages beneath the document root. Each section is enclosed within a `<Directory>` tag. Modify only the section for which access control is required.

Once these changes have been made, the web server must be restarted. This can be done either by sending a HUP signal to the master web server, or by cycling the web server with the `rc` files:

```
/etc/rc.d/init.d/httpd restart
```

Once the web server has reread its configuration files through a HUP or a restart, the security features will be enabled. To create a sample web page to test these features, execute the following commands as root:

```
mkdir /home/httpd/html/restrict
echo "<hr>HTML Rules<hr>" >
/home/httpd/html/restrict/test.html
```

This file can be viewed locally with the URL *http://127.0.0.1/restrict/test.html.* (Obviously, a qualified host name will be required for non-local browsers.)

To protect this file and everything in its directory, create the file shown in Listing 5.4 as `/home/httpd/html/restrict/.htaccess`.

Listing 5.4 *Access control with* `.htaccess`.

```
deny from all
allow from permitted.com
AuthType Basic
AuthUserFile /etc/httpd/htpasswd
AuthName "special directory"
require valid-user
satisfy any
```

After this file has been created, enter the following command:

```
/usr/bin/htpasswd -c /etc/httpd/htpasswd bogususer
```

The system will ask for a password. Enter one, then confirm it. Now examine the file `/etc/httpd/htpasswd`. It will be similar to this:

```
bogususer:TPNWusI5zZdqs
```

If all of these steps have been performed correctly, viewing the URL *http://127.0.0.1/restrict/test.html* with a browser will require a name and password.

The file above actually allows unrestricted access from any requests originating from *permitted.com* (which requires reverse DNS to function properly). An IP address can also be used in this position. If no unrestricted access is to be allowed, simply remove the `allow` line completely.

The `htpasswd` file can hold multiple accounts and passwords. To add another account and password to the file, enter the following command:

/usr/bin/htpasswd /etc/httpd/htpasswd realuser

Notice the lack of a `-c` option in the previous `htpasswd` command. The `htpasswd` file already exists; it does not need to be created again. After entering a password for this user, `/etc/httpd/htpasswd` will contain another line:

```
bogususer:TPNWusI5zZdqs
realuser:Mv19hxh2ff07k
```

A number of users with individual passwords may be added in this manner. The Apache documentation warns that access will become very slow if an `htpasswd` file grows large. The problem of large authorized users lists can be solved by moving the `htpasswd` data into a database. The Apache documentation recommends DBM files (which are not covered in this text), and authentication against a Sybase database is discussed in Chapter 7, "Database Servers."

As a final note, astute users might have noticed that the entries in an `htpasswd` file are similar to the `/etc/passwd` database (or `/etc/shadow`, if the `pwconv` utility has been executed) which holds information about all users. In fact, the same password encryption technique (DES, not MD5) is used in both files, and it is possible to move the password hashes freely from one file to the other.

An inexperienced administrator might be tempted to synchronize `/etc/passwd` and an `htpasswd` file, or make a call directly from an `.htaccess` to `/etc/passwd`. Be warned, however, that such a configuration is a welcome door for an attacker, and the practice is best avoided.

06

Database Servers

The administration of a Relational Database Management System (RDBMS) is not normally viewed as an enjoyable task by the general population of the Computer Science profession. The current technology behind such systems is more than twenty years old, and the standard database access language is now hindering the development of a true object-oriented database design. The World Wide Web, however, is generating renewed interest in database systems. In fact, to construct a web application that truly interacts with browser clients almost mandates the use of a database server.

An RDBMS enables the fast storage and retrieval of large amounts of information. The interface used to insert, manipulate, and extract data is called the Structured Query Language (SQL), and was developed by IBM for their DB2 database product in the 1970s.

Two database servers will be addressed in this text: PostgreSQL and Sybase. PostgreSQL, the successor to the Postgres RDBMS, implements a subset of ANSI-standard SQL and runs on a variety of UNIX platforms. Precompiled binaries for PostgreSQL are now shipped standard in Red Hat Linux 6.0. PostgreSQL was developed in a university environment, and the performance of the database at high loads is poor.

Sybase Adaptive Server Enterprise is a commercial RDBMS that has been available since 1988. Sybase is very powerful, but its administration is much more complex than that of PostgreSQL. It is available freely on Red Hat Linux with few restrictions. The RPM binaries for Sybase are on the CD included with this text in the `/sybase` directory. The implementation of a Sybase database will require much more planning than is required with PostgreSQL.

Without an interface to link it to the Web, however, a SQL database will be of little use. Middleware is required to meld HTML and SQL into a single format. This software will be discussed in the next chapter, which addresses web sites with dynamic content.

Installing PostgreSQL

If you are preparing for a fresh installation of Red Hat Linux 6.0, installation of PostgreSQL will be simple. Just select the SQL server from the "Components to Install" menu at setup time. Then, later in the setup, indicate that the PostgreSQL server should be started at boot in the "Services" menu. The software will be installed, a `postgres` user will be added as a DataBase Administrator (DBA), and startup scripts and links will be installed under `/etc/rc.d` to spawn the database server in the appropriate system run levels (supported by the UNIX `init` utility).

If the installed copy of Red Hat Linux 6.0 does not include the database components, they can be installed at a later time as long as access to the RPMs containing PostgreSQL can be obtained. The

RPMs can be found on the distribution CD included with this text (under RedHat/RPMS) or on the Red Hat FTP site. They can be installed and configured by running the following commands as root:

```
rpm -Uvh postgresql-6.4.2-3.i386.rpm
rpm -Uvh postgresql-clients-6.4.2-3.i386.rpm
rpm -Uvh postgresql-devel-6.4.2-3.i386.rpm
ntsysv
```

The `ntsysv` command will allow the selection of which system services are started at boot time (it creates links from files in `/etc/rc.d/init.d` to files in `/etc/rc.d/rcX.d`). If you want PostgreSQL to start at boot time, make sure that it is selected. It is important to note, however, that critical database system data must be initalized before the PostgreSQL subsystem can be used. Without this initialization, the `postmaster` daemon will not start. The steps required to initialize this data can be found below.

Establishing a PostgreSQL Database

The best way to learn to set up and use a DBMS is by following a set of consistent commands that initialize a database, populate it with some records and then issue queries against it. To this end, the following set of examples will create a database that implements a web-enabled shopping list.

Once PostgreSQL is installed, its system databases must be initialized. This will not be necessary on an upgrade installation where PostgreSQL was in active use, but it will be required if the database server has never been started before. If you are unsure if this step is necessary, startup the Postgres subsystem, as root, with the following command:

```
/etc/rc.d/init.d/postgresql restart
```

If this command fails, you will know that the databases were never initialized, and the following commands must be run. (Otherwise, they should be skipped.)

```
su - postgres
PGDATA=/var/lib/pgsql PGLIB=/usr/lib/pgsql initdb
exit
/etc/rc.d/init.d/postgresql start
```

Afterward, users should be created that will maintain the databases. Those users must also be registered with the PostgreSQL server.The commands below will add a user named `luser` to a Red Hat system, then register both `luser` and `nobody` with the database server. If a different account name than `luser` is desired, just substitute the modified name for `luser` in the rest of this chapter.

As the root user, issue the commands in Listing 6.1.

Listing 6.1 *Adding Postgres users.*

```
useradd luser
su - postgres
createuser luser
  Enter user's postgres ID or RETURN to use unix user ID:
500 -> (enter)
  Is user "luser" allowed to create databases (y/n) y
  Is user "luser" allowed to add users? (y/n) n
  createuser: luser was successfully added
createuser nobody
  Enter user's postgres ID or RETURN to use unix user ID:
99 -> (enter)
  Is user "nobody" allowed to create databases (y/n) n
  Is user "nobody" allowed to add users? (y/n) n
  createuser: nobody was successfully added
  don't forget to create a database for nobody
exit
```

The `useradd` command records a new user in the system password database (`/etc/passwd`). The **createuser** command adds a new PostgreSQL user. Don't forget to set the UNIX password for the `luser` account with the **passwd** command.

The user `nobody` needs to be registered with the database because the web server runs under this userid. PostgreSQL makes a strong association between the UNIX user and the database user, unlike Sybase where the two are completely separate. This action (i.e., adding `nobody` to the database) will enable the web server to run queries against the database server.

Next, login as `luser` and run the following command:

createdb shopping

This command creates a *database*. Older DBMS applications (like dBase and its derivatives) called tabular collections of data, *databases*. *Relations* could be established between these databases.

This is not so in PostgreSQL. In this new paradigm, databases contain *tables*, and these tables contain the tabular data. Relations are established between tables that lie within a database. The previous command (i.e., **createdb**) creates only the database; the tables are created in a later step.

Now, while logged in as `luser`, enter the following command to initiate the interactive SQL interpreter:

psql shopping

The SQL interpreter will print a welcome message:

```
Welcome to the POSTGRESQL interactive sql monitor:
Please read the file COPYRIGHT for copyright terms of
POSTGRESQL

   type \? for help on slash commands
   type \q to quit
   type \g or terminate with semicolon to execute query
You are currently connected to the database: shopping

shopping=>
```

SQL commands may be entered directly at the prompt. They may span many lines if necessary. The command is not issued until a semicolon is encountered.

Enter the following text at the prompt to create a table to hold the shopping list:

```
CREATE TABLE list (
    Item        TEXT,
    Vendorcode  INT,
    Quantity    INT);
```

This command creates a table named *list*, which is composed of three fields. The fields correspond to columns in a spreadsheet (although a PostgreSQL database can be orders of magnitude larger than the largest spreadsheets). The names of the fields are *item*, *vendorcode*, and *quantity*. The fields have an associated *data type*. For instance, the vendorcode and quantity fields are both defined as type integer (they can only contain numbers, not text). The item field is of type text, and it can be of any length.

SQL is not case-sensitive, so any combination of upper- and lower-case characters can be used with its commands. The style used here follows that of most popular tutorial texts on database design, which allows one to easily distinguish the SQL reserved words from the variable names.

The following command creates another table named "vendors" with two fields: one for integers, and the other for text.

```
CREATE TABLE vendors (
        Vendorcode  INT,
        Vendorname  TEXT);
```

At this point, the tables have been created and they are empty. The SQL `INSERT` command can be used to *populate* the tables with several values, as shown:

```
INSERT INTO vendors VALUES (100, 'Super Grocer');
INSERT INTO list VALUES ('Root Beer', 100, 3);
```

The previous insert syntax is valid and is very useful for one-time jobs. However, if columns are added to or removed from the tables, the above insert syntax will likely fail because of mismatches between the column and data types. An alternate syntax is available that can specify the columns into which data will be inserted. Any columns not mentioned will receive NULL values (if such values are allowed).

```
INSERT INTO vendors (vendorcode, vendorname)
   VALUES (101, 'General Department Store');
INSERT INTO vendors (vendorcode, vendorname)
   VALUES (102, 'General Auto Parts');
INSERT INTO list (item, vendorcode, quantity)
   VALUES ('Ice Cream', 100, 1);
INSERT INTO list (item, vendorcode, quantity)
   VALUES ('Napkins', 101, 50);
INSERT INTO list (item, vendorcode, quantity)
   VALUES ('Spark Plugs', 102, 4);
```

The data can be examined with the SQL `SELECT` command, shown here:

```
SELECT item, vendorcode, quantity FROM list;
```

The SQL interpreter should respond with:

```
  item       |vendorcode|quantity
  -----------+----------+--------
  Root Beer  |       100|       3
  Ice Cream  |       100|       1
  Napkins    |       101|      50
  Spark Plugs|       102|       4
  (4 rows)
```

Fields can be rearranged or omitted from the SELECT command by modifying the field names:

```
SELECT item, quantity FROM list;

  item       |quantity
  -----------+--------
  Root Beer  |       3
  Ice Cream  |       1
  Napkins    |      50
  Spark Plugs|       4
  (4 rows)
```

As an alternative, an asterisk can be used to indicate that all fields are desired from the SELECT query:

```
SELECT * FROM list;

  item       |vendorcode|quantity
  -----------+----------+--------
  Root Beer  |       100|       3
  Ice Cream  |       100|       1
  Napkins    |       101|      50
  Spark Plugs|       102|       4
  (4 rows)
```

An asterisk can be very useful when querying a database during interactive sessions. However, its use should be avoided in programs, as columns inserted into or removed from the database will change the physical order of the data returned. Specifying the desired columns will prevent this effect.

Notice in the previous table that the numerical vendorcodes are printed rather than the more useful vendornames. The latter are actually contained within the vendors table:

```
SELECT * FROM vendors;
```

```
vendorcode|vendorname
----------+-----------------------
       100|Super Grocer
       101|General Department Store
       102|General Auto Parts
(3 rows)
```

In the case of these two tables, however, the vendorcode field is not very useful. It would be much more appropriate to list the vendorname field from the vendors table when printing the list table. Such a thing is possible by establishing a *relation*:

```
SELECT list.item, vendors.vendorname, list.quantity
       FROM list, vendors
       WHERE list.vendorcode = vendors.vendorcode;

item       |vendorname              |quantity
-----------+------------------------+--------
Root Beer  |Super Grocer            |       3
Ice Cream  |Super Grocer            |       1
Napkins    |General Department Store|      50
Spark Plugs|General Auto Parts      |       4
(4 rows)
```

In the example above, the `FROM` clause specifies that two tables are to be used. The `WHERE` clause specifies the conditions for the relation. Relations such as these are called *joins* in SQL.

When two tables are used in a `SELECT` statement, such as the one above, the `tablename.fieldname` syntax is used to distinguish between the tables and fields.

There are many more options to the SQL `SELECT` statement—so many that `SELECT` is the most powerful command in the SQL language. Here is a slight variation on the previous example:

```
SELECT list.item, vendors.vendorname, list.quantity
       FROM list, vendors
       WHERE list.vendorcode = vendors.vendorcode
       ORDER BY item;

item       |vendorname              |quantity
-----------+------------------------+--------
Ice Cream  |Super Grocer            |       1
Napkins    |General Department Store|      50
Root Beer  |Super Grocer            |       3
Spark Plugs|General Auto Parts      |       4
(4 rows)
```

Here the `ORDER BY` clause causes the output to be sorted alphabetically by the "item" field.

It is also possible to use UNIX Regular Expressions in `SELECT` statements with PostgreSQL (a feat that not many commercial database servers can equal):

```
SELECT list.item, vendors.vendorname, list.quantity
       FROM list, vendors
       WHERE list.vendorcode = vendors.vendorcode
       AND list.item ~ '^[I-N]'
       ORDER BY item;

  item     |vendorname              |quantity
  ---------+------------------------+--------
  Ice Cream|Super Grocer            |       1
  Napkins  |General Department Store|      50
  (2 rows)
```

One interesting point about SQL join operations is that records in one table that will not join with records in the other table are omitted (although such records can be included with an *outer join*). If you run the following `INSERT` command:

```
INSERT INTO list (item, vendorcode, quantity)
   VALUES ('African Violet', 103, 1);
```

and then immediately follow it with the previous `SELECT` statement:

```
SELECT list.item, vendors.vendorname, list.quantity
       FROM list, vendors
       WHERE list.vendorcode = vendors.vendorcode
       ORDER BY item;
```

you will notice that the "African Violet" row in the "list" table was not printed. However, if you run the following command (and then rerun the `SELECT`):

```
INSERT INTO vendors (vendorcode, vendorname)
   VALUES (103, 'ACME Plant Store');
```

it will appear.

Records can be modified with the SQL of the following syntax:

```
UPDATE list SET item = 'African Violets' WHERE vendorcode = 103;
```

The above command modifies all records from vendor 103. There is only a single item in the table with this vendor, so the behavior in this case is correct. A more restrictive `WHERE` clause might be required were there additional records with the same vendor.

To delete rows from the database, use the SQL `DELETE` command:

```
DELETE FROM list WHERE item = 'African Violet';
DELETE FROM vendors WHERE vendorcode = 103;
```

Be careful. `DELETE FROM list` would wipe out all the data, leaving the table empty.

In a production environment, where tables contain a large number of rows, SQL operations may be faster if an *index* is defined. In this case, the commands to create the indexes are:

```
CREATE INDEX listtab ON list (vendorcode);
CREATE UNIQUE INDEX vendortab ON vendors (vendorcode);
```

Notice that a unique index is created on the vendors table, because each vendor will have a unique vendor code.

PostgreSQL keeps copies of modified or deleted rows in a database. This allows the database to be restored to the state it had at a previous date. Unfortunately, this also means that a large amount of storage could be consumed by inactive data. To clean your database of such inactive data, use the commands:

```
VACUUM list;
VACUUM vendors;
```

In the next section, the web server will be connecting to the database to perform `SELECT` operations. Under Red Hat Linux, the web server process runs under userid `nobody`. To grant this user permission to `SELECT` from the database, run the following commands:

```
REVOKE ALL ON list FROM nobody;
GRANT SELECT ON list TO nobody;
GRANT INSERT ON list TO nobody;
REVOKE ALL ON vendors FROM nobody;
GRANT SELECT ON vendors TO nobody;
GRANT ALL ON list TO luser;
GRANT ALL ON vendors TO luser;
```

The `REVOKE ALL` commands above remove all access permissions. Using such a `REVOKE` before a `GRANT` ensures that no previous permissions remain available to the user.

If you are finished with the SQL interpreter, you can log out of it by typing:

```
\q
```

The **pg_dump** command is a useful utility that allows easy backup and transport of PostgreSQL databases. It generates a text file composed of the SQL commands required to recreate a database. To dump the shopping database, use the shell command line:

pg_dump shopping > db.out

This file can be manipulated with a normal text editor. To reload the database, enter the shell command:

psql -e shopping < db.out

As a last point, `psql` uses the GNU Readline library. It is configured by default to accept Emacs keystrokes to edit the command line (that is, the up and down arrows cycle through the previous and next commands, Control-"A" moves to the beginning of the line, and so forth). Readline can be configured to use **vi** commands, if desired. Details can be found at the end of Chapter 1.

Installing Sybase

The Sybase Adaptive Server Enterprise RDBMS is much faster and more powerful than PostgreSQL, but it also requires much more planning and effort to install properly.

The Sybase server is included on the CD-ROM included with this book. It can be found in the `/sybase` directory. Sybase produces an HTML document with extensive documentation on the installation of Linux Sybase, but the document can be confusing, so the installation will be fully documented in this chapter.

The server software will require approximately 110MB of disk space. The documentation, if installed, requires another 40MB. Additional space must be allocated for user databases (this space must be set aside before the database is even created).

The RPM will install the server software in the `/opt` directory. Unless a separate file system has been created and mounted as `/opt`, this will place the Sybase server in the root file system. This is not a desirable location.

The `/home` directory is usually mounted as a separate file system. If a soft link from `/opt` to `/home` is placed in the root directory, the Sybase server software can be easily installed in `/home`. This location will also make the preparation of PHP slightly easier, as is explained in the next chapter.

Enter the following commands as the super user to set the link from `/opt` to `/home`:

cd /; ln -s home opt

The Sybase Adaptive Server Enterprise is installed by running the following command against the RPM:

rpm -Uvh sybase-ase-11.0.3.3-1.i386.rpm

The server license agreement will be displayed in the terminal window. The space bar can be used to page through the text. At the end of the license, the agreement must be accepted before installation can begin. To accept the agreement, enter:

Yes

The normal RPM software installation will commence. When it is completed, a prompt will be issued to create a *sybase* user and group. If the user and/or group already exists, it will not be affected (it is safe to answer yes if the server is being installed a second time). To add the sybase user and group, enter:

y

If the sybase group does not exist, a prompt will be issued to create it. To create the "sybase" group, enter:

y

If the sybase user does not exist, a prompt will be issued to create it. To create the sybase user, enter:

y

The system will prompt for a UNIX password for the sybase account in the usual way. After the password has been set for *sybase*, the installation of the server software is complete. If desired, the Sybase documentation can be installed with the following command:

rpm -Uvh sybase-doc-11.0.3.3-1.i386.rpm

To configure and activate the server with `sybinit`, enter the command:

su - sybase

A prompt will be issued to proceed with `sybinit`. To continue, enter:

y

The following menu will be displayed:

```
SYBINIT

1.  Release directory:  /home/sybase
2.  Edit / View Interfaces File
3.  Configure a Server product
4.  Configure an Open Client/Server product

Ctrl-a Accept and Continue, Ctrl-x Exit Screen, ? Help.

Enter the number of your choice and press return:
```

Enter **3** and press "Return" to configure the server. The following menu will be displayed:

```
CONFIGURE SERVER PRODUCTS

Products:

Product                 Date Installed      Date Configured
1.  SQL Server          10 Sep 1998 17:47
2.  Backup Server       10 Sep 1998 17:47

Ctrl-a Accept and Continue, Ctrl-x Exit Screen, ? Help.

Enter the number of your choice and press return:
```

Enter **1** and press "Return" to configure the SQL server.

```
NEW OR EXISTING SQL SERVER

1.  Configure a new SQL Server
2.  Configure an existing SQL Server
3.  Upgrade an existing SQL Server

Ctrl-a Accept and Continue, Ctrl-x Exit Screen, ? Help.

Enter the number of your choice and press Return:
```

Enter **1** and press "Return" to configure a new SQL server.

```
ADD NEW SQL SERVER
1.  SQL Server name:  SYBASE

Ctrl-a Accept and Continue, Ctrl-x Exit Screen, ? Help.

Enter the number of your choice and press return:
```

The name of the Sybase server must now be chosen. If several Sybase servers are to be installed on the local network, it is best to give each server a unique name (not the default name of `SYBASE`). However, if the server will *never* communicate with other Sybase database servers, it is convenient to leave the name as `SYBASE`.

If several Sybase servers must communicate, descriptions of all servers must be entered into a plain text file named `/home/sybase/interfaces`. Each Sybase server must have its own copy of the interfaces file, which is analogous to the `/etc/hosts` file.

To enter a new name, enter **1** and press "Return." Enter a new server name, and press "Return." Then hold the Control key and press "A" to continue.

To keep the server name *Sybase,* hold the Control key and press "A" to continue.

```
SQL SERVER CONFIGURATION

1.  CONFIGURE SERVER'S INTERFACES FILE ENTRY
Incomplete
2.  MASTER DEVICE CONFIGURATION
Incomplete
3.  SYBSYSTEMPROCS DATABASE CONFIGURATION
Incomplete
4.  SET ERRORLOG LOCATION
Incomplete
5.  CONFIGURE DEFAULT BACKUP SERVER
Incomplete
6.  CONFIGURE LANGUAGES
Incomplete
7.  CONFIGURE CHARACTER SETS
Incomplete
8.  CONFIGURE SORT ORDER
Incomplete
9.  ACTIVATE AUDITING
Incomplete

Ctrl-a Accept and Continue, Ctrl-x Exit Screen, ? Help.

Enter the number of your choice and press return:
```

Each step in the above menu must be completed before the SQL server can be activated. Some steps will require substantial configuration, while others will present settings that are normally only reviewed and confirmed.

To begin the configuration, enter **1** and press "Return."

```
SERVER INTERFACES FILE ENTRY SCREEN

    Server name:  SYBASE

1.  Retry Count:  0
2.  Retry Delay:  0
3.  Add a new listener service

Ctrl-a Accept and Continue, Ctrl-x Exit Screen, ? Help.

Enter the number of your choice and press return:
```

Enter **3** and press "Return" to configure the listener service for the SQL server.

```
EDIT TCP SERVICE

1.  Hostname/Address: gondor
2.  Port:
3.  Name Alias:
4.  Delete this service from the interfaces entry

Ctrl-a Accept and Continue, Ctrl-x Exit Screen, ? Help.

Enter the number of your choice and press return:
```

Enter **2** and press "Return" to configure the TCP port for the SQL server.

Enter **1433** for the port and press "Return."

Note

The Sybase documentation recommends port 7100 for the SQL server port. In Red Hat Linux 6.0, the font server for X-Windows runs at port 7100, which will result in a conflict if `xfs` is running. Do not configure Sybase to listen at port 7100, or conflicts will arise with X. Microsoft SQL Servers use port 1433, and selecting this port may ease the configuration of ODBC on Windows platforms.

Finally, hold the Control key and press "A" to continue.

When asked if the information is correct, answer **Y**.

To exit the "Server Interfaces File Entry menu," hold the Control key and press "A".

When asked if the interfaces file should be written, answer **Y**.

```
SQL SERVER CONFIGURATION

1.  CONFIGURE SERVER'S INTERFACES FILE ENTRY
Complete
2.  MASTER DEVICE CONFIGURATION
Incomplete
3.  SYBSYSTEMPROCS DATABASE CONFIGURATION
Incomplete
4.  SET ERRORLOG LOCATION
Incomplete
5.  CONFIGURE DEFAULT BACKUP SERVER
Incomplete
6.  CONFIGURE LANGUAGES
Incomplete
7.  CONFIGURE CHARACTER SETS
Incomplete
8.  CONFIGURE SORT ORDER
Incomplete
9.  ACTIVATE AUDITING
Incomplete

Ctrl-a Accept and Continue, Ctrl-x Exit Screen, ? Help.

Enter the number of your choice and press return:
```

Note that the first step is now complete. Enter **2** and press "Return" to configure the master device.

```
MASTER DEVICE CONFIGURATION

1.  Master Device:  /home/sybase/master.dat
2.  Size (Meg):  21

Ctrl-a Accept and Continue, Ctrl-x Exit Screen, ? Help.

Enter the number of your choice and press return:
```

Hold the Control key and press "A" to exit the master device configuration. Alternately, you may adjust the size or location of the master device with the options on the menu (unless you know why you want to change these options, it is safe to leave them at their default).

The following warning message will be issued:

```
WARNING: '/home/sybase/master.dat' is a regular file which
is not recommended for a Server device.
```

This warning can be ignored. Linux supports only regular files (not raw character mode devices). Press "Return' to pass the warning.

```
SQL SERVER CONFIGURATION

1.  CONFIGURE SERVER'S INTERFACES FILE ENTRY
Complete
2.  MASTER DEVICE CONFIGURATION
Complete
3.  SYBSYSTEMPROCS DATABASE CONFIGURATION
Incomplete
4.  SET ERRORLOG LOCATION
Incomplete
5.  CONFIGURE DEFAULT BACKUP SERVER
Incomplete
6.  CONFIGURE LANGUAGES
Incomplete
7.  CONFIGURE CHARACTER SETS
Incomplete
8.  CONFIGURE SORT ORDER
Incomplete
9.  ACTIVATE AUDITING
Incomplete

Ctrl-a Accept and Continue, Ctrl-x Exit Screen, ? Help.

Enter the number of your choice and press return:
```

Enter **3** and press "Return" to configure the system procedures database.

```
SYBSYSTEMPROCS DATABASE CONFIGURATION

1.  sybsystemprocs database size (Meg):  16
2.  sybsystemprocs logical device name:  sysprocsdev
3.  create new device for the sybsystemprocs database:  yes
4.  physical name of new device:  /home/sybase/sybprocs.dat
5.  size of the new device (Meg):  16

Ctrl-a Accept and Continue, Ctrl-x Exit Screen, ? Help.

Enter the number of your choice and press return:
```

Hold the Control key and press "A" to exit the system procedures database configuration. Alternately, you may adjust the size or location of the system procedures database and device with the options on the menu (unless you want to add stored procedures in the future, it is safe to leave the settings at their default).

```
SQL SERVER CONFIGURATION

1.  CONFIGURE SERVER'S INTERFACES FILE ENTRY
Complete
2.  MASTER DEVICE CONFIGURATION
Complete
3.  SYBSYSTEMPROCS DATABASE CONFIGURATION
Complete
4.  SET ERRORLOG LOCATION
Incomplete
5.  CONFIGURE DEFAULT BACKUP SERVER
Incomplete
6.  CONFIGURE LANGUAGES
Incomplete
7.  CONFIGURE CHARACTER SETS
Incomplete
8.  CONFIGURE SORT ORDER
Incomplete
9.  ACTIVATE AUDITING
Incomplete

Ctrl-a Accept and Continue, Ctrl-x Exit Screen, ? Help.

Enter the number of your choice and press return:
```

Emter **4** and press "Return" to configure the error log.

```
SET ERRORLOG LOCATION

1.  SQL Server errorlog:  /home/sybase/install/errorlog

Ctrl-a Accept and Continue, Ctrl-x Exit Screen, ? Help.

Enter the number of your choice and press return:
```

Hold the Control key and press "A" to exit the error log configuration. Alternately, you may adjust the location of the error log with the options on the menu.

```
SQL SERVER CONFIGURATION

1.  CONFIGURE SERVER'S INTERFACES FILE ENTRY
Complete
2.  MASTER DEVICE CONFIGURATION
Complete
3.  SYBSYSTEMPROCS DATABASE CONFIGURATION
Complete
4.  SET ERRORLOG LOCATION
Complete
5.  CONFIGURE DEFAULT BACKUP SERVER
Incomplete
6.  CONFIGURE LANGUAGES
Incomplete
7.  CONFIGURE CHARACTER SETS
Incomplete
8.  CONFIGURE SORT ORDER
Incomplete
9.  ACTIVATE AUDITING
Incomplete

Ctrl-a Accept and Continue, Ctrl-x Exit Screen, ? Help.

Enter the number of your choice and press return:
```

Enter **5** and press "Return" to configure the backup server.

```
SET THE SQL SERVER'S BACKUP SERVER

1.  SQL Server Backup Server name:  SYB_BACKUP

Ctrl-a Accept and Continue, Ctrl-x Exit Screen, ? Help.

Enter the number of your choice and press return:
```

If you have changed the name of your Sybase server, then you should change the name of the backup server as well.

When the name of the backup server is configured, hold the Control key and press "A" to exit.

```
SQL SERVER CONFIGURATION

1.  CONFIGURE SERVER'S INTERFACES FILE ENTRY
Complete
2.  MASTER DEVICE CONFIGURATION
Complete
```

```
3.  SYBSYSTEMPROCS DATABASE CONFIGURATION
Complete
4.  SET ERRORLOG LOCATION
Complete
5.  CONFIGURE DEFAULT BACKUP SERVER
Complete
6.  CONFIGURE LANGUAGES
Incomplete
7.  CONFIGURE CHARACTER SETS
Incomplete
8.  CONFIGURE SORT ORDER
Incomplete
9.  ACTIVATE AUDITING
Incomplete

Ctrl-a Accept and Continue, Ctrl-x Exit Screen, ? Help.

Enter the number of your choice and press return:
```

Enter **6** and press "Return" to configure the server language.

```
CONFIGURE LANGUAGES

    Current default language:  us_english
    Current default character set:  ISO 8859-1 (Latin-1) -
Western European 8-b
character set.
    Current sort order:  Binary ordering, for the ISO
8859/1 or Latin-1 charact (iso_1).

Select the language you want to install, remove, or
designate as the default language.

Language          Installed?  Remove   Install   Make default
1.  us_english       yes         no       no          yes
2.  chinese          no          no       no          no
3.  french           no          no       no          no
4.  german           no          no       no          no
5.  japanese         no          no       no          no
6.  spanish          no          no       no          no

Ctrl-a Accept and Continue, Ctrl-x Exit Screen, ? Help.

Enter the number of your choice and press return:
```

Unless you are bilingual, hold the Control key and press "A" to exit.

```
SQL SERVER CONFIGURATION

1.  CONFIGURE SERVER'S INTERFACES FILE ENTRY
Complete
2.  MASTER DEVICE CONFIGURATION
Complete
3.  SYBSYSTEMPROCS DATABASE CONFIGURATION
Complete
4.  SET ERRORLOG LOCATION
Complete
5.  CONFIGURE DEFAULT BACKUP SERVER
Complete
6.  CONFIGURE LANGUAGES
Complete
7.  CONFIGURE CHARACTER SETS
Incomplete
8.  CONFIGURE SORT ORDER
Incomplete
9.  ACTIVATE AUDITING
Incomplete

Ctrl-a Accept and Continue, Ctrl-x Exit Screen, ? Help.

Enter the number of your choice and press return:
```

Enter **7** and press "Return" to configure the character sets.

```
CONFIGURE CHARACTER SETS

    Current default language:  us_english
    Current default character set:  ISO 8859-1 (Latin-1) -
Western European 8-b character set.
    Current sort order:  Binary ordering, for the ISO
8859/1 or Latin-1 charact (iso_1).

Select the character set you want to install, remove, or
designate as the defauset.aracter
                                                     Make
Character set           Installed?  Remove  Install  default
1. ASCII, for use with unsp  yes      no       no       no
2. Code Page 437, (United S  no       no       no       no
3. Code Page 850 (Multiling  no       no       no       no
4. ISO 8859-1 (Latin-1) - W  yes      no       no       yes
5. Macintosh default charac  no       no       no       no
6. Hewlett-Packard propriet  no       no       no       no

Ctrl-a Accept and Continue, Ctrl-x Exit Screen, ? Help.

Enter the number of your choice and press return:
```

Hold the Control key and press "A" to exit.

```
SQL SERVER CONFIGURATION

1.  CONFIGURE SERVER'S INTERFACES FILE ENTRY
Complete
2.  MASTER DEVICE CONFIGURATION
Complete
3.  SYBSYSTEMPROCS DATABASE CONFIGURATION
Complete
4.  SET ERRORLOG LOCATION
Complete
5.  CONFIGURE DEFAULT BACKUP SERVER
Complete
6.  CONFIGURE LANGUAGES
Complete
7.  CONFIGURE CHARACTER SETS
Complete
8.  CONFIGURE SORT ORDER
Incomplete
9.  ACTIVATE AUDITING
Incomplete

Ctrl-a Accept and Continue, Ctrl-x Exit Screen, ? Help.

Enter the number of your choice and press return:
```

Enter **8** and press "Return" to configure the sort order.

```
CONFIGURE SORT ORDER

    Current default language:  us_english
    Current default character set:  ISO 8859-1 (Latin-1) -
Western European 8-b
character set.
    Current sort order:  Binary ordering, for the ISO
8859/1 or Latin-1 charact
(iso_1).

Select a sort order.

Sort Order
Chosen
1.  Binary ordering, for the ISO 8859/1 or Latin-1
character set (is  yes
```

```
2.  General purpose dictionary ordering.
no
3.  Spanish dictionary ordering.
no
4. Spanish case and accent insensitive dictionary order.
no
5.  Spanish case insensitive dictionary order.
no
6. Dictionary order, case insensitive, accent insensitive.
no
7.  Dictionary order, case insensitive.
no
8. Dictionary order, case insensitive with preference.
no

Ctrl-a Accept and Continue, Ctrl-x Exit Screen, ? Help.

Enter the number of your choice and press return:
```

Hold the Control key and press "A" to exit.

```
SQL SERVER CONFIGURATION

1.  CONFIGURE SERVER'S INTERFACES FILE ENTRY
Complete
2.  MASTER DEVICE CONFIGURATION
Complete
3.  SYBSYSTEMPROCS DATABASE CONFIGURATION
Complete
4.  SET ERRORLOG LOCATION
Complete
5.  CONFIGURE DEFAULT BACKUP SERVER
Complete
6.  CONFIGURE LANGUAGES
Complete
7.  CONFIGURE CHARACTER SETS
Complete
8.  CONFIGURE SORT ORDER
Complete
9.  ACTIVATE AUDITING
Incomplete

Ctrl-a Accept and Continue, Ctrl-x Exit Screen, ? Help.

Enter the number of your choice and press return:
```

Enter **9** and press "Return" to configure server auditing.

```
ACTIVATE AUDITING

1.  Install auditing:  no
2.  sybsecurity database size (Meg):  5
3.  sybsecurity logical device name:  sybsecurity
4.  create new device for the sybsecurity database:  no

Ctrl-a Accept and Continue, Ctrl-x Exit Screen, ? Help.

Enter the number of your choice and press return:
```

Unless you want to configure auditing and are aware of the storage requirements, hold the Control key and press "A" to exit.

```
SQL SERVER CONFIGURATION

1.  CONFIGURE SERVER'S INTERFACES FILE ENTRY
Complete
2.  MASTER DEVICE CONFIGURATION
Complete
3.  SYBSYSTEMPROCS DATABASE CONFIGURATION
Complete
4.  SET ERRORLOG LOCATION
Complete
5.  CONFIGURE DEFAULT BACKUP SERVER
Complete
6.  CONFIGURE LANGUAGES
Complete
7.  CONFIGURE CHARACTER SETS
Complete
8.  CONFIGURE SORT ORDER
Complete
9.  ACTIVATE AUDITING
Complete

Ctrl-a Accept and Continue, Ctrl-x Exit Screen, ? Help.
Enter the number of your choice and press "Return":
```

The configuration of the SQL server is now complete. Hold the Control key and press "A" to activate the server.

When prompted to "Execute the SQL Server Configuration Now?" answer **Y**.

The master device warning will be repeated. It can be ignored. Press "Return" to skip past it.

The system will issue the following messages as the server is configured:

```
Running task: create the master device.
Building the master device
..........Done
Task succeeded: create the master device.
Running task: update the SQL Server runserver file.
Task succeeded: update the SQL Server runserver file.
Running task: boot the SQL Server.
waiting for server 'SYBASE' to boot...
waiting for server 'SYBASE' to boot...
Task succeeded: boot the SQL Server.
Running task: create the sybsystemprocs database.
sybsystemprocs database created.
Task succeeded: create the sybsystemprocs database.
Running task: install system stored procedures.
...........................................................
..................
...........................................................
..................
........................Done
Task succeeded: install system stored procedures.
Running task: set permissions for the 'model' database.
Done
Task succeeded: set permissions for the 'model' database.
Running task: set the default character set and/or default
sort order for the SQL Server.
Setting the default character set to iso_1
Sort order 'binary' has already been installed.
Character set 'iso_1' is already the default.
Sort order 'binary' is already the default.
Task succeeded: set the default character set and/or
default sort order for the SQL Server.
Running task: set the default language.
Setting the default language to us_english
Language 'us_english' is already the default.
Task succeeded: set the default language.

Configuration completed successfully.
Press <return> to continue.
```

Press "Return" to continue to the next phase of the server installation.

```
NEW OR EXISTING SQL SERVER

1.  Configure a new SQL Server
2.  Configure an existing SQL Server
3.  Upgrade an existing SQL Server

Ctrl-a Accept and Continue, Ctrl-x Exit Screen, ? Help.

Enter the number of your choice and press return:
```

Hold the Control key and press "A" to exit this screen.

```
CONFIGURE SERVER PRODUCTS

Products:
Product                Date Installed      Date Configured
1.  SQL Server         10 Sep 1998 17:47   08 Nov 1998 13:25
2.  Backup Server      10 Sep 1998 17:47

Ctrl-a Accept and Continue, Ctrl-x Exit Screen, ? Help.

Enter the number of your choice and press return:
```

Hold the Control key and press "A" to exit this screen.

```
SYBINIT

1.  Release directory:  /home/sybase
2.  Edit / View Interfaces File
3.  Configure a Server product
4.  Configure an Open Client/Server product

Ctrl-a Accept and Continue, Ctrl-x Exit Screen, ? Help.

Enter the number of your choice and press return:
```

The next step will add an interface description for the backup server. Enter **2** and press "Return" to add the interface entry.

```
INTERFACES FILE TOP SCREEN

Interfaces File:

1.  Add a new entry
2.  Modify an existing entry
3.  View an existing entry
4.  Delete an existing entry

Ctrl-a Accept and Continue, Ctrl-x Exit Screen, ? Help.

Enter the number of your choice and press return:
```

Enter **1** and press "Return" to configure the backup server interface file entry.

```
CREATE NEW INTERFACES FILE ENTRY
1.  Server name:

Ctrl-a Accept and Continue, Ctrl-x Exit Screen, ? Help.

Enter the number of your choice and press return:
```

The name of the backup server must be entered. Enter **1** and press "Return" to add the new server name. Enter the name **SYB_BACKUP** (or the name that you have chosen for your backup server) and press "Return." Hold the Control key and press "A" to accept the name.

```
SERVER INTERFACES FILE ENTRY SCREEN

    Server name:  SYB_BACKUP

1.  Retry Count:  0
2.  Retry Delay:  0
3.  Add a new listener service

Ctrl-a Accept and Continue, Ctrl-x Exit Screen, ? Help.

Enter the number of your choice and press return:
```

At this menu, enter **3** and press "Return" to add a listener for the backup server.

```
EDIT TCP SERVICE

1.  Hostname/Address: gondor
2.  Port:
3.  Name Alias:
4.  Delete this service from the interfaces entry

Ctrl-a Accept and Continue, Ctrl-x Exit Screen, ? Help.

Enter the number of your choice and press return:
```

Enter **2** and press "Return" to configure the TCP port for the backup server.

Enter **1434** for the port and press "Return."

Finally, hold the Control key and press "A" to continue.

When asked if the information is correct, answer **Y**.

To exit the "Server Interfaces File Entry menu," hold the Control key and press "A."

When asked if the `interfaces` file should be written, answer **Y**.

```
INTERFACES FILE TOP SCREEN

Interfaces File:

1.  Add a new entry
2.  Modify an existing entry
3.  View an existing entry
4.  Delete an existing entry

Ctrl-a Accept and Continue, Ctrl-x Exit Screen, ? Help.

Enter the number of your choice and press return:
```

Hold the Control key and press "A" to leave the "Interfaces" menu.

```
SYBINIT

1.  Release directory:  /home/sybase
2.  Edit / View Interfaces File
3.  Configure a Server product
4.  Configure an Open Client/Server product

Ctrl-a Accept and Continue, Ctrl-x Exit Screen, ? Help.

Enter the number of your choice and press return:
```

Now that the backup server is defined in the `interfaces` file, it must be configured and activated. Enter **3** and press "Return."

```
CONFIGURE SERVER PRODUCTS

Products:

Product             Date Installed      Date Configured
1.  SQL Server      10 Sep 1998 17:47   08 Nov 1998 13:25
2.  Backup Server   10 Sep 1998 17:47

Ctrl-a Accept and Continue, Ctrl-x Exit Screen, ? Help.

Enter the number of your choice and press return:
```

Enter **2** and press "Return" to configure the backup server.

```
NEW OR EXISTING BACKUP SERVER

1.  Configure a new Backup Server
2.  Configure an existing Backup Server

Ctrl-a Accept and Continue, Ctrl-x Exit Screen, ? Help.

Enter the number of your choice and press return:
```

Enter **1** and press "Return" to configure a new backup server.

```
ADD NEW BACKUP SERVER

1.  Backup Server name:  SYB_BACKUP

Ctrl-a Accept and Continue, Ctrl-x Exit Screen, ? Help.

Enter the number of your choice and press return:
```

If the name of the backup server is correct, hold down the Control key and press "A".

```
BACKUP SERVER CONFIGURATION

1.  Backup Server errorlog:
/home/sybase/install/backup.log
2.  Enter / Modify Backup Server interfaces file
information
3.  Backup Server language:  us_english
4.  Backup Server character set:  iso_1
5.  Backup Server tape configuration file:
/home/sybase/backup_tape.cfg

Ctrl-a Accept and Continue, Ctrl-x Exit Screen, ? Help.

Enter the number of your choice and press return:
```

Hold down the Control key and press "A" to start the backup server.

When asked if the backup server should be configured, answer **Y**.

The system will issue the following messages as the server is configured:

```
Running task: update the Backup Server runserver file.
Task succeeded: update the Backup Server runserver file.
Running task: boot the Backup Server.
waiting for server 'SYB_BACKUP' to boot...
Task succeeded: boot the Backup Server.
```

```
Configuration completed successfully.
Press <return> to continue.
```

The last step that remains is to configure the system libraries. Press “Return” to proceed.

```
NEW OR EXISTING BACKUP SERVER

1.  Configure a new Backup Server
2.  Configure an existing Backup Server

Ctrl-a Accept and Continue, Ctrl-x Exit Screen, ? Help.

Enter the number of your choice and press return:
```

Hold down the Control key and press “A” to return to the previous menu.

```
CONFIGURE SERVER PRODUCTS

Products:

Product              Date Installed       Date Configured
1.  SQL Server       10 Sep 1998 17:47    08 Nov 1998 13:25
2.  Backup Server    10 Sep 1998 17:47    08 Nov 1998 17:41

Ctrl-a Accept and Continue, Ctrl-x Exit Screen, ? Help.

Enter the number of your choice and press return:
```

Hold down the Control key and press “A” to return to the previous menu.

```
SYBINIT

1.  Release directory:  /home/sybase
2.  Edit / View Interfaces File
3.  Configure a Server product
4.  Configure an Open Client/Server product

Ctrl-a Accept and Continue, Ctrl-x Exit Screen, ? Help.

Enter the number of your choice and press return:
```

Enter **4** and press “Return” to configure the Sybase libraries.

```
CONFIGURE CONNECTIVITY PRODUCTS

Products:

Product                     Date Installed    Date Configured
1. Open Client Library      10 Sep 1998 17:4
2. Open Server Library      10 Sep 1998 17:4
3. Embedded SQL/C Precomp 10 Sep 1998 17:4

Ctrl-a Accept and Continue, Ctrl-x Exit Screen, ? Help.

Enter the number of your choice and press return:
```

Enter **1**. Then press "Return" three times to configure the client library.

Enter **2**. Then press "Return" three times to configure the server library.

Enter **3**. Then press "Return" three times to configure the embedded SQL for C system.

```
CONFIGURE CONNECTIVITY PRODUCTS

Products:

Product                   Date Installed    Date Configured
1. Open Client Library  10 Sep 1998 17:4  08 Nov 1998 17:4
2. Open Server Library  10 Sep 1998 17:4  08 Nov 1998 17:5
3. Embedded SQL/C Precomp10 Sep 1998 17:4  08 Nov 1998 17:5

Ctrl-a Accept and Continue, Ctrl-x Exit Screen, ? Help.

Enter the number of your choice and press return:
```

All tasks within `sybinit` are now complete. Hold down the Control key and press "A" two times to exit the `sybinit` utility.

When `sybinit` has exited to a shell prompt, exit from the prompt to return to superuser status.

Following are three steps that can be taken to further configure Sybase Adaptive Server Enterprise 11.0.3.3 on Linux:

In `/etc/profile`, add the following lines after the first PATH statement:

```
SYBASE=/home/sybase
export SYBASE
PATH="$PATH:$SYBASE/bin"
```

This will allow all users to run Sybase server programs without specifying the full path.

The Sybase servers will not be automatically started at system boot. To configure them to start in this manner, run the following commands as the super user:

```
cd /etc/rc.d/rc3.d
ln -s ../init.d/sybase S85sybase
ln -s ../init.d/sybase K15sybase
cd /etc/rc.d/rc5.d
ln -s ../init.d/sybase S85sybase
ln -s ../init.d/sybase K15sybase
```

The Sybase server startup scripts leave inactive shells in the process table. To remove these inactive processes for peak efficiency, add the command **exec** to the first line that does not begin with a pound sign (#) to all of the `RUN` files in `/home/sybase/install` (with the default server names, the files will be `RUN_SYBASE` and `RUN_SYB_BACKUP`).

The interactive SQL interpreter that is shipped with Sybase (called `isql`) is not as powerful as some open-source tools that have become available. In particular, the `sqsh` SQL shell for Sybase includes support for GNU Readline and XWindows. The `sqsh` home page is at *http://www.voicenet.com/~gray/sqsh.html* and a copy of the source and a binary are included in the `sybase` directory of the CD that accompanies this text. Copy the `sqsh` binary to a location that is visible in the shell path (`$SYBASE/bin` is a good location). It should be noted that the manual page will not be installed if the package is not built.

A bug in the older versions of the Linux kernel prevented network connections to the Sybase server from working properly. This bug was fixed in 2.0.36 prepatch 7, which is included in Red Hat Linux 5.2. Red Hat 6.0, with the Linux 2.2 kernel, should never have this problem. However, if Sybase is installed on an older system (such as Red Hat Linux 5.1), network connections will not work properly unless the kernel is upgraded. If an older system is being used, it must have kernel 2.0.36 for proper Sybase network operation.

The Sybase ASE package requires the GNU C library (`glibc`). The Sybase server will not run on systems with the older C library (`libc5`), but there are a set of CT-Lib client libraries available for these platforms (`libc5` platforms include Red Hat Linux 4.2, Slackware 3.2, etc.). The DB-Lib library is specifically *not* available. These libraries will enable older Linux systems to access any TCP/IP-enabled Sybase server, and they are included in the `sybase/oldlibs` directory on the CD-ROM that accompanies this text.

The best way to shut down the Sybase server is with the following command:

```
# /home/sybase/bin/isql -U sa -S SYBASE
1 shutdown
2 go
Server SHUTDOWN by request.
The SQL Server is terminating this process.
DB-LIBRARY error:
        Unexpected EOF from SQL Server.
```

If the `sqsh` SQL interpreter is installed, then the following shell command can be used to shut down the server:

```
echo -e "shutdown SYB_BACKUP \n go \n shutdown \n go \n" | \
/usr/local/bin/sqsh -S SYBASE -U sa -P sapass
```

Please note that when the password is changed for the Sybase `sa` account in the next section, that password must be provided above. Substitute the appropriate server name for the `-S` parameter, if it is not SYBASE, and the path to the `sqsh` binary.

The above shutdown methods are much safer than passing `stop` as an argument to the `/etc/rc.d/init.d/sybase` script. Allowing the server to be shut down by this script can have adverse effects.

Warning

One specific problem associated with using the `/etc/rc.d/init.d/sybase` script to shut down the Sybase server is that `IDENTITY` columns will increase by the burn factor; neither identity columns nor the burn factor are discussed in this text. Substitution of the `sqsh` syntax for the `killproc` call in `/etc/rc.d/init.d/sybase` is recommended if the script is to be used to shut down Sybase.

Sybase Devices

Unlike PostgreSQL, Sybase will not natively use space in a Linux file system (no matter what the type—`ext2fs` or otherwise). In a

UNIX environment, the preferred approach to Sybase data storage is a raw character-mode disk partition—effectively a partition made with `fdisk` that is formatted and utilized directly by Sybase.

Linux does not support the use of character-mode disk partitions. Fortunately, Sybase also supports the use of *device* files—standard files created anywhere in the file system (not to be confused with the I/O device files in the `/dev` directory). Sybase device files are initialized and formatted by Sybase, both in the `sybinit` installer and in the interactive SQL interpreter.

The drawback to placing Sybase database files within the file system is that write operations are buffered. Sybase can write data to its device files and receive a confirmation of the write, but then find that Linux has buffered the data and the write has not actually taken place at all. In the case of a server crash, data which Sybase confirmed as safely committed to the media is actually lost.

It is possible to use a raw disk partition (such as `/dev/sdb1`) as a Sybase device file, but these partitions are block-mode devices and will be buffered. At this time, there is no character-mode storage that would bring higher-reliability to Linux Sybase ASE. This situation will be rectified with the latest commercial release of Sybase for Linux.

Sybase Configuration

It is unfortunate that Sybase is shipped with default settings that will quickly destroy the server if they are not changed.

Sybase is shipped with a single default device called the *master.* If the master device becomes full, the server will crash. The first thing that the DBA should do is create a new set of devices for database storage, select one of the new devices as the default storage device, then remove the default storage designation from the master device.

Some recommend that no default devices be selected. This will force an explicit device selection when databases are created, and will ensure that those who create databases make conscious decisions about the allocation of storage.

Performance can be greatly improved when devices are created on physically separate disk drives, especially in high-utilization environments.

The size of Sybase devices is specified in 2KB blocks (1MB = 512 blocks).

Sybase configuration changes are made with the Sybase `isql` (Interactive SQL) utility—or `sqsh`, if it was installed. `isql` can be invoked with this command:

```
isql -U sa -S SYBASE
```

If `sqsh` is used with the same arguments, an interactive SQL session will be initiated that is supported by GNU Readline (for command repetition) and XWindows.

The `-U` option selects the account under which to login. The `-S` option selects the server (it must be defined in the interfaces file). This option can be omitted if the server is named `SYBASE`, since this server name is assumed by default. If the shell cannot find the `isql` binary, enter its full path (`/home/sybase/bin/isql` or `/opt/sybase/bin/isql`, or the location for `sqsh`). You will be prompted for a password before the SQL session begins; there is no initial password for the `sa` account, so just press "Return."

The version number of the Sybase server can be printed with the following commands:

```
select @@version
go
```

```
SQL Server/11.0.3.3/P/Linux Intel/Linux 2.0.36
   i586/1/OPT/Thu Sep 10 13:42:44 CEST 1998
```

The following commands, which will add a new 20MB default device and remove the master device from the default device list, should be entered at the `isql` prompt:

```
disk init name="gendev",
  physname="/home/sybase/gendev.dat",
  vdevno=2,
  size=10240
go
sp_diskdefault master, defaultoff
go
sp_diskdefault gendev, defaulton
go
```

At this point, a password should be set for the `sa` account, and additional users can be created. These users can be granted permission to create databases. Some DBAs are hesitant to grant such privileges to their users, and prefer to create all databases themselves and transfer ownership afterwards.

You might also notice the annoyingly repetitive **go** command. Sybase uses **go** in the same way that PostgreSQL uses the semicolon. It is possible to configure the sqsh interpreter to use a semicolon if the **go** becomes intolerable.

Please note that Sybase users have absolutely nothing to do with UNIX accounts. In fact, Sybase runs under many non-UNIX operating systems that have no support for UNIX logins. The commands below create a set of users similar to the PostgreSQL examples earlier in this chapter:

```
sp_password NULL, sapass
go
sp_addlogin luser, luserpass
go
sp_adduser luser
go
grant create database to luser
go
sp_addlogin nobody, nobodypass
go
sp_adduser nobody
go
```

A Sybase database has two main types of storage: data areas and transaction logs. Data areas contain the data associated with tables and indexes. Transaction logs contain the sequential changes to the database which form a complete audit trail.

Database backups are normally two-phase. Occasional complete database backups are augmented by more regular backups of transactions. In the event that the database must be restored from the backup media, the complete database is restored first, then the subsequent incremental transactions are restored.

Making a backup of the transaction log will cause the log to be cleared. If the transaction log becomes full, no more changes to the database can take place. The transaction log can be immediately cleared by issuing the SQL command **dump transaction with no_log**, but this invalidates all incremental backups; a complete database dump must then be performed to ensure data integrity (this will also produce a stern warning in the error log). Data backups include data only. A data backup will not clear the transaction log.

The data areas and transaction logs can share the same space on a device, or they can be allocated separately. However, if they share the same space, the transaction log can never be backed up separately from the database. All backups will be complete database backups; incremental transaction log backups will not be allowed.

Enter the following to create a 5MB device for transaction logs:

```
disk init name="gentran",
  physname="/home/sybase/gentran.dat",
  vdevno=3,
  size=2560
go
quit
```

The rest of the commands in this example can be run as user `luser`. Use **isql** to log in as `luser`:

```
isql -U luser -S SYBASE
```

To create a shopping database similar to the one discussed earlier in this chapter which utilizes the devices created with the previous commands, enter the following at the `isql`prompt:

```
CREATE DATABASE shopping ON gendev=20 LOG ON gentran=5
go
```

Please note that the sizes listed above are in megabytes, unlike the 2KB page size used by `disk init`.

The Sybase `luser` account can be modified to use the shopping database by default:

```
sp_modifylogin luser, defdb, shopping
go
```

To finish creating a database similar to the one created in the PostgreSQL examples earlier in this chapter, enter the sequence of commands shown in Listing 6.2.

Listing 6.2 *Creating databases.*

```
USE shopping
go
CREATE TABLE list (
     item            VARCHAR(32)     NULL,
     vendorcode      INT             NULL,
     quantity        INT             NULL)
go
```

```
CREATE TABLE vendors (
     vendorcode      INT             NULL,
     vendorname      VARCHAR(32)     NULL)
go
INSERT INTO vendors (vendorcode, vendorname)
   VALUES (100, 'Super Grocer')
go
INSERT INTO vendors (vendorcode, vendorname)
   VALUES (101, 'General Department Store')
go
INSERT INTO vendors (vendorcode, vendorname)
   VALUES (102, 'General Auto Parts')
go
INSERT INTO list (item, vendorcode, quantity)
   VALUES ('Root Beer', 100, 3)
go
INSERT INTO list (item, vendorcode, quantity)
   VALUES ('Ice Cream', 100, 1)
go
INSERT INTO list (item, vendorcode, quantity)
   VALUES ('Napkins', 101, 50)
go
INSERT INTO list (item, vendorcode, quantity)
   VALUES ('Spark Plugs', 102, 4)
go
CREATE CLUSTERED INDEX listtab ON list (vendorcode)
go
CREATE UNIQUE CLUSTERED INDEX vendortab ON vendors
(vendorcode)
go
GRANT SELECT ON list TO nobody
go
GRANT INSERT ON list TO nobody
go
GRANT SELECT ON vendors TO nobody
go
SELECT list.item, vendors.vendorname, list.quantity
        FROM list, vendors
        WHERE list.vendorcode = vendors.vendorcode
        ORDER BY item
go
```

If the preceding sequence of commands is entered, Sybase will respond with:

```
item                     vendorname                quantity
------------------------ ------------------------- --------
Ice Cream                Super Grocer                     1
Napkins                  General Department Store        50
Root Beer                Super Grocer                     3
Spark Plugs              General Auto Parts               4

(4 rows affected)
```

One specific indexing feature should be discussed in the above example. The above commands create a *clustered* index on each table. A clustered index in Sybase orders the data in the table in the method specified in the index creation statement. The important thing to note about clustered indexes is that the space released by `SQL DELETE` statements is not reused unless a clustered index is defined. Only a single clustered index can be defined for a table (the data can only be organized one way). Clustered indexes can be removed from a table with a `SQL DROP INDEX` command. Normal indexes can be created by omitting the `CLUSTERED` keyword.

Sybase also has a utility called `bcp` that can be used to copy database data in and out of operating system files. However, `bcp` is beyond the scope of this book.

Also note that Sybase supports outer joins, as demonstrated by the following example:

```
INSERT INTO list (item, vendorcode, quantity)
   VALUES ('African Violet', 103, 1)
go
SELECT list.item, vendors.vendorname, list.quantity
        FROM list, vendors
        WHERE list.vendorcode *= vendors.vendorcode
        ORDER BY item
go
item                   vendorname                 quantity
---------------------- -------------------------- --------
African Violet         NULL                              1
Ice Cream              Super Grocer                      1
Napkins                General Department Store         50
Root Beer              Super Grocer                      3
Spark Plugs            General Auto Parts                4
```

Note the *= in the `WHERE` clause of the above select. It allows *all* rows of the first table to be included, regardless of the existence of a matching entry in the secondary table. The =* relation reverses the effect. The command below will add a vendor to obviate the need for the outer join:

```
INSERT INTO vendors (vendorcode, vendorname)
  VALUES (103, 'ACME Plant Store')
go
```

Sybase databases can be updated with normal SQL syntax:

```
UPDATE list SET item = 'African Violets' WHERE vendorcode = 103;
```

Occasionally, the transaction logs for the shopping database should be cleared. This is done with the following:

```
dump tran shopping
go
```

This command will dump the transaction log to the default backup device (the **sp_helpdevice** command can be called to list the available devices). The transaction log will be cleared when the dump is complete. It is perfectly safe to run this command while the server is being accessed by other users.

```
dump tran shopping with truncate_only
go
```

This command will clear the transaction log without actually running a backup. Don't use this command if you have critical data integrity concerns.

```
dump database shopping
go
```

This command will dump the entire database out to the default backup device. The dump file can only be read by Sybase servers of the same release running on the same hardware platform.

Note The transaction log will *not* be cleared during this process. Dump the transaction log separately.

07

Dynamic Content Web Services

This chapter presents two of the main technologies for putting active content on the Web—Apache ModPerl and PHP.

For information systems requiring global visibility, the Web is an obvious choice. The Web has achieved such ubiquity that there simply are no reasonable alternatives. The Hypertext Markup Language (HTML), however, has one very serious weakness—its static nature. It was intended to be a method for sharing documents, not an interactive medium. As demands for increased sophistication mount, developers have focussed on technologies to overcome the static nature of the Web. Technologies such as Java, ActiveX, and XML represent the recent attempts to extend the power of the Web.

Perl is a text processing language that has recently developed database extensions and ModPerl—a special version that can be included within the Apache web server. The PHP language is deeply rooted in C and Awk and has always had a primary focus on the efficient use of SQL databases.

The information presented within this chapter is intended for Intel-based systems running Red Hat Linux 6.0. Much of the same information will be applicable to other platforms, however, as all of the software discussed here (Sybase, PostgreSQL, PHP 3.0) has been ported to a wide variety of UNIX implementations.

PHP

PHP (Professional Home Pages), the successor to PHP/FI, is a web utility that has enjoyed a great deal of popularity. It allows a C-like programming language with SQL extensions to be directly embedded within HTML documents, transforming them into active content. The software has recently been through a complete rewrite with a development emphasis upon performance. PHP requires no extensions to the browser, as it relies upon the CGI interface.

PHP supports a number of database servers in addition to Sybase and PostgreSQL. These include Adabas, mSQL, MySQL, Oracle, and ODBC. PHP now also supports LDAP directory services and the IMAP mail protocol. More information about PHP is available in the documentation at the developer's site—*http://www.php.net*.

Installing PHP

PHP is available from the PHP website or in the `sybase/php-3.0.12.tar.gz` file on the CD-ROM included with this text. You must use this file, or a later version if one is available.

There are two ways to configure PHP. It can be set up as a CGI binary, or as a module loaded at run-time for a supported Web server (Apache, the Netscape servers, and Microsoft IIS).

Loading PHP as an Apache module has a number of benefits. With the CGI approach, the entire PHP parser is loaded, executed and then terminated every time a browser accesses PHP on the server. When loaded as a module, on the other hand, the PHP parser becomes an integrated part of the Apache run-time environment. Because the PHP memory image is not loaded and destroyed by each access, the performance of the module configuration is significantly better. A module configuration will also permit much greater flexibility in the placement and access of PHP source files on the server. When used as a module, no reference to a `cgi-bin` directory is required in a URL; PHP application files can be placed anywhere within the web server document root.

However, there have been a number of security updates to the Apache Web server issued by Red Hat. Each time such an update occurs, the PHP-enabled Web server must be rebuilt from source. Such an arrangement can quickly become tedious. If the system is upgraded at a later date to a new version of Red Hat Linux, a rebuild of the web server will probably be necessary.

In compiling PHP as a CGI binary, PHP is built in such a way that it is entirely separate from Web server installation. Updates to the Web server can be applied without fear of disturbing PHP. This configuration should be appropriate for all but the busiest Web sites.

Running PHP as a CGI binary, however, could create a serious security problem. Apache allows files (named `.htaccess` by default) to limit access to Web pages to specific IP addresses or to users who supply a valid username-password combination. The CGI version of PHP does *not* honor `.htaccess` files. If installed as a

CGI binary, it can be used to read every Web page under the server's document root or users' directories (which lie in the `public_html` directory within the users' home accounts), regardless of the access control that has been specified in `.htaccess`. Luckily, this is not an issue with the Apache module version of PHP.

Ultimately, users who are not overly concerned with the security of their Web server's directory tree and who do not anticipate high volume usage of PHP-enabled Web pages, should install the CGI version of the parser. All others should take the extra time to install PHP as an Apache module.

This chapter will assume the safer (if more arduous) approach to the preparation of the PHP-enabled web server daemon. The steps required to prepare PHP as an Apache module follow. The script in Listing 7.1 must be run by root. It assumes that the PHP binary distribution (`php-3.0.12.tar.gz`) and the source RPM for Apache (`apache-1.3.6-7.src.rpm`) are in the current directory. A good place to start this build is in root's home directory (`/root`, also known by BASH as `~root`). This is a temporary space used to build Apache; it can be deleted once the new daemon is installed. Both the PHP and Apache source files are included on the attached CD-ROM in the `sybase` directory. RPM build methods are not used because they are not as convenient. A binary RPM version of `mod_php` exists, but it lacks Sybase support. The source is built outside of RPM to localize the build area.

There is some importance in the database selection options of the PHP configuration. In Listing 7.1, the script includes support for both Sybase and PostgreSQL. To remove support for PostgreSQL, remove the `--with-pgsql` directive. To remove support for Sybase, remove the `--with-sybase-ct` directive. If Sybase has not been installed in `/home/sybase`, as was suggested in the previous chapter, the installation directory must be specified as an option (e.g., `--with-sybase-ct=/opt/sybase`).

Listing 7.1 *Building Apache with PHP.*

```
#!/bin/sh
/etc/rc.d/init.d/httpd stop
mkdir apache
cd apache
rpm2cpio ../apache-1.3.6-7.src.rpm | cpio -i
tar xvzf apache_1.3.6.tar.gz
cd apache_1.3.6
for x in ../*.patch
do
     patch -p1 < $x
done
CFLAGS="-O2" LDFLAGS="-s" ./configure --prefix=/usr \
               --with-layout=RedHat \
               --enable-module=all \
               --disable-rule=WANTHSREGEX \
               --disable-module=auth_dbm \
               --with-perl=/usr/bin/perl
cd ../..
tar xvzf php-3.0.12.tar.gz
cd php-3.0.12
# Remove the "--with-pgsql" line below to disable PostgreSQL.
# Remove the "--with-sybase-ct" line below to disable Sybase support.
LDFLAGS="-s" CFLAGS="-O3 -I/usr/include/pgsql" ./configure --disable-debug
\
               --with-system-regex \
               --with-pgsql \
               --with-sybase-ct \
               --with-apache=../apache/apache_1.3.6
make
make install
cd ../apache/apache_1.3.6
CFLAGS="-O2" LDFLAGS="-s" ./configure --prefix=/usr \
               --with-layout=RedHat \
               --enable-module=all \
               --disable-rule=WANTHSREGEX \
               --disable-module=auth_dbm \
               --with-perl=/usr/bin/perl \
               --activate-module=src/modules/php3/libphp3.a
make
cd src
cp -f httpd /usr/sbin
echo 'AddType application/x-httpd-php3 .php3' >> /etc/httpd/conf/srm.conf
echo 'AddType application/x-httpd-php3 .phtml' >> /etc/httpd/conf/srm.conf
```

```
cd /etc/httpd/conf
sed 's/^LoadModule/#LoadModule/
s/^ClearModule/#ClearModule/
s/^AddModule/#AddModule/' httpd.conf > httpd.conf.avecphp
mv httpd.conf httpd.conf.sansphp
mv httpd.conf.avecphp httpd.conf
cd
/etc/rc.d/init.d/httpd start
```

The above script may take a great deal of time to run (from ten minutes to over an hour, depending upon the speed of the system). A copy of the script has been placed in the `sybase/PREP-APACHE.sh` file on the CD-ROM included in this text.

If the CGI configuration of PHP is desired, it can be prepared by root with the commands in Listing 7.2.

Listing 7.2 *Building the standalone (CGI) PHP.*

```
tar xvzf php-3.0.12.tar.gz
cd php-3.0.12
# Remove the "--with-pgsql" line below
# to disable PostgreSQL.
# Remove the "--with-sybase-ct" line below
# to disable Sybase support.
LDFLAGS="-s" CFLAGS="-O3 -I/usr/include/pgsql" ./configure --disable-debug \
             --with-pgsql \
             --with-sybase-ct \
             --with-system-regex
make
cp php /home/httpd/cgi-bin
```

Using SELECT from the Web

This section assumes that you have a firm working knowledge of HTML. If this is not the case, you might want to review the NCSA Beginner's Guide to HTML at *http://www.ncsa.uiuc.edu/General/Internet/WWW/HTMLPrimer.html.*

If you have installed a PHP-enabled web server and have entered the database commands described in the previous chapter, you are ready to build web pages that use SQL.

PHP and its earlier namesake, PHP/FI, use a C-like structured programming language that is embedded directly within HTML. PHP is used as a document preprocessor (much like the preprocessing stage of a C-compiler, except that it is much more powerful).

If you are using PostgreSQL, copy the HTML in Listing 7.3 into a file on your system named `/home/httpd/html/dbprint.php3`.

Listing 7.3 *Simple PostgreSQL Select from PHP.*

```
<HTML>
<HEAD>
<TITLE>View Database Records</TITLE>
</HEAD>
<BODY>

<DIV ALIGN="center">

<P>View Database Records</P>

<TABLE BORDER>

<TR>
<TH>item</TH>
<TH>vendorname</TH>
<TH>quantity</TH>
</TR>

<?PHP

        $conn = pg_Connect("", "", "", "", "shopping");

        if (!$conn) {
                echo "</table>An error occurred.\n";
                exit;
        }

    $result = pg_Exec($conn,
       "SELECT list.item, vendors.vendorname, list.quantity
               FROM list, vendors
               WHERE list.vendorcode = vendors.vendorcode
                        ORDER BY list.item;");

        if (!$result) {
                echo "</table>An error occurred.\n";
                exit;
        }

        $num = pg_NumRows($result);
        $i = 0;

        while ($i < $num) {
                echo "<TR><TD>";
```

```
                    echo pg_Result($result, $i, "item");
                    echo "</TD><TD>";
                    echo pg_Result($result, $i, "vendorname");
                    echo "</TD><TD>";
                    echo pg_Result($result, $i, "quantity");
                    echo "</TD></TR>";
                    $i++;
            }

            pg_FreeResult($result);
            pg_Close($conn);
?>

</TABLE>

</BODY>
</HTML>
```

The above PHP code extracts each vendorname in alphabetical order and prints it to the browser with a prefix of `OPTION` (as is required by the `SELECT` tag).

Noticing the `ORDER BY` clause in the above `SELECT` statement, an index on vendors.vendorname might be useful if the "vendors" table grows large.

The SQL-enabled document can be viewed with the URL *http://127.0.0.1/dbform.php3* (the URL for a CGI implementation of PHP would be *http://127.0.0.1/cgi-bin/php/dbform.php3*). The Fully Qualified Domain Name (FQDN) can be substituted for localhost to view the page from browsers that are running on different hosts.

Assuming that everything runs smoothly, and you created and populated the databases as described in the previous chapter, the display shown in Figure 7.1 should be presented.

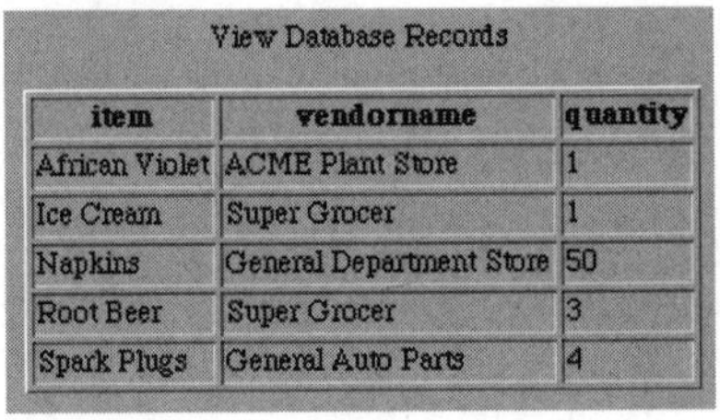

View Database Records

item	vendorname	quantity
African Violet	ACME Plant Store	1
Ice Cream	Super Grocer	1
Napkins	General Department Store	50
Root Beer	Super Grocer	3
Spark Plugs	General Auto Parts	4

Figure 7.1 *Output of dbprint.php3.*

PHP also has a directive that is similar to Server Side Includes (SSI) which is supported by most popular Web servers. If the command `include("/some/path/to/a/file.html")` is encountered in a PHP block, the specified file will be inserted and parsed by PHP. There is even a `phpIncludePath` variable that can be set that will allow the Web developer to dispense with path names. Conventional SSI directives will not be processed with the CGI version of PHP. URL locations on different hosts can also be included, such as `include ("http://www.redhat.com")`.

The CGI version of PHP can load files in users' home directories with URLs of the form

http://127.0.0.1/cgi-bin/php/~luser/dbprint.php3

The algorithm and syntax of the above HTML example are relatively simple. They are taken almost directly from the PHP/FI documentation.

Notice first the enclosing `<?PHP` and `?>` tags that surround the non-HTML language. These mark the beginning and end respectively of PHP language statements. You may insert PHP statements delimited by these markers as many times as you like in your HTML file.

These PHP statements do the following:

`pg_Connect()`
: Establishes a connection to the grocery database on the local server. It would be possible to place the PostgreSQL database server on a separate host. If such a thing were done, the target host would be entered here

`pg_Exec()`
: Executes a SQL query and stores the output in a variable named `$result`

`pg_NumRows()`
: Returns the number of rows extracted from the table by the previous SELECT

`while loop`
: Extracts and prints (using `echo`) the results, row by row, with the `pg_Result()` function call

`pg_FreeResult()`
: Discards the contents of the previous `pg_Exec`, which can be important when running several consecutive large queries.

`pg_Close()`
: Closes the connections and releases the buffer memory.

If the CGI version of PHP is prepared, the binary can be used as a script interpreter that can be called from the shell. Consider the variant of the previous script found in Listing 7.4.

Listing 7.4 *Running PHP scripts from the shell.*

```
#!/usr/local/bin/php -f
<?PHP

        $conn = pg_Connect("", "", "", "", "shopping");

        if (!$conn) {
                echo "An error occurred.\n";
                exit;
        }

    $result = pg_Exec($conn,
       "SELECT list.item, vendors.vendorname, list.quantity
               FROM list, vendors
               WHERE list.vendorcode = vendors.vendorcode
                        ORDER BY list.item;");

        if (!$result) {
                echo "An error occurred.\n";
                exit;
        }

        $num = pg_NumRows($result);
        $i = 0;

        while ($i < $num) {
                echo pg_Result($result, $i, "item");
                echo "\t";
                echo pg_Result($result, $i, "vendorname");
                echo "\t";
                echo pg_Result($result, $i, "quantity");
                echo "\n";
                $i++;
        }

        pg_FreeResult($result);
        pg_Close($conn);
?>
```

If the CGI version of PHP is placed in `/usr/local/bin`, this script can be executed directly from the shell. For this reason, administrators often build PHP both as an Apache module and as a CGI. Notice specifically that `/usr/local/bin` cannot be accessed by the web server, so the CGI security issues do not apply. If you are installing the CGI version of PHP for shell scripts, do not put a copy in `/home/httpd/cgi-bin`, or in any other position which would allow execution by the web server.

Listing 7.5 shows how calls to a Sybase database can be executed.

Listing 7.5 *Simple Sybase Select from PHP.*

```
<HTML>
<HEAD>
<TITLE>View Database Records</TITLE>
</HEAD>
<BODY>

<DIV ALIGN="center">

<P>View Database Records</P>

<TABLE BORDER>

<TR>
<TH>item</TH>
<TH>vendorname</TH>
<TH>quantity</TH>
</TR>

<?PHP
        error_reporting(1);

  $conn = sybase_connect("SYBASE", "nobody", "nobodypass");

        sybase_select_db("shopping",$conn);

        if (!$conn) {
                echo "</table>An error occurred.\n";
                exit;
        }

    $rc = sybase_query(
       "SELECT list.item, vendors.vendorname, list.quantity
               FROM list, vendors
               WHERE list.vendorcode = vendors.vendorcode
                        ORDER BY list.item",$conn);
```

```
        if (!$rc) {
                echo "</table>An error occurred.\n";
                exit;
        }

        while ($result = sybase_fetch_array($rc)) {

// The alternate syntaxes of the following two lines
// are both legal.

                echo "<TR><TD>$result[item]";
                echo "</TD><TD>" . $result["vendorname"];

                echo "</TD><TD>$result[quantity]";
                echo "</TD></TR>";
        }

        sybase_free_result($rc);
        sybase_close($conn);

?>

</TABLE>

</BODY>
</HTML>
```

The syntax used for the above Sybase example relies upon a PHP `fetch_array()` function. The `fetch_array()` functions return *associative arrays,* which allow the `$result[]` array elements to be addressed directly by column name, in addition to the numeric offsets. The only weakness to this approach is that if two tables have columns of the same name; the second such column cannot be addressed by the associative array. Sybase does have a method to rename a column, however:

```
SELECT "newname" = list.item, vendors.vendorname,
list.quantity
     FROM list, vendors
     WHERE list.vendorcode = vendors.vendorcode
          ORDER BY list.item
```

Using the preceding Sybase SQL syntax, the "item" column could be addressed within PHP as `$results["newname"]`.

Sybase also generates warning messages within PHP when the active database is changed (with the call to `sybase_select_db("shopping",$conn)` above). The call to `error_reporting(1)` suppresses these messages. A Sybase login can be set to use a specific database by default by calling the `sp_modifylogin` stored procedure as was discussed in the previous chapter. If the login is set appropriately, the calls to `sybase_select_db()` and `error_reporting(1)` can be omitted.

Using INSERT from the Web

This section assumes that you have a firm working knowledge of HTML forms. If this is not the case, you might want to review the NCSA Guide to Fill-Out-Forms at *http://www.ncsa.uiuc.edu/SDG/Software/Mosaic/Docs/fill-out-forms/overview.html.*

There are two main sections of HTML that will be used (in our example) to add records to the database. First, an HTML form must be constructed so that the information can be easily entered by the browser. Second, the information must be returned and processed by PHP in order to add it to the table.

The implementation of the form, and specifically the vendor field, presents a design dilemma. The `SELECT` form tag is the most obvious HTML form element to use to present a pre-defined vendor list. Should this list be hard-coded in the HTML? If another vendor is added to the "vendors" table, the HTML will not be automatically updated, and users will not be able to enter data against the new vendor. The form elements for the vendor `SELECT` tag could alternately be generated by PHP each time the form is accessed. The drawback to this method is that the server load will be increased.

Another approach would be to generate the HTML for the form whenever the "vendors" table is updated. This could be accomplished in a variety of ways, some of which stem from the fact that the CGI version of PHP can be called from a Unix shell prompt as well as from a CGI environment.

The second alternative is presented below; each time the page for the data-entry form is accessed, PHP uses a SQL `SELECT` to obtain the data from the "vendors" table to build the HTML `SELECT` list.

To implement this example, copy the HTML in Listing 7.6 on page 186 into a file on your system named `/home/httpd/html/dbform.php3`.

Listing 7.6 *Preparing a form with PostgreSQL.*

```
<HTML>
<HEAD>
<TITLE>Insert Database Record</TITLE>
</HEAD>
<BODY>

<DIV ALIGN="center">

<H1>Add Database Record</H1>

<FORM METHOD="post" ACTION="dbinsert.php3">

<TABLE BORDER="0">

<TR>
<TD>New Item:</TD>
<TD><INPUT NAME="item"></TD>
</TR>

<TR>
<TD>Vendor:</TD>
<TD><SELECT NAME="vendor" SIZE="1">

<?PHP

        $conn = pg_Connect("", "", "", "", "grocery");

        if (!$conn) {
                echo "An error occurred.\n";
                exit;
        }

        $rc = pg_Exec($conn,
                "SELECT vendorcode, vendorname
                        FROM vendors
                        ORDER BY vendorname;");

        if (!$rc) {
                echo "An error occurred.\n";
                exit;
        }

      $num = pg_Numrows($rc);
      $i = 0;
```

```
     while ($i < $num) {
          echo "\n<OPTION VALUE=\"" .
               pg_Result($rc, $i, "vendorcode") .
               "\">" .
               pg_Result($rc, $i, "vendorname");
          $i++;
     }

        pg_FreeResult($result);
        pg_Close($conn);
?>

</SELECT></TD>
</TR>

<TR>
<TD>Quantity:</TD>
<TD><INPUT NAME="quantity"></TD>
</TR>


</TABLE>

<INPUT TYPE="submit">

</FORM>

</BODY>
</HTML>
```

Noticing the ORDER BY clause in the above SELECT statement, you should conclude that an index on vendors.vendorname might be useful if the "vendors" table grows large.The above PHP code extracts each vendorname in alphabetical order and prints it to the browser with an OPTION prefix (as is required by the HTML SELECT tag). The numerical vendor code is recorded as the value to be passed if the respective vendor name is passed.

The SQL-enabled document can be viewed with the URL *http://127.0.0.1/dbform.php3* (the URL for a CGI implementation of PHP would be *http://127.0.0.1/cgi-bin/php/dbform.php3*).

Assuming that everything runs smoothly, an HTML form such as the one shown in Figure 7.2 should be presented.

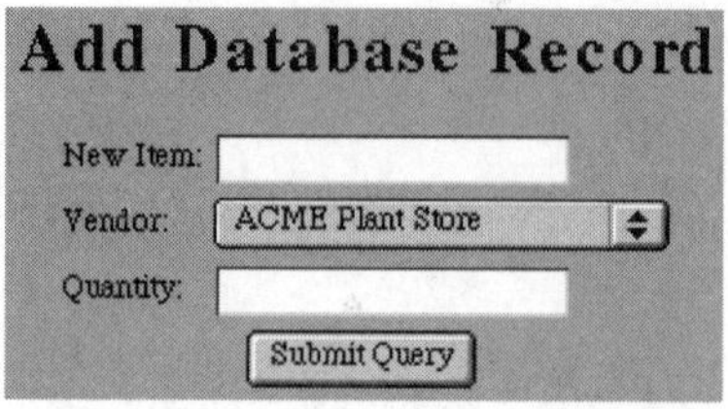

Figure 7.2 *Output of dbform.php3.*

Listing 7.7 exhibits what the Sybase version of `dbform.php3` might look like.

Listing 7.7 *Preparing a form with Sybase.*

```
<HTML>
<HEAD>
<TITLE>Insert Database Record</TITLE>
</HEAD>
<BODY>

<DIV ALIGN="center">

<H1>Add Database Record</H1>

<FORM METHOD="post" ACTION="dbinsert.php3">

<TABLE BORDER>

<TR>
<TD>New Item:</TD>
<TD><INPUT NAME="item">
</TR>

<TR>
<TD>Vendor:</TD>
<TD><SELECT NAME="vendor" SIZE="1">

<?PHP
   error_reporting(1);

   $conn = sybase_connect("SYBASE", "nobody", "nobodypass");

   sybase_select_db("shopping",$conn);
```

```
    if (!$conn) {
        echo "An error occurred.\n";
        exit;
    }

    $rc = sybase_query(
        "SELECT vendorcode, vendorname
            FROM vendors
            ORDER BY vendorname", $conn);

    if (!$rc) {
        echo "An error occurred.\n";
        exit;
    }

    while ($result = sybase_fetch_array($rc)) {
        echo "<OPTION VALUE=\"$result[vendorcode]\">$result[vendorname]";
    }

    sybase_free_result($rc);
    sybase_close($conn);
?>

</SELECT></TD>
</TR>

<TR>
<TD>Quantity:</TD>
<TD><INPUT NAME="quantity"></TD>
</TR>


</TABLE>

<INPUT TYPE="submit">

</FORM>

</BODY>
</HTML>
```

Now that the “front end” is complete, a “back end” must be implemented. The HTML in Listing 7.8 on page 190 should be copied into a file on the system named `/home/httpd/html/dbinsert.php3`.

Listing 7.8 *Database insertions with PostgreSQL.*

```
<HTML>
<HEAD>
<TITLE>Confirm Database Insert</TITLE>
</HEAD>
<BODY>

<DIV ALIGN="center">

<?PHP

        $conn = pg_Connect("", "", "", "", "shopping");

        if (!$conn) {
                echo "An error occurred.\n";
                exit;
        }

        pg_Exec($conn,
             "INSERT INTO list (item, vendorcode, quantity)
                   VALUES ('$item', $vendor, $quantity);");

        pg_Close($conn);
?>

Database Updated

</BODY>
</HTML>
```

With complete information for the item, vendorcode, and quantity fields of the "list" table, the data can then be inserted by the `pg_Exec()` call.

Notice that the *vendor* variable name given to the HTML `SELECT` tag in `dbform.php3` is available to PHP in `dbinsert.php3`. The same is true of the *item* and *quantity* form elements that are used in the `pg_Exec()`. PHP carries variable information into the form action without any intervention from the developer.

Notice the format of the SQL `INSERT` statement, in that it lists the field names that are respectively associated with the `VALUES` clause. This type of SQL `INSERT` should always be used in development; it will allow greater changes to the table structure without the necessity of recoding. Any fields not referenced in the `INSERT` will be populated with NULL values if the table format will allow it.

The above PHP performs the SQL insert transactions and sends a confirmation message to the browser. If these `.php3` files were describing a high-production data entry interface, it might be useful to copy (or `include()`) `dbform.php3` onto the end of `dbinsert.php3` so that the form is continually presented.

The Sybase version of `dbinsert.php` is presented in Listing 7.9.

Listing 7.9 *Database insertions with Sybase.*

```
<HTML>
<HEAD>
<TITLE>Confirm Database Insert</TITLE>
</HEAD>
<BODY>

<DIV ALIGN="center">

<?PHP
        error_reporting(1);

  $conn = sybase_connect("SYBASE", "nobody", "nobodypass");

        sybase_select_db("shopping",$conn);

        if (!$conn) {
                echo "An error occurred.\n";
                exit;
        }

     sybase_query(
        "INSERT INTO list (item, vendorcode, quantity)
             VALUES ('$item', $vendor, $quantity)", $conn);

        sybase_close($conn);
?>

Database Updated

</BODY>
</HTML>
```

For another example of PHP, an authentication mechanism similar to an `.htaccess` file will be demonstrated that authenticates against a Sybase database.

Place the code in Listing 7.10 on page 192 in `/home/httpd/html/auth.php3`.

Listing 7.10 *Web authentication with a Sybase database.*

```
<?php

   error_reporting(1);

   if(!isset($PHP_AUTH_USER))
   {
      Header("WWW-Authenticate: Basic realm=\"PHP Auth\"");
          Header("HTTP/1.0 401 Unauthorized");
          echo "You must log in to access these pages.\n";
          exit;
   }
   else
   {
    $link=sybase_connect("SYBASE", "nobody", "nobodypass");

          sybase_select_db("security",$link);

          $rc = sybase_query("SELECT password
                      FROM auth
                      WHERE name='$PHP_AUTH_USER'", $link);

          /* should be 1 row */
          if(sybase_num_rows($rc) != 1)
          {
      Header("WWW-Authenticate: Basic realm=\"PHP Auth\"");
      Header("HTTP/1.0 401 Unauthorized");
      echo "Attempt to log in as $PHP_AUTH_USER failed.\n";
      exit;
          }

          $row = sybase_fetch_array($rc);

          if($PHP_AUTH_PW != $row[password])
          {
      Header("WWW-Authenticate: Basic realm=\"PHP Auth\"");
      Header("HTTP/1.0 401 Unauthorized");
      echo "Attempt to log in as $PHP_AUTH_USER failed.\n";
               exit;
          }

          sybase_close($link);

// $PHP_AUTH_USER and $PHP_AUTH_PW are global and authenticated.
     }
?>
```

The above example relies upon a database named *security* which contains a table named "auth" (although another database and/or table name could be substituted if they had a similar format). The "auth" table must contain name and password entries in *clear text.*

Another PHP document could make use of the authentication subroutine by using the `include()` directive to read it. As an example, examine the PHP document in Listing 7.11.

Listing 7.11 *Calling the authentication subroutine.*

```
<?php

include("auth.php3");

?>

<HTML>
<HEAD>
<TITLE>Authenticated Document</TITLE>
</HEAD>
<BODY>

<?php

echo "some sensitive data";

?>

</BODY>
</HTML>
```

Any attempt to load this document would cause a password prompt to be presented.

The example in Listing 7.12 shows that PHP has applications outside the realm of databases. Assume HTML of the following form:

Listing 7.12 *File upload with HTML.*

```
<html>
<body>
<form enctype="multipart/form-data" action=".upload.php3"
method=post>
<input type="hidden" name="MAX_FILE_SIZE" value="10000000">
Send this file:<input name="userfile" type="file">
<input type="submit" value="Send File">
</form>
</body>
</html>
```

The PHP in Listing 7.13 will take a file passed by the web browser and store it on the server.

Listing 7.13 *Processing a file upload with PHP.*

```
<html>
<body>

<?php

if (is_file("/home/httpd/html/upload/$userfile_name"))
            echo "The file $userfile_name already exists;
            pick another name.";
else
{
    $f1 = fopen("$userfile","r");

    if(!$f1)
    {
        echo "File not received properly.";
        exit();
    }

    $f2 =

      fopen("/home/httpd/html/upload/$userfile_name","w");

    if(!$f2)
    {
        echo "File could not be created.";
        exit();
    }

    while($buffer = fread($f1, 1024))
        fwrite($f2, $buffer);

    fclose($f1);
    fclose($f2);

  echo "The file $userfile_name was successfully stored.";
}

?>

</body>
</html>
```

The above script will allow files to be placed in the `/home/httpd/html/upload` directory. The directory must have write permissions for nobody (one way to accomplish this would be to put the directory in the group nobody and assign group write permissions). The maximum size of the file upload is controlled not by the HTML above, but by the upload_max_filesize PHP configuration directive in /usr/local/lib/php3.ini. The default maximum file size is 2 megabytes.

Apache mod_perl

mod_perl is a special version of the perl interpreter that can be included within the Apache web server. mod_perl enables dramatic speed improvements on the execution of Perl scripts from a web environment.

The RPM version of mod_perl documented here will not work with the Apache-PHP configuration documented earlier in this chapter; it must be installed on the stock Apache RPM distribution. It would be highly unwise to run both PHP and mod_perl at the same time, as the binary image of the web server would be huge. If the functionality of both packages is required, it might be preferable to configure two separate web servers, running at different ports, with the appropriate modules installed in each.

A mod_perl RPM image is included with Red Hat Linux, but it is not installed by default. It can be found in the RedHat/RPMS/mod_perl-1.19-2.i386.rpm file on the CD-ROM included with this text. Enter the commands shown in Listing 7.14 to install it.

Listing 7.14 *Installing mod_perl for Apache.*

```
/etc/rc.d/init.d/httpd stop

rpm -Uvh mod_perl-1.19-2.i386.rpm

echo 'LoadModule perl_module        modules/libperl.so
AddModule mod_perl.c

<Files ~ "\.pl$">
SetHandler perl-script
PerlHandler Apache::Registry
Options ExecCGI
</Files>

PerlSendHeader On' >> /etc/httpd/conf/httpd.conf

/etc/rc.d/init.d/httpd start
```

At this point, perl scripts that are placed in the document root will take advantage of `mod_perl`. To test `mod_perl`, create the perl script in Listing 7.15.

Listing 7.15 *Testing mod_perl.*

```
echo '#!/usr/bin/perl

print "Content-type: text/html\n\n";

print $ENV{"GATEWAY_INTERFACE"};
print "<br>";
print $ENV{"MOD_PERL"};' > /home/httpd/html/ptest.pl
```

Then load this script with a URL of *http://127.0.0.1/ptest.pl* in a web browser. The output should be:

```
CGI-Perl/1.1
mod_perl/1.19
```

`mod_perl` can be *much* more destructive than PHP with improper perl source code. Read the documentation produced by the following commands to learn about programming structure limitations imposed by `mod_perl`:

```
perldoc cgi_to_mod_perl
perldoc mod_perl_traps
```

`mod_perl` is *not* for novice or irreverent perl programmers. Such developers will be much better advised to pursue PHP.

Pg Perl

The PostgreSQL interface to perl is included in the PostgreSQL packages on Red Hat Linux 6.0 (it is actually in `postgresql-clients-6.4.2-3.i386.rpm`).

The perl interface is relatively straightforward and is completely documented in the online manual page (use the command `man Pg` to access it).

Listing 7.16 is a script to access the contents of the shopping database from within perl.

Listing 7.16 *An example of Pg Perl.*

```
#!/usr/bin/perl

use Pg;

$conn = Pg::connectdb("dbname = shopping");

$result = $conn-exec("SELECT list.item, vendors.vendorname,
list.quantity
                     FROM list, vendors
                     WHERE list.vendorcode = vendors.vendorcode
                     ORDER BY list.item;");

$ntuples = $result->ntuples;

for($i=0; $i < $ntuples; $i++)
{
      $item = $result-getvalue($i, 0);
      $vendorname = $result-getvalue($i, 1);
      $quantity = $result-getvalue($i, 2);
      print "$quantity\t$item\t$vendorname\n";
}
```

Please notice that the user running the script is the PostgreSQL user who will attempt to access the database. In the examples in the last two chapters, only `luser` and `nobody` have such permissions, so the script will fail for everyone else.

sybperl

The preeminent perl connection tool for Sybase databases is the `sybperl` distribution written by Michael Peppler. The `sybperl-2.10_02.tar.gz` home page can be found at *http://www.mbay.net/~mpeppler/* (which doubles as the author's personal home page). Additionally, Michael Peppler has written a DBI/DBD Perl interface for Sybase, but these interfaces are still in an alpha release, so they are not included here.

The script below builds only Sybase CT-Lib support for perl. Support for the older Sybase DB-Lib, and the utilities based upon it (such as the BCP routines), is not built because there are conflicts with various DBM packages. The resolution of these conflicts is beyond the scope of this text.

Listing 7.17 is a script to build `sybperl-2.10_02`. The source package can be obtained from the CD-ROM included with this text in `sybase/sybperl-2.10_02.tar.gz` or from Michael Peppler's web site. Please note that if Sybase was not installed in `/home/sybase` as server name `SYBASE` with an administrator's password of *sapass*, then the script below must be modified to reflect these changes. To build `sybperl`, enter the following commands as root. (The versions documented below take a *long* time to compile—over seventeen minutes on a P166. Do not interrupt them.)

Listing 7.17 *Compiling Sybperl.*

```
#!/bin/sh
tar xvzf sybperl-2.10_02.tar.gz
cd sybperl-2.10_02
sed 's/^SYBASE=.*$/SYBASE=\/home\/sybase/
s/^DBLIBVS=.*$/DBLIBVS=0/' CONFIG > CONFIG.NEW
mv -f CONFIG.NEW CONFIG
sed 's/PWD=/PWD=sapass/
s/SRV=.*$/SRV=SYBASE/' PWD > PWD.NEW
mv -f PWD.NEW PWD
perl Makefile.PL
make
make test
make install
```

Assuming that perl is enabled with the CT-Lib functions of Sybperl, the script in Listing 7.18 will fetch a SQL query from Sybase when run from a shell.

Listing 7.18 *An example call to Sybperl.*

```
#!/usr/bin/perl

# Load the Sybase::CTlib module:
use Sybase::CTlib;

# Allocate a new Database 'handle':
$dbh = new Sybase::CTlib 'luser', 'luserpass', 'SYBASE';

# Select the target database:
$dbh-ct_sql("use shopping");
```

```
# Send the query to the server:
$dbh-ct_execute("SELECT list.item, vendors.vendorname,
list.quantity
                 FROM list, vendors
                 WHERE list.vendorcode = vendors.vendorcode
                 ORDER BY list.item");

# Retrieve the result sets
while($dbh-ct_results($restype) == CS_SUCCEED) {

   # Skip non-fetchable results:
   next unless $dbh-ct_fetchable($restype);

   # Retrieve actual data rows:
   while(($item, $vendorname, $quantity) = $dbh-ct_fetch) {
        print "$quantity\t$item\t$vendorname\n";
    }
}
```

The script could easily be modified to run from an HTML context.

08

Samba Services and Windows Connectivity

The prevalence of the Microsoft Windows platform is most distressing for UNIX enthusiasts. For a long time, UNIX was so much more powerful than Windows that the PC platform could be ignored completely; Windows could play no role in enterprise computing. But times have changed and powerful applications have made their homes on Windows, for better or for worse. The UNIX world must occasionally play a role in Windows networking, and Samba over TCP/IP will let you do just that.

The NetBIOS networking environment began as a joint project of Microsoft and IBM. It originally made use of a non-routable protocol (NetBEUI) that was intended only for small computer networks. NetBIOS itself was subsequently reimplemented over TCP/IP. NetBIOS over TCP/IP still bears the limitations of its original design (i.e., WINS). Its union with TCP/IP could never be described as harmonious. Still, Microsoft has promoted this overworked protocol as the "Common Internet File System," and it is rare that NetBIOS can be entirely ignored in the networked enterprise, however unfortunate that may be.

Samba is a free implementation of NetBIOS over TCP/IP for UNIX. While there are problems with the design (it forks too many processes), Samba has seen enterprise-class usage and has withstood the associated challenges. The goal of the Samba project is to reproduce the entire network functionality of Windows NT within UNIX (which includes the ability to function as a domain controller).

With RedHat Linux, Samba is an optional component that can be selected during system installation. If it is installed, the Linux system will be a fully operational NetBIOS file server when the system boots for the first time.

Caution The original Samba release in Red Hat 6.0 had a security problem. Be certain that you are running the samba-2.0.5a-1.i386.rpm release, or later.

Note If you use Samba, its author would like you to send him a pizza. The Samba web site at *http://www.samba.org* has information on how this might be accomplished. It can be a challenge; he lives in Australia. (And no, the author of this text has not yet sent his pizza, but will if he should have the misfortune of working in Windows in the future.)

Samba and Password Encryption

Microsoft doesn't like Samba. They have good reason not to like it. Recent performance improvements in Samba have made it faster than the default configuration of Windows NT for file and print services on most hardware.

In fact, Microsoft dislikes Samba so much that they made password changes to the Windows NT Service Pack 3 to prevent it from sharing unencrypted passwords with a Samba server. Samba's default settings are for unencrypted passwords, but these settings can be modified to circumvent this dastardly mischievousness.

The new encrypted passwords are not compatible with the DES format used in `/etc/passwd` or `/etc/shadow`, so Samba must have its own distinct password file when encrypted passwords are enabled. If connecting with either Windows NT Service Pack 3 or higher (or Windows 98 or higher), encrypted passwords must be implemented before these clients will function. This is done by removing the comments from the following two lines (they are lines 65 and 66 in `/etc/smb.conf`):

```
encrypt passwords = yes
smb passwd file = /etc/smbpasswd
```

The Samba server must then be restarted by running the following command as root:

/etc/rc.d/init.d/smb restart

When this is done, no users will be allowed to login to the Samba server. Each user must be individually added to the new `/etc/smbpasswd` file by root. The method for doing so follows:

```
# smbpasswd -a luser
New SMB password:
Retype new SMB password:
```

The username `luser` must exist in the `/etc/passwd` database when the command is executed. When it is executed, the `/etc/smbpasswd` will be created with contents similar to the following:

```
# Samba SMB password file
luser:500:5EDBBAA6F82E9DD9AAD3B435B51404EE:
F908E55FD20399082E5ADEB9792D27D1:
/home/luser:/bin/bash
```

Once the root user has created the entries in `/etc/smbpasswd`, individual users can change their Samba password by running the **smbpasswd** command with no arguments.This procedure must be executed for each user on the system. On a new system, it should be part of the routine to establish a new user account.

On an older system where many accounts already exist, however, it might not be practical to migrate each individual user in this way. In that case, there is a (rather awkward) method to migrate such users *en masse*.To migrate an existing non-encrypted password file into /etc/smbpasswd, *do not* set the encryption option in /etc/smb.conf. First execute the following command as root:

cat /etc/passwd | /usr/bin/mksmbpasswd.sh /etc/smbpasswd
chmod 600 /etc/smbpasswd

This operation will create an entry for each user in /etc/smbpasswd. They will have the following form:

```
luser:500:XXXXXXXXXXXXXXXXXXXXXXXXXXXXXXXX:
XXXXXXXXXXXXXXXXXXXXXXXXXXXXXXXX:
:/home/luser:/bin/bash
```

These entries have no password, and users cannot change them.

The following options must then be added to /etc/smb.conf:

```
update encrypted = yes
smb passwd file = /etc/smbpasswd
```

The Samba server must then be restarted by running the following command as root:

/etc/rc.d/init.d/smb restart

At this point, users can login to Samba using *older, unencrypted clients* (such as Windows 95), and the /etc/smbpasswd file will be populated with the encrypted passwords as the users connect.

When the migration is complete, the option

```
update encrypted = yes
```

contained in /etc/smb.conf can be replaced with:

```
encrypt passwords = yes
```

Samba will then switch to the encrypted versions only, and the newer clients can login.

A migration such as the one discussed above will require planning, timing, and forethought, especially for a large enterprise. It should be initiated several months before these newer clients enter a Samba network.

Mapping Users

Windows 95 and 98 differ substantially from Windows NT in their ability to make use of network resources. Windows NT will allow the user to change his login identity for a particular server; Windows 95 and 98 will allow only a single login identity for all network resources to be entered at boot/login time. This becomes extremely inconvenient when a user logged into a Windows network wishes to connect to their account on a Samba system and the names used in each environment are different.

Because of this, it is sometimes convenient to translate an incoming username to a different UNIX user. To do so, uncomment line 79 in `/etc/smb.conf`:

```
username map = /etc/smbusers
```

Then populate `/etc/smbusers` with the translations:

```
# Unix_name = SMB_name1 SMB_name2 ...
#root = administrator admin
#nobody = guest pcguest smbguest
1user = FunnyWindowsUser
user2 = WindowsUser2 Otheruser diewindowsdie
```

The `root` and `nobody` users are not commented out of the `/etc/smbusers` file included in the standard Samba RPM distribution. It is advisable to remove them, unless a valid reason for these user mappings can be demonstrated.

Samba and the Master Browser

In a Windows NT network, a centralized computer is responsible for maintaining a list of NetBIOS servers and their browsable shares. This computer is called the *master browser.* If the Windows NT network has a *Domain Controller,* then the Domain Controller is the master browser for the network. If there is no Domain Controller, the Windows NT Server computers will hold an *election.* The results of the election will determine which Windows NT system will be the master browser. If no Windows NT Server systems are available, Windows NT Workstation computers will converse and allocate one of their number as the master browser.

When improperly configured, Samba can repeatedly force these elections upon the network in an attempt to become the master browser, causing great contention with the true master browser.

To halt this behavior, append the following to `/etc/smb.conf`:

```
domain master = no
local master = no
preferred master = no
os level = 0
```

Samba Server Components

The `/etc/smb.conf` file contains a number of important parameters and example configurations. An option that deserves consideration is the workgroup name:

```
workgroup = MYGROUP
```

This name should be changed to the desired domain name or workgroup name for the network.

It is possible that a client will not be able to see a Samba server because it lies on the far side of a router. If you have this problem, create an `LMHOSTS` file on the client to direct queries for a particular IP. The proper location for this file depends upon the Windows variant being used; it lies in the `\windows` directory on Windows 95 and 98. For NT, look for the file `LMHOSTS.SAM` (which is a sample `LMHOSTS` file with demonstrations of many of the common configurations); `LMHOSTS` should be placed in the same directory as the sample file.

To allow the client to see the Samba server, the `LMHOSTS` entry would have the following form:

```
1.2.3.4 remotehost #PRE
```

The `#PRE` instructs windows to "preload" the entry, making it available before dynamic lookups are performed. If the `LMHOSTS` file is modified, it can be reloaded into Windows by issuing `nbtstat -R` from a DOS prompt. If `LMHOSTS` files become inconvenient because of a large number of clients, the use of a WINS server (either on Samba or NT) should be investigated, especially in conjunction with DHCP (See Chapter 2: Basic Networking for more details).

Samba has a number of options for WINS services; start with `smb.conf` for details.

It is also possible that a client will not be able to connect to the Samba server because the wrong protocols have been loaded. Samba requires TCP/IP support on the client, which is not loaded by default on some versions of Windows (Windows 95 specifically). To enable Windows 95 or 98 to use Samba resources, you must load *Client for Microsoft Networks* and TCP/IP in the Network section of the Control Panel. Consult a Windows networking text for more details.

File Services

By default, as soon as the Samba server is activated, users can mount their home directories as drive letters on their Windows systems by using a share of the form

```
\\remotehost\luser
```

where `remotehost` is the remote Red Hat Samba server, and `luser` is any user on that host.

Should this behavior not be desired, remove the following section from `/etc/smb.conf`:

```
[homes]
   comment = Home Directories
   browseable = no
   writable = yes
```

To create a public browsable area, add an entry of the following form:

```
# A publicly accessible directory, but read only, except
for people in
# the "staff" group
[public]
   comment = Public Stuff
   path = /home/samba
   public = yes
   writable = yes

   printable = no
   write list = @staff
```

In order to create a set of users able to write to such a directory, an entry for `staff` must be created and populated with the selected users in `/etc/group`, and those users must correspond to user entries in `/etc/passwd`. Note also that the directory permissions must also be set to writable for the `staff` group, as UNIX permissions will still apply.

The following example demonstrates the "valid users" directive, an alternative to using groups:

```
# The following two entries demonstrate how to share a
directory so that two
# users can place files there that will be owned by the
specific users. In this
# setup, the directory should be writable by both users and
should have the
# sticky bit set on it to prevent abuse. Obviously this
could be extended to
# as many users as required.
[myshare]
   comment = Mary's and Fred's stuff
   path = /usr/somewhere/shared
   valid users = mary fred
   public = no
   writable = yes
   printable = no
   create mask = 0765
```

Illustrated below is the procedure for mapping these server resources on Windows clients. First, in Windows 98 or Windows 95, right-click on the "My Computer" icon. From this menu, select "Map Network Drive" (Figure 8.1).

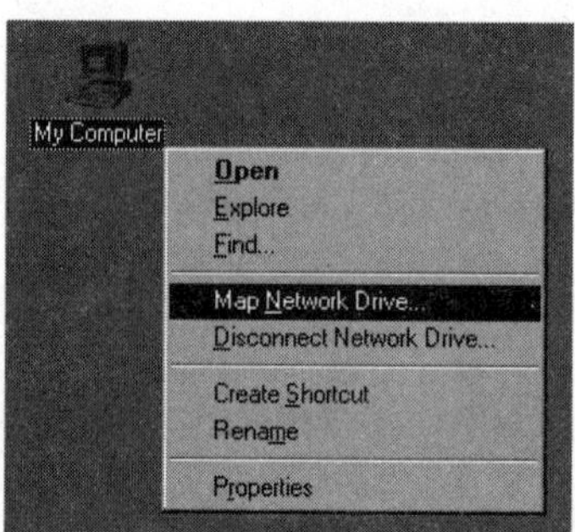

Figure 8.1 *Windows 95/98 – Map Network Drive.*

Select an empty virtual drive and enter the share to be mapped (Figure 8.2).

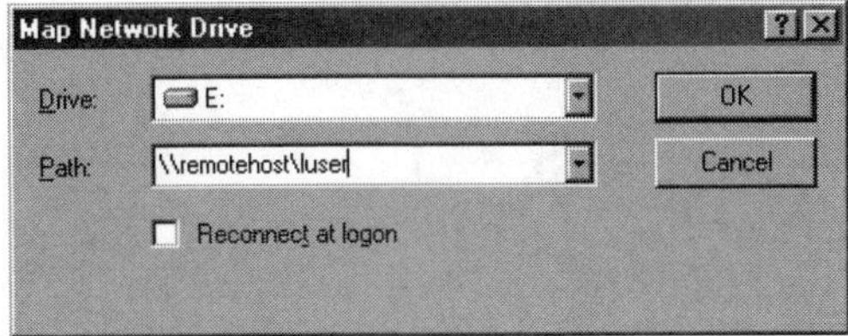

Figure 8.2 *Windows 95/98 – Map Network Drive – Detail.*

Provide the server password to complete the connection (Figure 8.3).

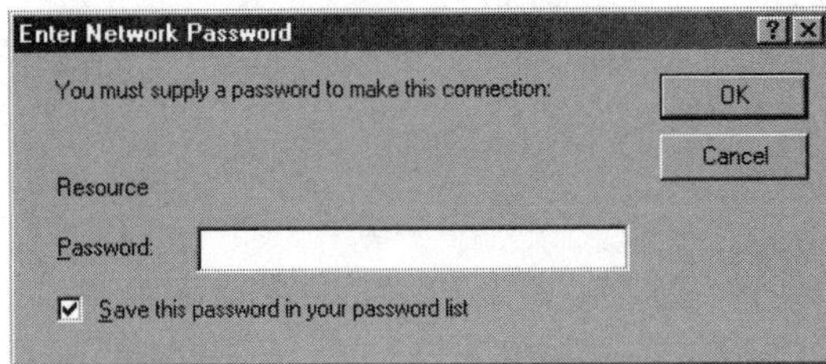

Figure 8.3 *Windows 95/98 – Password dialog box.*

The procedure in Windows NT is slightly different (Figure 8.4).

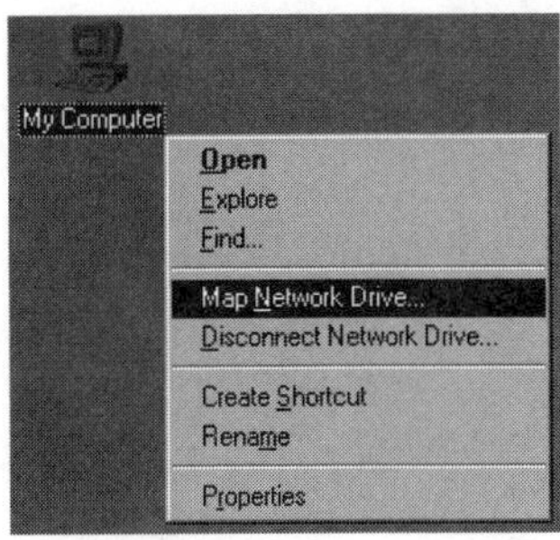

Figure 8.4 *Windows NT – Map Network Drive.*

Windows NT allows the user to "Connect As" (Figure 8.5), a feature sorely lacking in the Windows 95/98 releases.

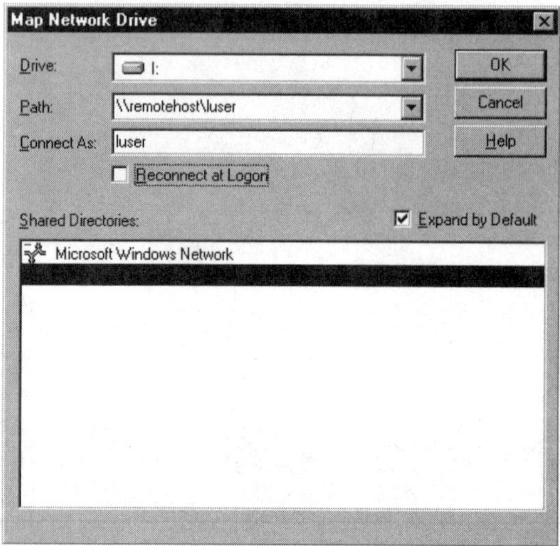

Figure 8.5 *Windows NT – Map Network Drive – Detail.*

Provide the server password to complete the connection (Figure 8.6).

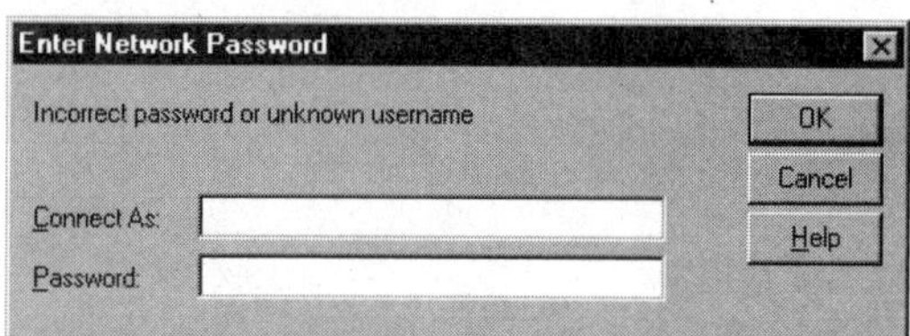

Figure 8.6 *Windows NT – Password dialog box.*

Print Services

By default, all system printers are shared through Samba. This behavior is controlled by the following lines in `/etc/smb.conf`:

```
# if you want to automatically load your printer list
rather
# than setting them up individually then you'll need this
   printcap name = /etc/printcap
   load printers = yes
```

Remove this section if this is not the desired behavior.

If it is removed, the following example from `/etc/smb.conf` can be used to share an individual printer:

```
# A private printer, usable only by fred. Spool data will
be placed in fred's
# home directory. Note that fred must have write access to
the spool directory,
# wherever it is.
[fredsprn]
   comment = Fred's Printer
   valid users = fred
   path = /homes/fred
   printer = freds_printer
   public = no
   writable = no
   printable = yes
```

You can also specify the print command that should be used.

```
[laser]
comment = Laser Printer
path = /var/spool/samba
printer driver = "Generic Laser"
print command = lpr -P lp1 %s
public = no
writable = no
printable = yes
```

Note It has occasionally been observed with the Red Hat RPM versions of Samba that all methods of sharing printers fail except for this last example, where the print command is directly specified. If you have trouble, specify the print command explicitly as demonstrated here.

NetBIOS Client Services for Linux

Linux can participate as a client in Windows NT networks. It can access both file and printer shares.

File Services

If a remote NT or 95/98 server is running TCP/IP and has available shares, these shares can be accessed via the **smbmount** command (please note that the standard **mount** command is not used for this purpose).

The following command, when run by root, mounts a share called `data` on the remote host `nthost` on the local `/mnt` directory:

```
smbmount //nthost/data -c 'mount /mnt'
```

This command will first prompt for a password, then mount the share off `/mnt`.

This command assumes that there is a "root" user defined on the remote NT system, and that `nthost` is visible on the local network.

A different remote user name for accessing the remote host can be specified with the `-U` option:

```
smbmount //nthost/data -U luser -c 'mount /mnt'
```

Should the remote host not be easily visible on the local network, the `-I` option can be used to specify a host name or IP address:

```
smbmount //nthost/data -I nthost.com -c 'mount /mnt'
```

The file permissions model on NT servers is usually much different from UNIX. If the NT server is using a FAT file system, there are no permissions on files. If the server is using NTFS, its security model is actually more flexible than UNIX, but it is not compatible. Options can be specified that control the user, group, file mode, and directory mode that Linux will assign the mounted file system:

```
smbmount //nthost/data -U luser -I nthost.com \
-c 'mount /mnt -u 500 -g 500 -f 644 -d 755'
```

An alternate form of the command is sometimes more effective:

```
smbmount //nthost/data /mnt -U luser -I nthost.com \
-u 500 -g 500 -f 644 -d 755
```

The author has seen the syntax of each example used on Red Hat Linux 6.0.

Print Services

Adding a Windows printer as a Linux system printer is relatively straightforward. As the root user under XWindows, run the following command:

```
printtool
```

The Print System Manager will appear, as shown in Figure 8.7.

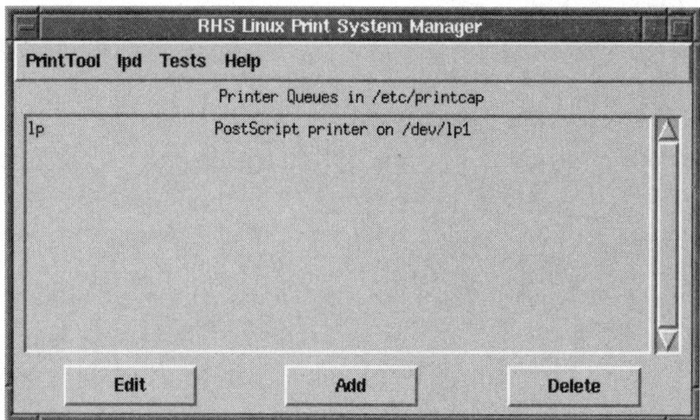

Figure 8.7 *Red Hat Linux Print System Manager.*

Select the "Add" button, and the dialog box in Figure 8.8 will be presented.

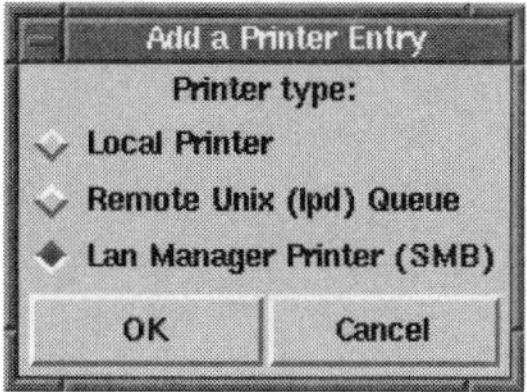

Figure 8.8 *Printer type.*

Select "Lan Manager Printer" and click "OK." Click "OK" on the warning dialog box (Figure 8.9 on page 214) to continue.

Add the relevant information to the dialogs (Figure 8.10) and click "OK." The Print System Manager is now configured (Figure 8.11).

Any user should now be able to send output to the Windows printer with a command such as:

lpr -Plp0 /etc/passwd

If the NT printer has been installed as the default printer `lp`, the `-P` option above is unnecessary.

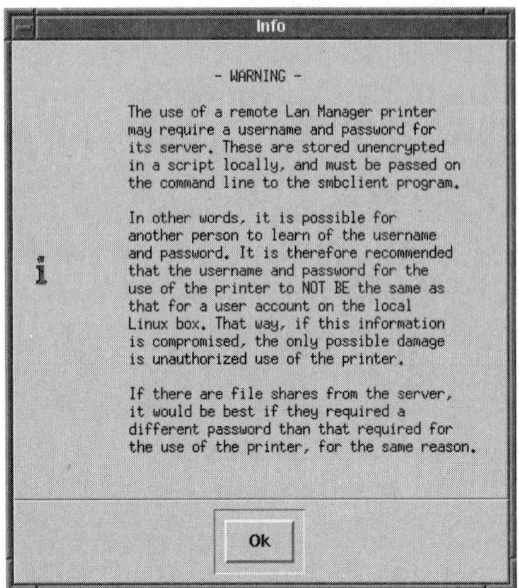

Figure 8.9 *Security Warning.*

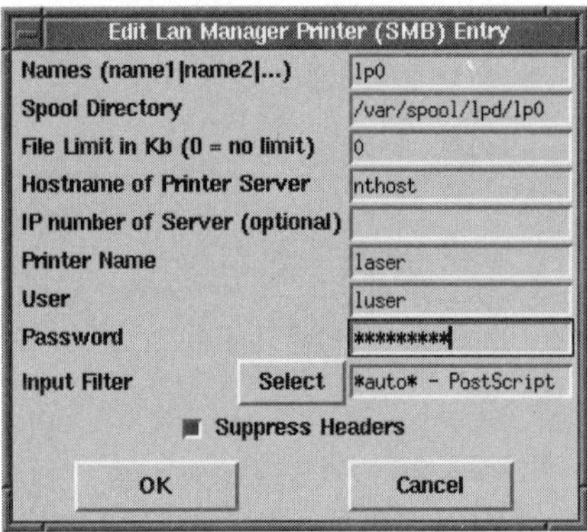

Figure 8.10 *SMB Printer Configuration.*

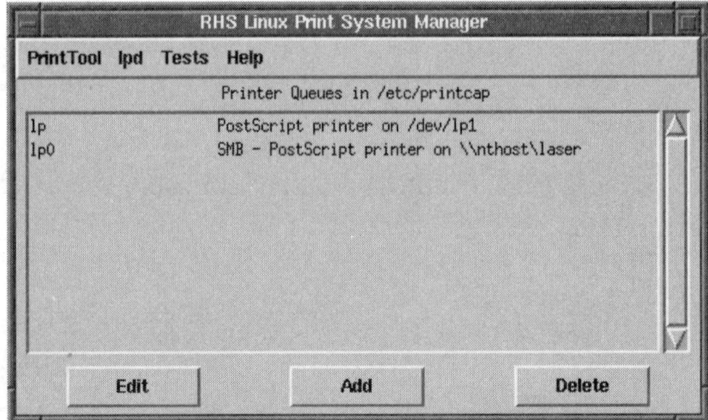

Figure 8.11 *Red Hat Linux Print System Manager.*

It is also possible to use a simple shell script to print to remote Windows printers. Record the following shell script in the file `winprint`:

```
#!/bin/sh
SERVER="NTHOST"
SERVICE="PRINTER"
USER="luser"
PASSWORD="secret"
(
echo "print -"
cat $*
) | /usr/bin/smbclient "\\\\$SERVER\\$SERVICE" $PASSWORD -U
$SERVER -N
```

An example of using the `winprint` script could be:

```
winprint /etc/passwd /etc/group /etc/hosts
```

There is one extremely important point to make about these SMB printers. The username and passwords that are entered in the Print System Manager dialog boxes are saved and then sourced directly into a shell script.

Because of this, a password of *" ";rm –rf /* could be potentially disastrous. To be safe, limit the sharenames, usernames, and passwords to alphanumeric characters (*[A-Za-z0-9]*).

09

The GIMP

The GNU Image Manipulation Program (GIMP) is a powerful imaging tool that is included with Red Hat Linux. One of the intentions of the GIMP is to reproduce most of the features and functionality of sophisticated image manipulation software in an application that is under the General Public License (GPL). This chapter will provide a brief introduction to the GIMP, with demonstrations of layers and selections.

The GIMP is not a Linux-only application. Far from it, the GIMP runs on most other UNIX platforms, and a Win32 port also exists.

Work on the GIMP has also spawned other projects with profound influence on the Linux community. The GIMP ToolKit (GTK), in particular, has risen out of the GIMP to become the heart of the GNOME project, which is the strongest contender for the Linux desktop.

Free Fonts for the GIMP

The GIMP uses the fonts available with XWindows. The X fonts included by Red Hat are complete, but lack many of the stylized typefaces that graphic artists have come to expect.

Information is available at *http://www.gimp.org/fonts.html* about font resources for the GIMP. In particular, the Freefonts and Sharefonts can be downloaded and added to the Xserver to vastly increase the available typefaces. These extra fonts can be downloaded from *ftp://ftp.gimp.org/pub/gimp/fonts*. These fonts can also be found in the /fonts directory on this text's included CD-ROM.

Assuming that `freefonts-0.10.tar.gz` has been stored in the root user's home directory, the archive can be loaded into the Xserver with the following commands:

```
cd /usr/X11R6/lib/X11/fonts
tar xvzf ~/freefonts-0.10.tar.gz
chown -R root.root freefont
cd /etc/X11/fs
awk '
/fonts\/Type1/ { print; print
"\t/usr/X11R6/lib/X11/fonts/freefont,"}
! /Type1/
' config config.new
mv config config.without_free
mv config.new config
/etc/rc.d/init.d/xfs restart
```

After this script has been executed, enter the following command from within XWindows to see all the new available fonts:

```
xlsfonts | grep free
```

Examine the /usr/X11R6/lib/X11/fonts/freefont directory after installation. Read the license files for any fonts you use continuously, and follow the instructions found there. The shareware fonts are also easily installed, although they have more strenuous licensing issues.

Assuming that sharefonts-0.10.tar.gz has been stored in the root user's home directory, the archive can be loaded into the Xserver with the following commands:

```
cd /usr/X11R6/lib/X11/fonts
tar xvzf ~/sharefonts-0.10.tar.gz
chown -R root.root sharefont
cd /etc/X11/fs
awk '
/fonts\/Type1/ { print; print
"\t/usr/X11R6/lib/X11/fonts/sharefont,"}
! /Type1/
' config config.new
mv config config.without_share
mv config.new config
/etc/rc.d/init.d/xfs restart
```

After these commands have been executed, enter the following command from within XWindows to see all the new available fonts:

```
xlsfonts | grep share
```

One last font collection that can be installed is the URW collection of standard fonts (these fonts are the standard fonts found on many Postscript printers). Assuming that urw-fonts.tar.gz has been stored in the root user's home directory, the archive can be loaded into the Xserver with the following commands (there is also a URW RPM that can be used):

```
cd /usr/X11R6/lib/X11/fonts
tar xvzf ~/urw-fonts.tar.gz
chown -R root.root URW
cd /etc/X11/fs
awk '
/fonts\/Type1/ { print; print "\t/usr/X11R6/lib/X11/fonts/URW,"}
! /Type1/
' config config.new
mv config config.without_urw
mv config.new config
/etc/rc.d/init.d/xfs restart
```

A Session with GIMP

To run GIMP, start XWindows, open a terminal window, and run the command **gimp**. GIMP may also be started with tools available in the XWindow manager (but there are so many such window managers that it would be impossible to document all possible methods here). When a user starts up GIMP for the first time, the dialog boxes shown in Figure 9.1 and Figure 9.2 are displayed.

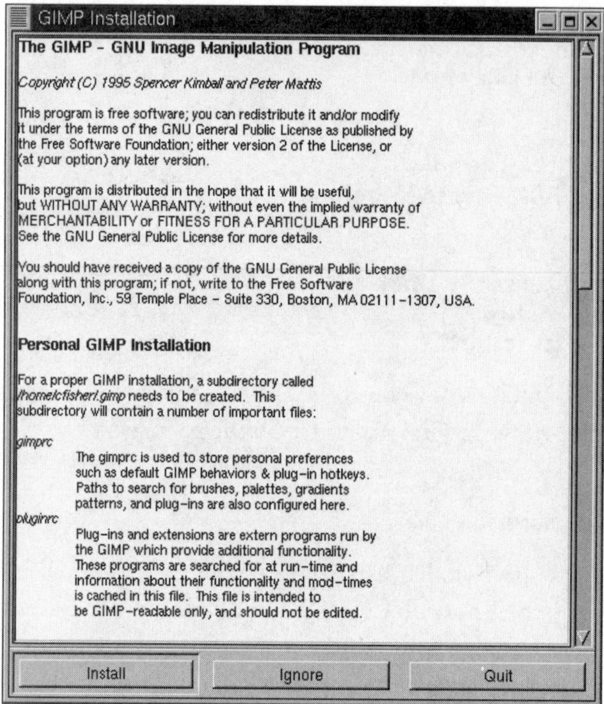

Figure 9.1 *GIMP Installation.*

The window in Figure 9.1 indicates that a number of GIMP components will be installed in the user's home directory. Press "Install" to continue.

From the Installation Log window (Figure 9.2), press "Continue" to proceed with starting the GIMP. The GIMP welcome window will then be displayed (see Figure 9.3).

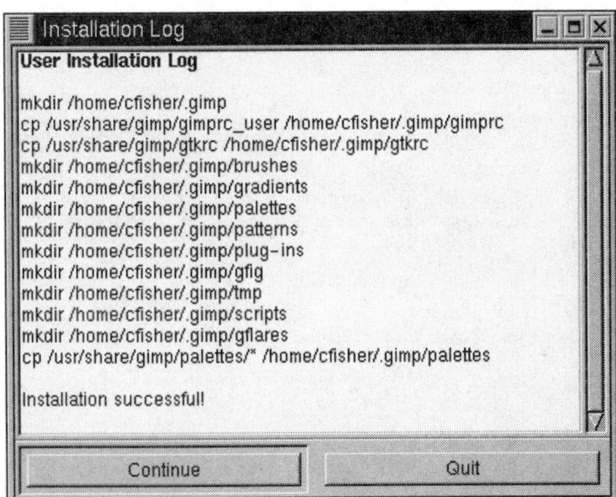

Figure 9.2 *Installation Log.*

Figure 9.3 *GIMP Startup.*

It may take some time to initialize all the GIMP components in the above dialog box. The next time the user starts the GIMP, it will not take so long to initialize. When preparations are complete, the two windows shown in Figure 9.4 on page 222 will appear.

The GIMP Tip of the Day window can be safely closed.

> **Note**
> Feel free to browse for more tips before closing.

The remaining tool window is the control panel for the GIMP, and we will use it to create a new, blank image.

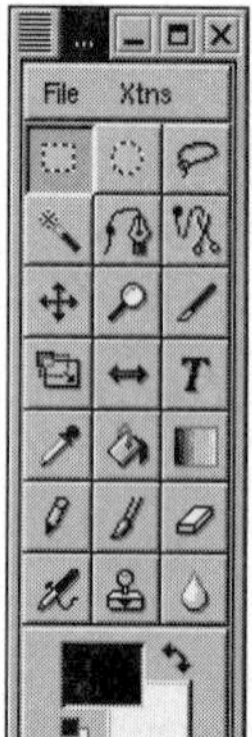

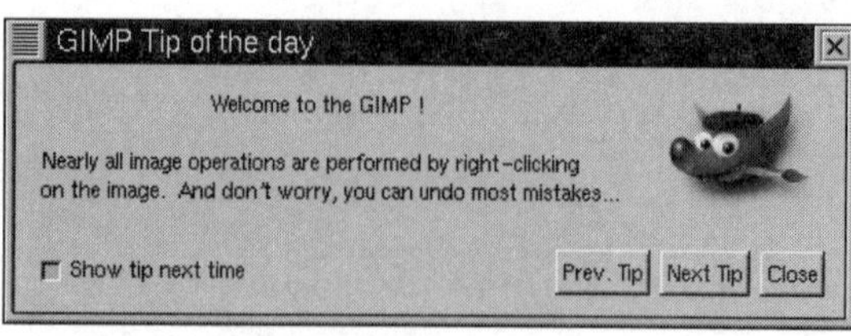

Figure 9.4 *Control Panel and GIMP Tip of the day.*

Select the "File/New" option on the GIMP control panel. An image creation dialog box will appear (see Figure 9.5).

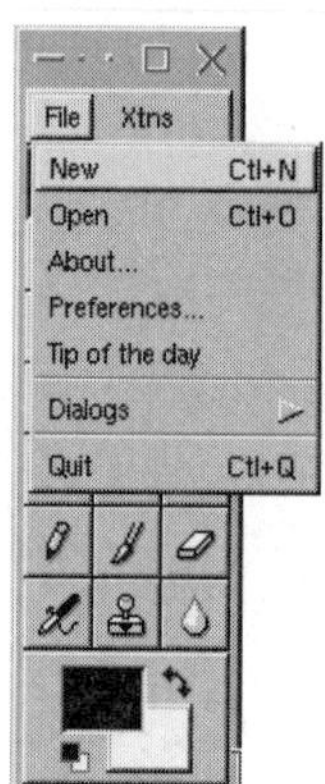

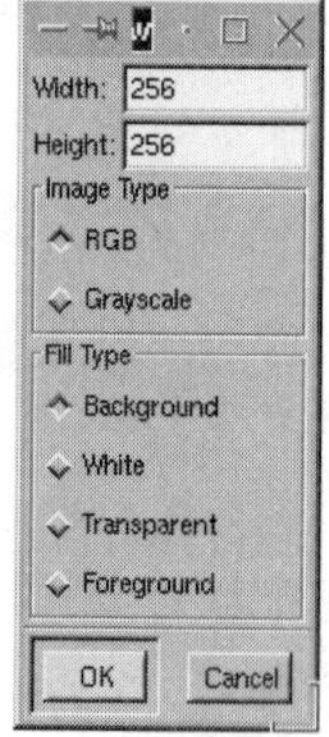

Figure 9.5 *Creating a new image using the New Image dialog box.*

Click the "OK" button to create the image with default settings. The blank image will appear in a new window, similar to what is shown in Figure 9.6.

We are going to apply a *gradient fill* to the blank image. Before doing so, we should set new foreground and background colors. To change the foreground color, double-click on the large, black rectangle at the bottom of the GIMP control panel. A color selection dialog should appear (see Figure 9.7).

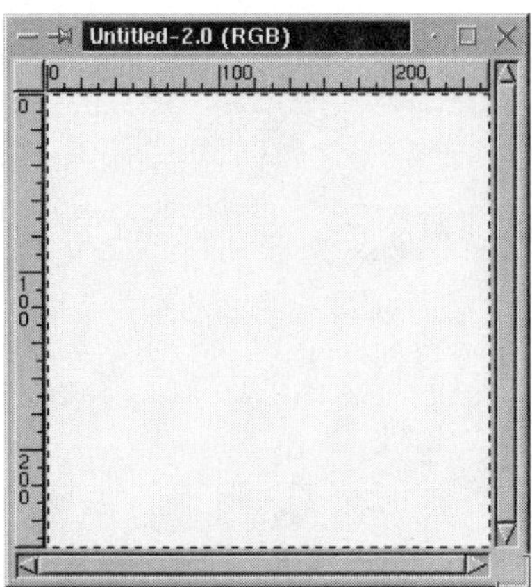

Figure 9.6 *A blank image.*

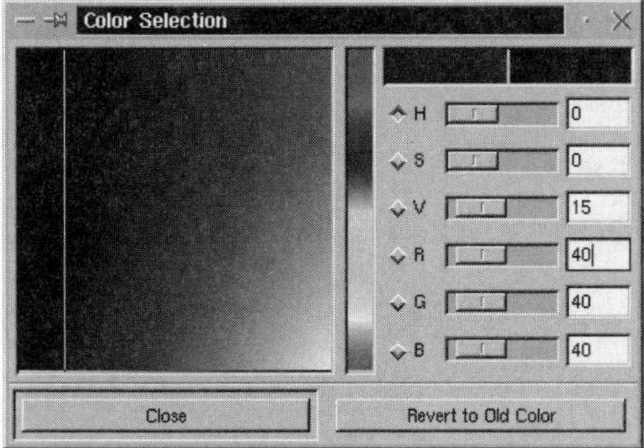

Figure 9.7 *Foreground color selection.*

In this example, manual entries have been made in the RGB color components to select a very dark shade of grey. The *RGB color model* says that all visible colors are made up of combinations of the three primary colors (red, green, and blue). When red, green, and blue colors are used in the same intensity, a pure shade of grey will result, as it has here. The other color model, *HSV* (hue, saturation and brightness), is not discussed here, but is obvious from the dialog that achieving a grey color in the HSV model is done by setting the first two components (the *hue* and *saturation*) to zero. When all three RGB values of the foreground color have been set to 40, double-click on the large white rectangle at the bottom of the GIMP control panel to set the background color. The color selection dialog box will show white. Change it to a light shade of grey with 200 for each red, green, and blue component as shown in Figure 9.8.

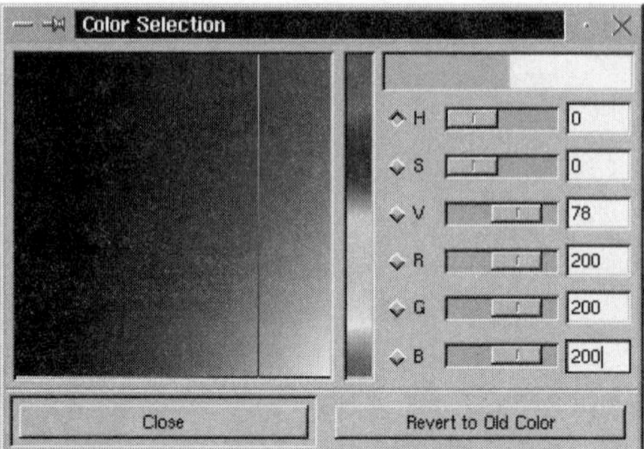

Figure 9.8 *Background color selection.*

Once the background color has been set, close the color selection dialog box, then select the gradient fill tool on the GIMP control panel, shown in Figure 9.9 in its selected state. (Notice also that the foreground and background colors have changed.) Double-click on the gradient fill tool button. Its tool options dialog box will also appear (see Figure 9.9).

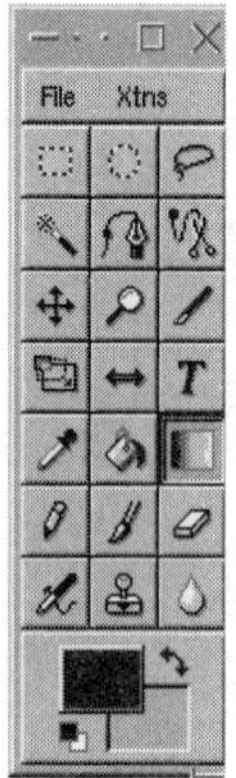

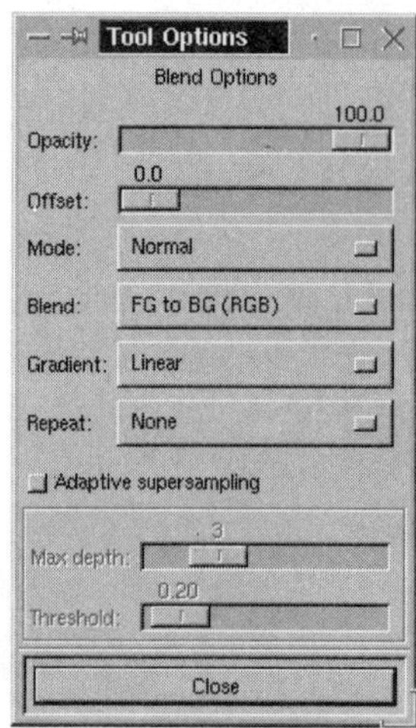

Figure 9.9 *Gradient fill tool and gradient fill options dialog box.*

We aren't going to change any of these options, but it is important to see that most tools have a tool options dialog box. Close the dialog box after it has been examined. Then, select the blank image again. Click and drag from left to right within it to draw a line similar to the one in Figure 9.10.

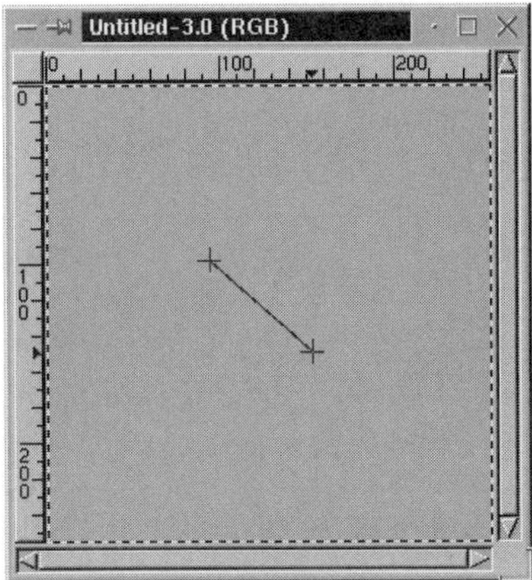

Figure 9.10 *Drawing a gradient fill.*

When the line has been drawn and the mouse button released, a *gradient fill* will be generated (see Figure 9.11).

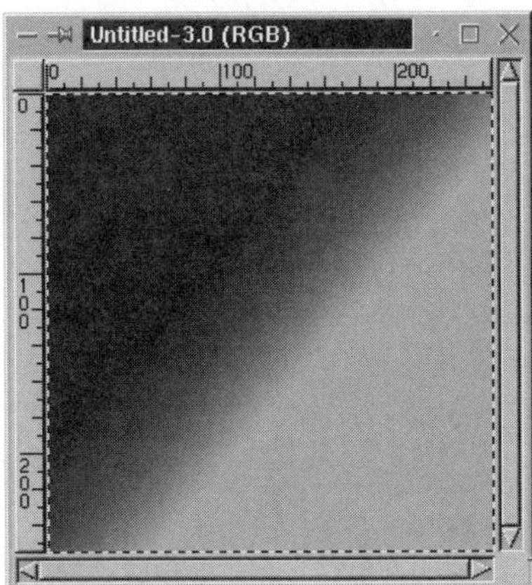

Figure 9.11 *Gradient fill.*

The colors used in this fill gradually change from one shade to another—the general behavior of a gradient fill. Now, we are going to generate a tile pattern upon this fill for an even more interesting background. Within the image, right-click the mouse and select "Filters/Artistic/Mosaic" as shown in Figure 9.12.

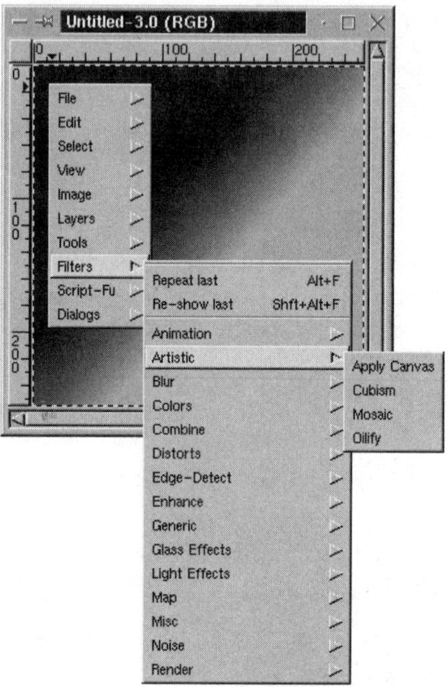

Figure 9.12 *Preparing for a mosaic effect.*

The dialog box shown in Figure 9.13 will appear. Click "OK" to use the default options. The GIMP will compute for a moment, then transform our image into something like the one shown in Figure 9.14.

The mosaic pattern has been applied to our background image. Now, we are ready to apply some art to the foreground. First we will generate some text with artistic effects. From the GIMP control panel, choose "Xtns/Script-Fu/Logos/Cool Metal" as shown in Figure 9.15 on page 228.

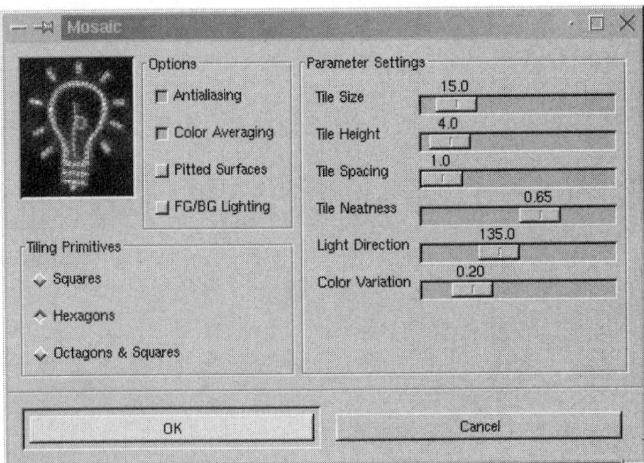

Figure 9.13 *Mosaic effect dialog box.*

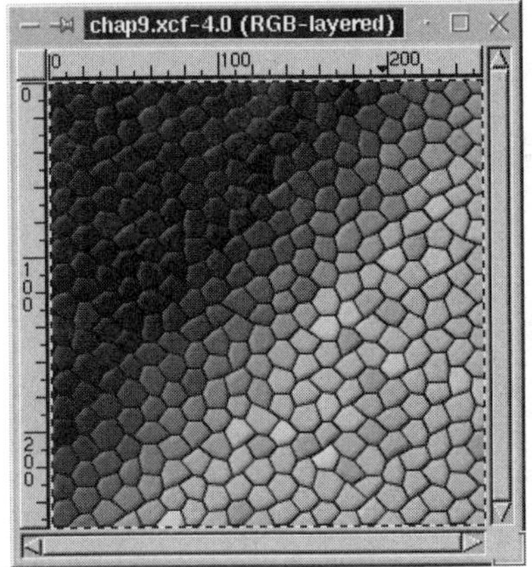

Figure 9.14 *The completed mosaic.*

Change the "Text String" option to "GIMP" and the point size to "50." If the free fonts have not been loaded, change the font to "Charter." Select "OK," and the image shown in Figure 9.16 on page 228 will be generated.

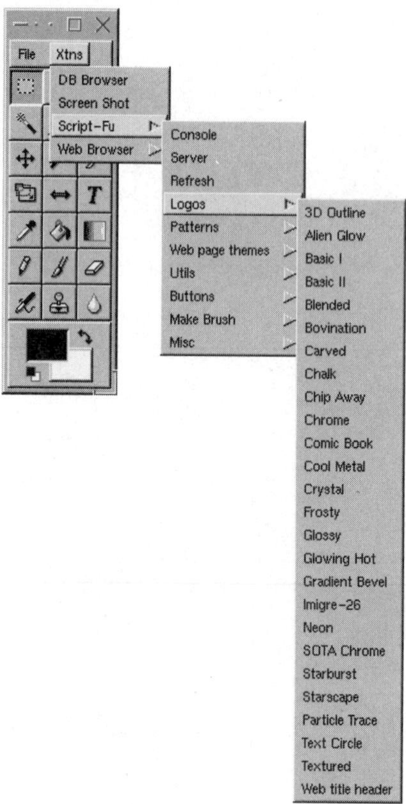

Figure 9.15 *Special font effects: Cool Metal.*

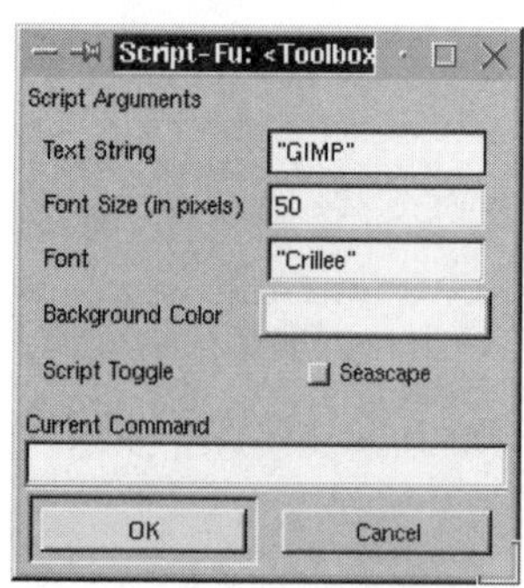

Figure 9.16 *Cool Metal dialog box and resulting text image.*

We are ready at this point to move the text string into our original image. It will offset the mosaic background rather well. Open the Layers & Channels dialog box by right-clicking in the image and selecting "Dialogs/Layers & Channels..." as shown in Figure 9.17.

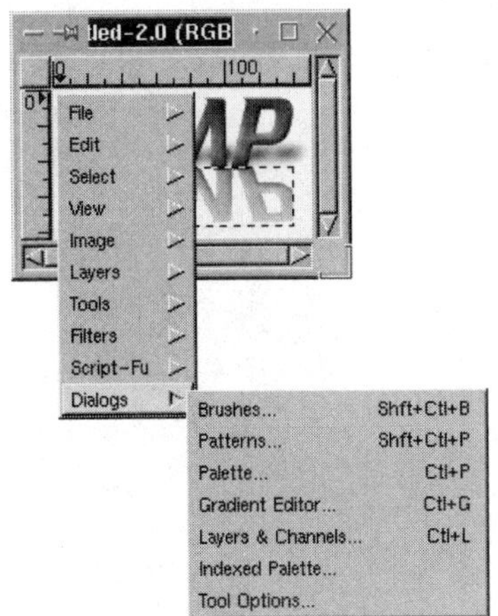

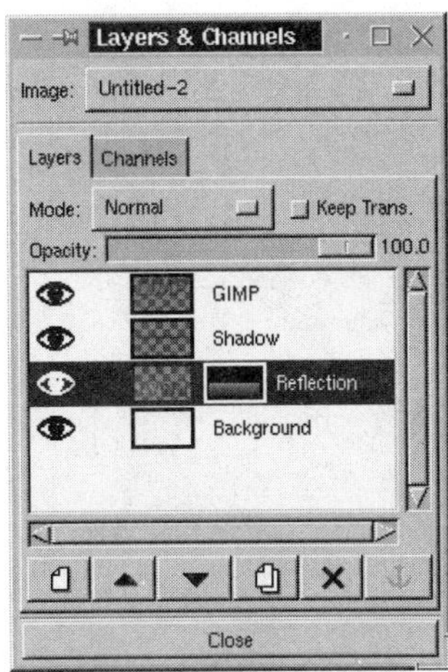

Figure 9.17 *Opening the Layers & Channels dialog box.*

Click on the eyeball on the background layer. This turns the background layer off. The image will be displayed without the background. Feel free to experiment by clicking the eyeballs of the other layers, but do not proceed until all layers are visible except the background (see Figure 9.18).

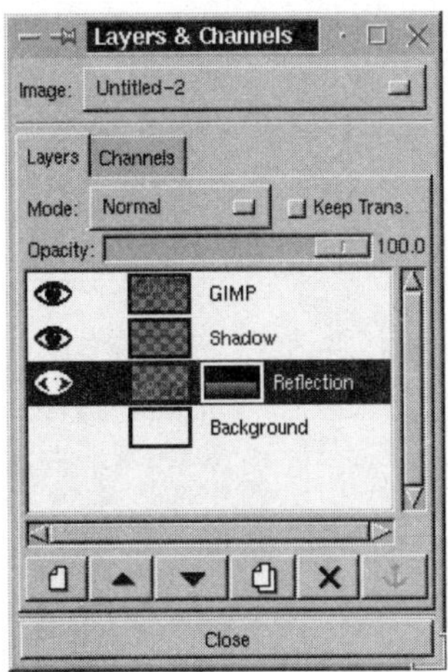

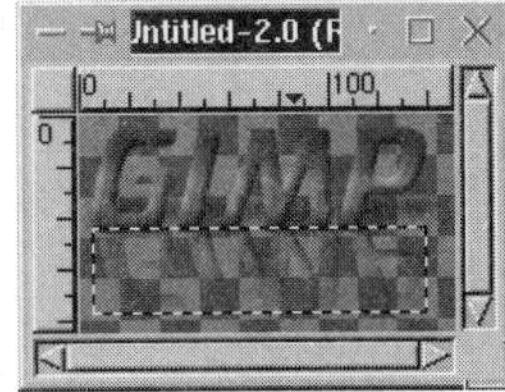

Figure 9.18 *Toggling visibility to make the background invisible.*

Next, ensure the reflection layer is selected (by left-clicking on it), then right-click it to bring up the layer options menu. Select "Merge Visible Layers" to flatten the three remaining layers into one. A layer-merging dialog box will be presented. Click "OK" to use the default options (see Figure 9.19).

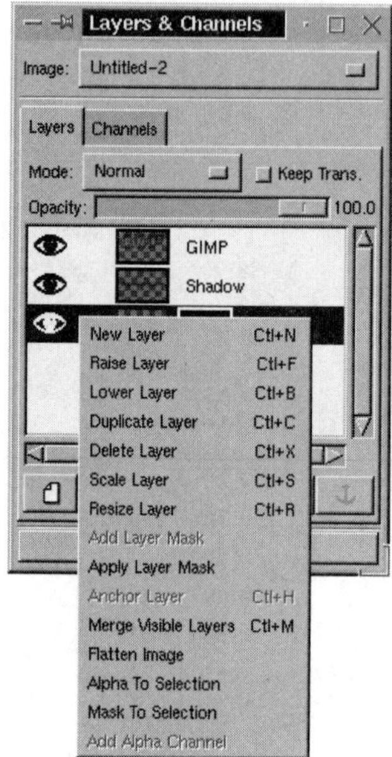

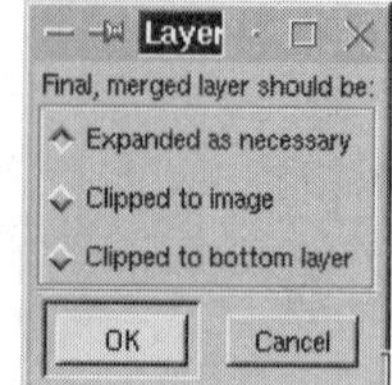

Figure 9.19 *Merging layers with the layer merging dialog box.*

When the layers are merged, the GIMP and Shadow layers will be deleted, and their contents will be combined with the Reflection layer. The reflection area in the image will no longer be selected (see Figure 9.20).

Right-click in the image and select the "Edit/Copy" menu option to prepare the text for transport into the original mosaic image (see Figure 9.21).

Once the image has been copied into the clipboard, select the "File/Close" menu option to destroy the text image, and then select the "Close" option in the confirmation dialog box that is presented (see Figure 9.22).

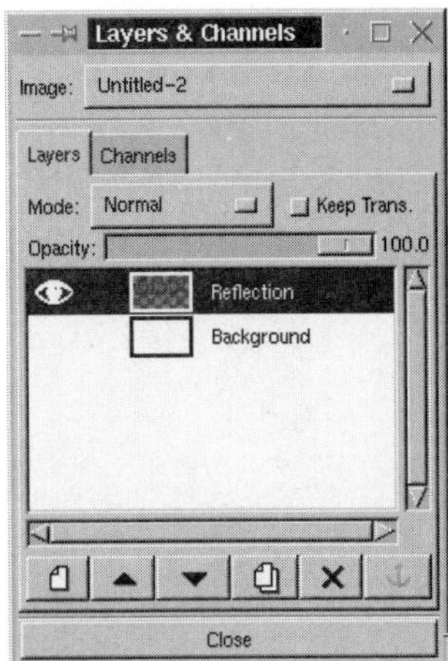

Figure 9.20 *Merged image resulting from layer merging.*

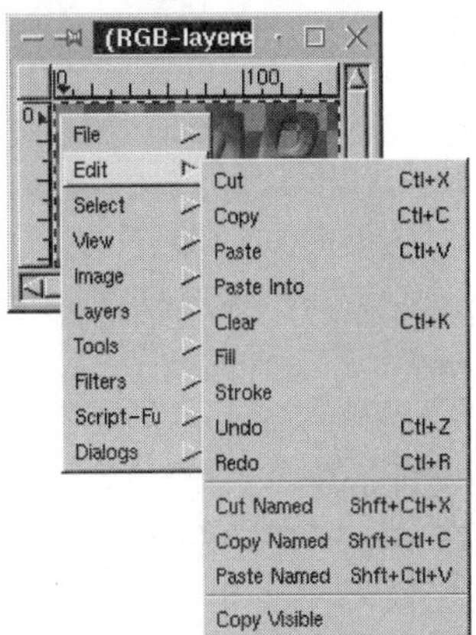

Figure 9.21 *Copying a layer's contents.*

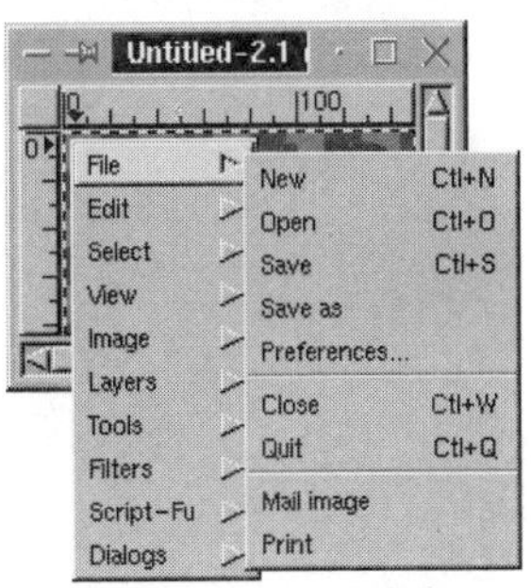

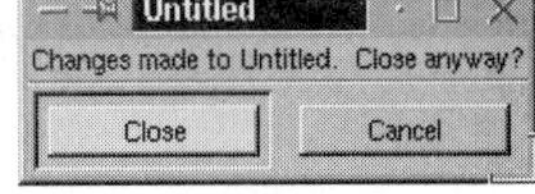

Figure 9.22 *Closing & confirming the text image.*

When the text image is closed, the Layers & Channels dialog box should automatically revert to the original mosaic image. We want to create a new layer in the mosaic image, so click on the button in the lower left corner that has a picture of a white piece of paper with the edge folded (it is highlighted in the Layers & Channels dialog box in Figure 9.23). Doing so will present the New Layer dialog box. Press "Enter" in this dialog box to create a new layer with default settings.

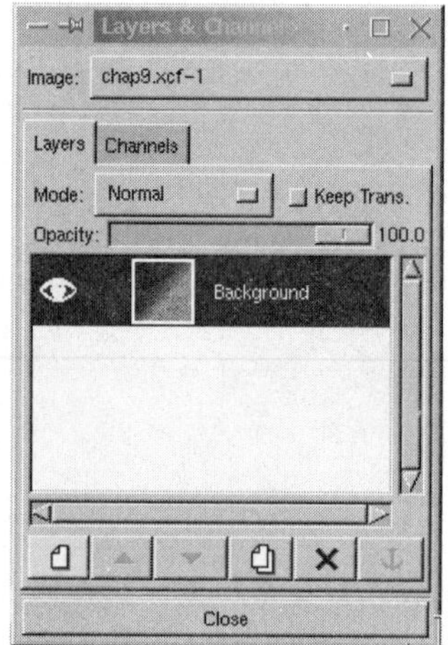

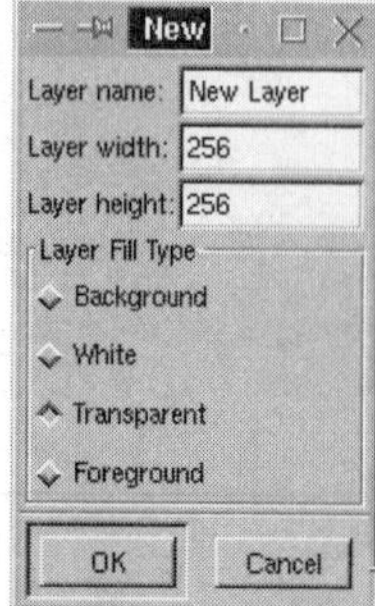

Figure 9.23 *Creating a new layer using the new layer dialog box.*

Now, within the image, right-click and select "Edit/Paste" (see Figure 9.24).

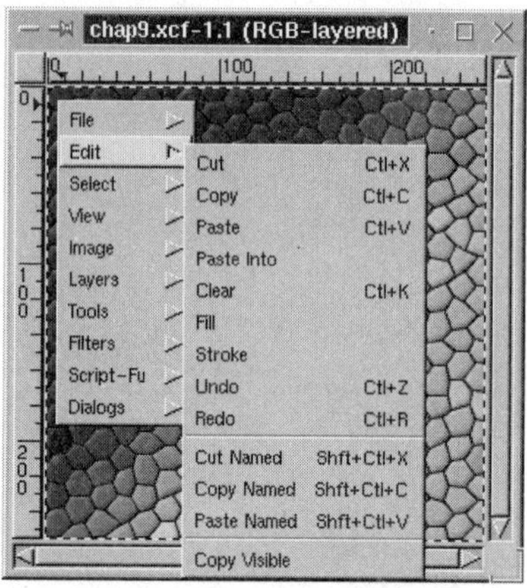

Figure 9.24 *Pasting the text.*

The text should appear in the center of the image, as shown in Figure 9.25. When pasted this way, the material becomes a *floating selection,* not based in any layer (although it will shortly merge with the active layer).

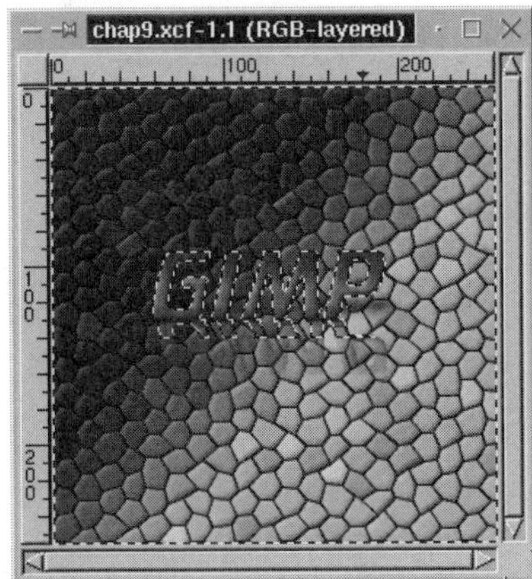

Figure 9.25 *Paste results.*

Select the mover tool on the GIMP control panel (it is shown selected in Figure 9.26). Next, click on the text and drag it to the upper left corner of the screen.

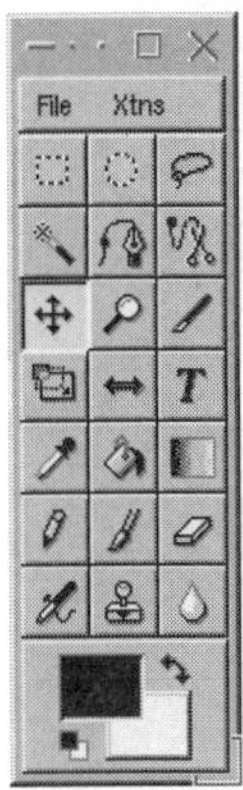

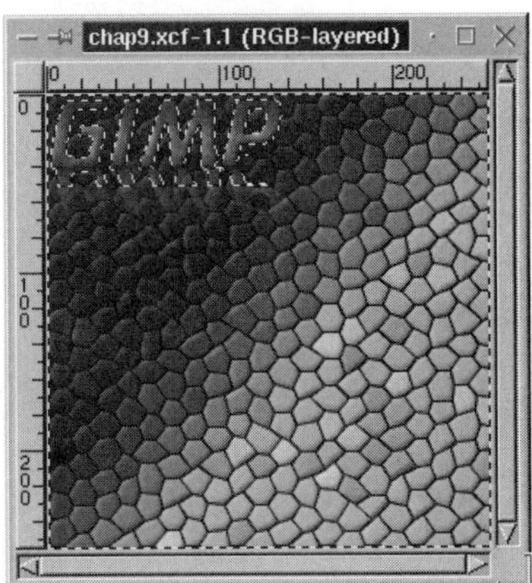

Figure 9.26 *Moving the floating selection with the mover tool.*

Notice that the Layers & Channels dialog box has a floating selection. Click once with the mover tool in the (approximate) center of the image, and the floating selection will merge with the new layer (which is active), as shown in Figure 9.27.

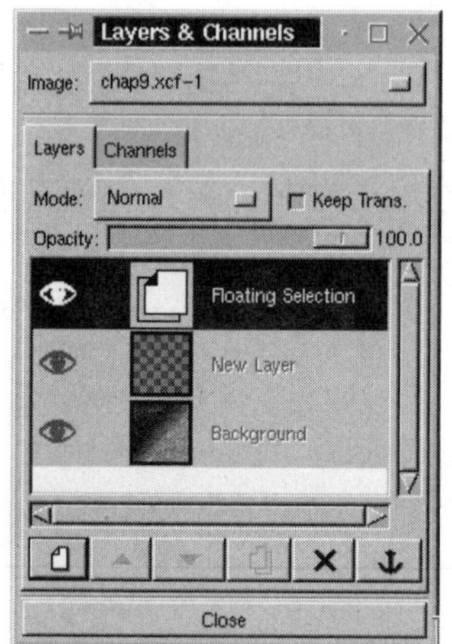

Figure 9.27 *Floating section before and after merging.*

Adjust the Opacity slider. As it is adjusted, the text becomes more transparent. Move the slider to various positions all across the dial to see the different opacity results (Figure 9.28).

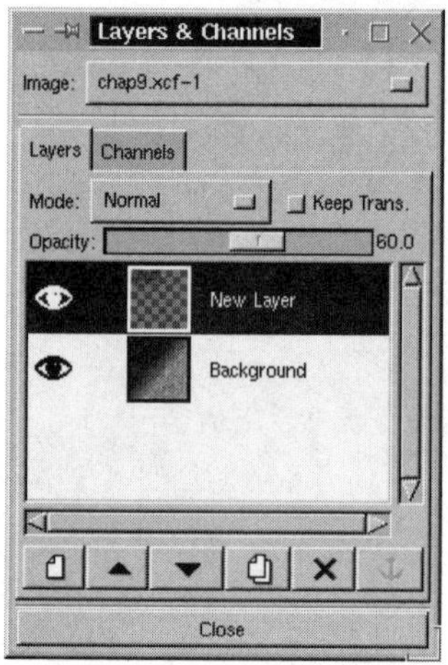

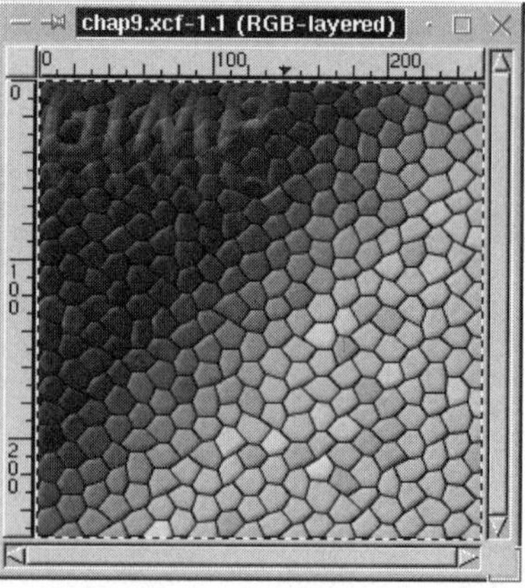

Figure 9.28 *Layer opacity results.*

Return the opacity to 100% and click on the elliptical selection tool in the GIMP control panel (it is shown selected in Figure 9.29). Then draw an ellipse in the middle of the right side of the image.

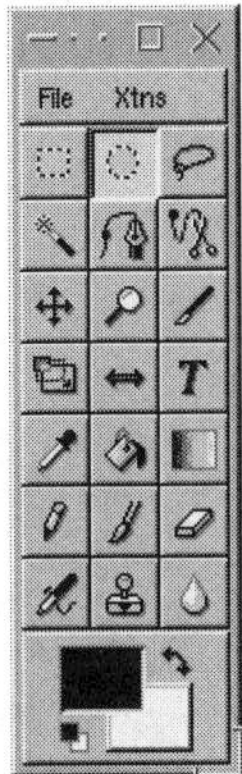

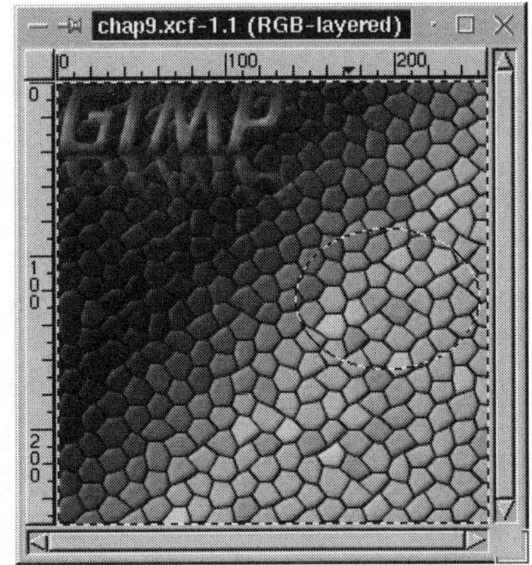

Figure 9.29 *Elliptical selection tool.*

Within the ellipse, we will generate a *Super Nova* effect Right-click in the image and select "Filters/Light Effects/Super Nova" (see Figure 9.30).

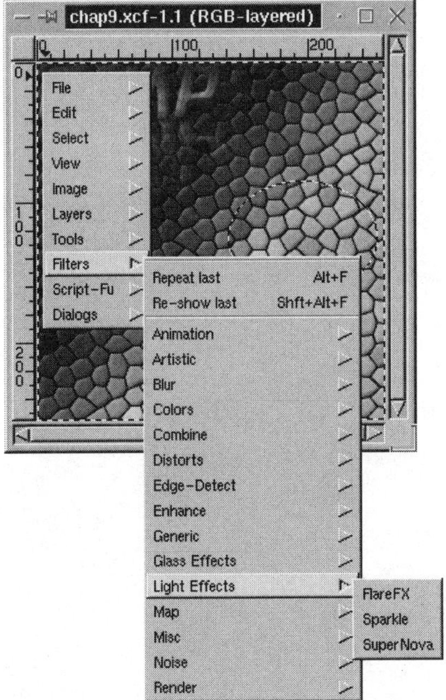

Figure 9.30 *The Super Nova effect.*

Move the center of the Super Nova so that it is in the approximate center of the ellipse selected earlier, then press "OK." The Super Nova effect will be generated (see Figure 9.31).

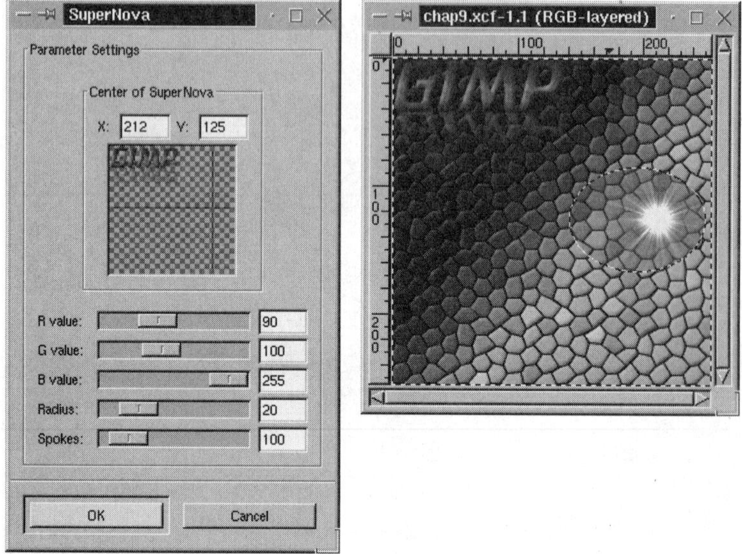

Figure 9.31 *Super Nova dialog box.*

The "Edit/Undo" option (obtained by right-clicking on the image) can be used to remove the Super Nova effect. The "Edit/Redo" option will bring it back. Try these options now.

Note Filters and effects apply *only to the current selection.* We could have used another mosaic pattern, or any other filter, but these filters would be bounded to the confines of the elliptical selection area.

Next, select the text tool from the GIMP control panel. Move the mouse to a lower portion of the image and left-click. The text tool dialog box will be presented (see Figure 9.32). Select the Caligula typeface, then enter the text "Is Fun!" in the large white text area at the bottom of the dialog box. Finally, click "OK."

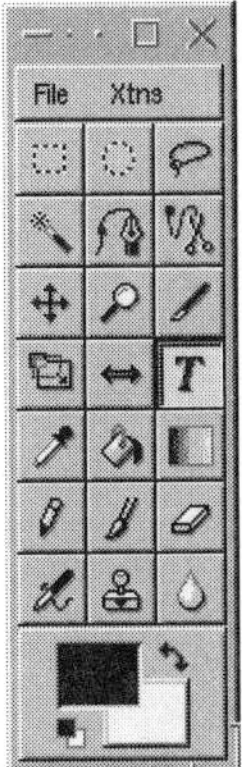

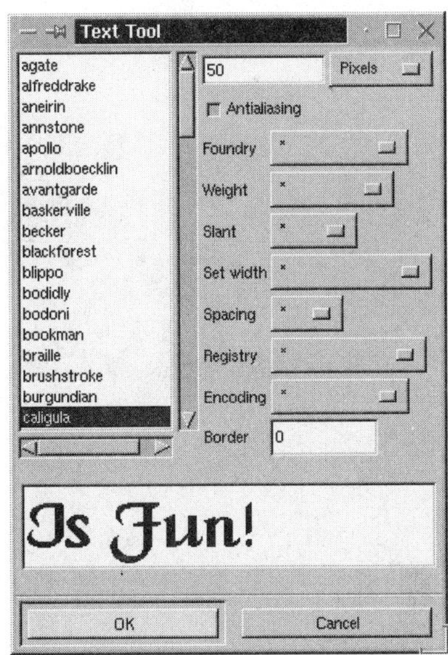

Figure 9.32 *The text tool dialog box.*

The text will appear somewhere in the image. Next, select the mover tool from the GIMP control panel and reposition the text at the lower right corner (see Figure 9.33).

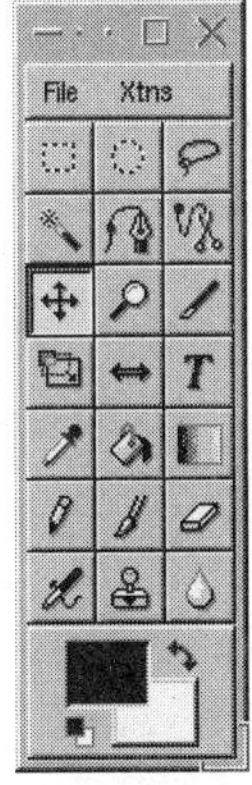

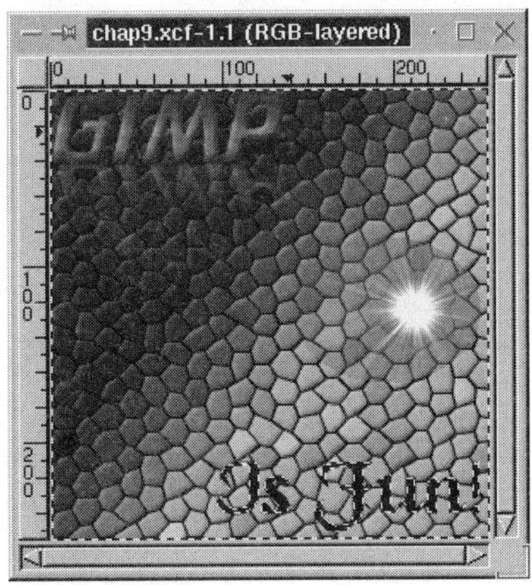

Figure 9.33 *Moving the text by using the mover tool.*

Click in another area of the image to merge the text with the active layer (see Figure 9.34).

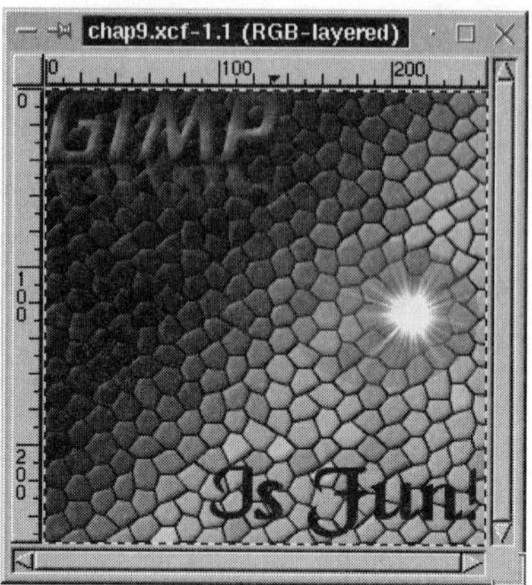

Figure 9.34 *The completed image.*

Now save the image. This is a good time to discuss graphics file formats and their limitations (although a thorough discussion is beyond the scope of this text). To save an image with all layer information intact, use the GIMP *XCF* file format. XCF files can be very large, because they store multiple layers with transparency data.

XCF files, however, are not used for graphics on web pages. The two common web graphics formats are *JPEG* (which uses a lossy compression format based on the discrete cosine transform) and *GIF* (which is a lossless format based on the Ziv-Lempel-Welch compression algorithm; while it is lossless, it is limited to 255 colors per image). The *PNG* graphic format is also becoming popular.

Note

> When a non-GIMP native format is used, *only the active layer will be saved.* Therefore, when saving graphics for the web in one of these formats, merge all the layers prior to writing the image.

First, save the image below using XCF format. Right-click on the image and select "File/Save" (see Figure 9.35).

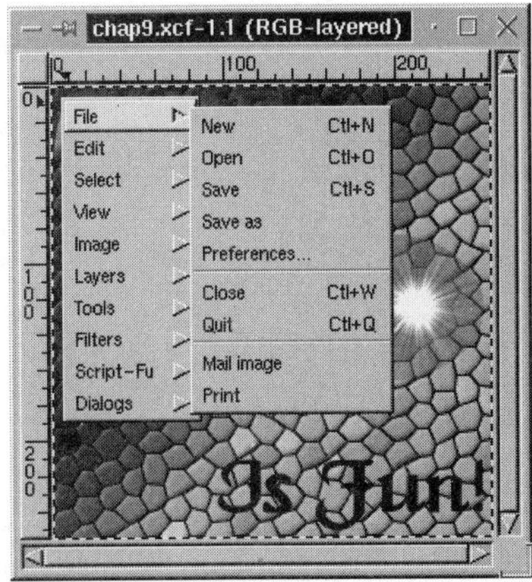

Figure 9.35 *Saving an image.*

Then, select XCF for the file type and enter a name in the text area at the bottom (see Figure 9.36). Make sure the file name ends in ".xcf".

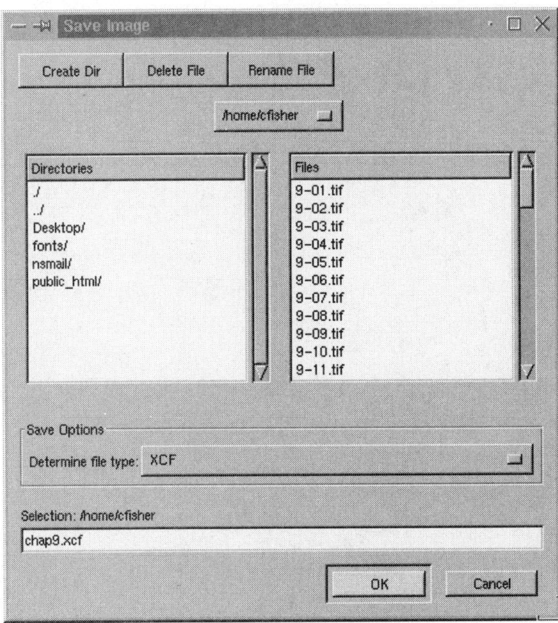

Figure 9.36 *The Save Image dialog box—XCF.*

To save this image as a JPEG, first merge all the layers. Right-click on the image and select "Layers/Flatten Image" (see Figure 9.37).

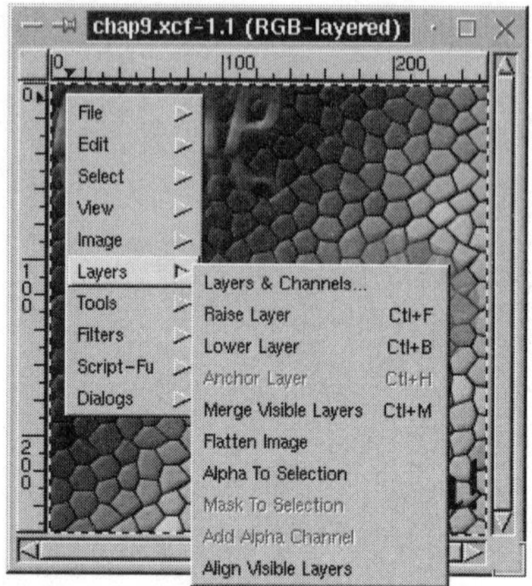

Figure 9.37 *Flattening the layers.*

Then select JPEG for the file type and enter a name in the text area at the bottom (see Figure 9.38). Make sure the file name ends in ".jpg".

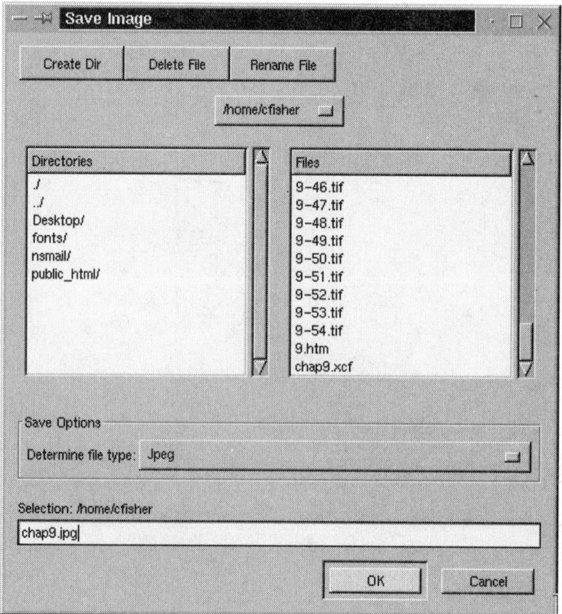

Figure 9.38 *The Save Image dialog box—JPEG.*

The JPEG compression settings dialog box will appear (see Figure 9.39). Press "OK" to select the default compression settings.

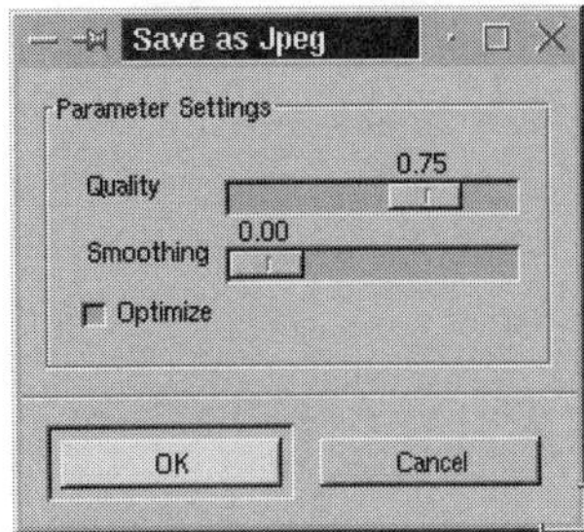

Figure 9.39 *JPEG compression options.*

This concludes our introduction to the GIMP. There is a great deal more to discover. This tutorial is specifically sparse on the subject of selections. We have not covered freehand selections, selections with Bezier curves, fuzzy selections, intelligent scissors, or selecting by color, nor have additive selections been addressed. The XCF image above can be found in the `/fonts` directory on the CD-ROM included with this text.

Other Imaging Tools

A few other applications can complement the use of the GIMP.

Electric Eyes is an application based upon the GIMP ToolKit (GTK). It is intended for displaying large sequences of images. Its image-editing functions are very limited, and it has bugs.

ImageMagick is a much older suite of imaging tools. It has an image-viewing tool called `display`. Type **display** at a shell to start it. A modified version of the `display` tool, called `animate`, displays a sequence of images quickly. A particularly useful component is the `convert` utility, which allows images to be converted between different formats directly from the shell, without starting XWindows. For example, the command **convert a.jpg GIF:a.gif** converts a JPEG file called "a.jpg" into GIF format. The following shell script converts all TIFF files in a directory to JPEG images (and was used in the production of this text):

```
for x in *.tif; do convert $x JPG:`echo $x | sed 's/tif$/jpg/'`; done
```

XV-3.10a is the oldest and one of the most powerful graphics utilities. For some reason, it is no longer included in Red Hat Linux 6.0. An RPM version, which works well in 6.0, can still be found in Red Hat Linux 5.2.. XV has many strengths and is second only to the GIMP in functionality. XV was used to create all of the screen captures in this text. Let's hope that Red Hat brings this application back in the next release.

10

Rebuilding the Linux Kernel

Basic to most UNIX environments is the configuration of the kernel, and Red Hat Linux is no exception. The Linux kernel used by Red Hat can be manipulated both through run-time configuration directives and through a complete rebuild of its operating environment. This chapter will concentrate upon the kernel build environment and the methods required to generate an operational kernel.

The Linux kernel is distinctive among major commercial UNIX variants because the complete source code for the kernel is available and generally included in most major Linux distributions. If you are curious about a particular Linux implementation detail, you can look at the source. If you have a special need that requires modification of the kernel, you can apply a patch and build your own special version of Linux.

This is not to say that building a kernel is a *required* step in the administration of a Linux system. No application mentioned in this text mandates a kernel with special features; the generic kernel left on your system by the installer contains everything that is required. While older Linux implementations commonly required custom kernels (especially in the days before kernel modules) in order to work properly, recent improvements in Linux have obviated much of the need for customization. A Linux administrator who insists on a custom kernel without a specific reason is behind the times. There are times, however, when kernel reconfigurations might be needed.

Since security vulnerabilities were found in the 2.2.5 kernel shortly after Red Hat Linux 6.0 was released, any production Linux installation based on the 2.2 kernel series should be upgraded to a patched kernel. This can be done with a complex set of steps involving RPM, or by building a new kernel. Both methods are outlined below.

It is more important to build custom kernels for servers with Internet exposure than for workstations. It is also easier, since servers generally do not have sound cards or other hardware that increase kernel complexity.

The Linux kernel is usually stored in a file called `vmlinuz`, in the root directory of the system. Red Hat Linux 6.0, however, puts the kernel in the `/boot` directory under a different name (such as `vmlinuz-2.2.5-15`). The kernel is loaded at boot time. As it boots, the kernel probes the system and configures basic hardware settings. It then loads a program called `init`, which continues the boot process. (The boot sequence is not documented in this text.) While portions of the kernel can be loaded or removed at will, the only way to switch to a completely different kernel image is to reboot.

Throughout this text, there is an implicit understanding that i386 architecture is in use. We now make that assertion explicit—the slight differences in preparing and booting kernels for Alpha and Sparc architectures are not discussed here.

Installing the Kernel Source

The Linux kernel is written in C and requires a C compiler in the development environment. A copy of the kernel source (version 2.2.12) is included in the `/linux` directory on the CD-ROM that accompanies this book. It is encoded with the `bzip2` compression utility. This `bzip2` utility is not installed by default, but an RPM package for installing it is available in the standard distribution of Red Hat Linux 6.0. If you do not know how to install such packages, you are *definitely* not ready to build a new kernel. Read the RPM section of Chapter 1 for information on installation.

When building a kernel, it is very easy to make a mistake that will prevent a system from booting. Kernel builds are not for the inexperienced. An emergency boot disk, created at installation time, is *mandatory.* For an inexperienced administrator, it is not a question of whether or not a future kernel build will render the system incapable of booting—it's a question of *when* it will.

Assuming that the CD-ROM included with this text is mounted on the `/cdrom` directory, the kernel source can be unpacked with the following sequence of commands:

```
cd /usr/src
rm -f linux
bzip2 -cd /cdrom/linux/linux-2.2.12.tar.bz2 | tar xvf -
chown -R root.root linux
cd linux
```

Once the 2.2.12 kernel source is installed, you should check for newer versions of the kernel on-line. Two popular Linux kernel sites are *http://www.kernel.org* and *http://www.kernelnotes.org*. If there are new kernel versions available, download and apply the patch files to bring your kernel source up-to-date. The patches are applied with a command of the form:

```
cd /usr/src/linux; bzip2 –cd ~/patch-2.2.x.bz2 | patch –p1
```

FTP access to *kernel.org* is facilitated by the use of country codes. Administrators in the United States, for example, should use the *ftp.us.kernel.org* address to download kernel patches from the `/pub/linux/kernel/v2.2` directory. Users in the United Kingdom should use *ftp.uk.kernel.org*, and Canadians should use *ftp.ca.kernel.org*, etc.

Note

It should not be necessary to download the entire kernel source package. Use the patches, as they are much smaller and accomplish the same thing (i.e., they will update your source code to the newer release).

The kernel source is also available in RPM format in the standard Red Hat distribution, but the use of the Linux kernel source RPMs is *not recommended.* The RPM versions do not include the entire source distribution. Source patches will commonly fail to work properly with these versions.

Navigating "make config"

There is one valuable piece of advice for users considering the use of the `make config` command to configure the kernel—*don't!* The `make config` command has been supplanted by the much easier `make menuconfig`, which is the most flexible of the kernel build configuration utilities. `make xconfig` is also useful, but since it requires XWindows, it is not covered in this text.

Enter the following command to configure the build options for the Linux kernel:

make menuconfig

A menu similar to that in Listing 10.1 will appear.

Each menu option composes a major subsection of the kernel configuration parameters. Within these subsections, individual options can be enabled or disabled. Most options, as they are enabled, cause extra code to be compiled into the kernel. This makes the binary kernel image larger.

Most of these options can be built in one of two ways. They can either be compiled directly into the kernel binary, or they can be built as modules (which can be loaded and removed from the kernel at will). Some configuration options cannot be prepared as modules, and others can be used *only* as modules. Most, however, can be used either way.

Listing 10.1 *Linux Kernel v2.2.12 Configuration.*

```
************************************************************************
************************* Main Menu ************************************
* Arrow keys navigate the menu.  <Enter> selects submenus --->.        *
* Highlighted letters are hotkeys. Pressing <Y> includes, <N> excludes,*
* <M> modularizes features.  Press <Esc><Esc> to exit, <?> for Help.   *
* Legend: [*] built-in  [ ] excluded  <M> module  < > module capable   *
************************************************************************
* *            Code maturity level options  --->                     * *
* *            Processor type and features  --->                     * *
* *            Loadable module support  --->                         * *
* *            General setup  --->                                   * *
* *            Plug and Play support  --->                           * *
* *            Block devices  --->                                   * *
* *            Networking options  --->                              * *
* *            SCSI support  --->                                    * *
* *            Network device support  --->                          * *
* *            Amateur Radio support  --->                           * *
* *            IrDA subsystem support  --->                          * *
* *            ISDN subsystem  --->                                  * *
* *            Old CD-ROM drivers (not SCSI, not IDE)  --->          * *
* *            Character devices  --->                               * *
* *            Filesystems  --->                                     * *
* *            Console drivers  --->                                 * *
* *            Sound  --->                                           * *
* *            Kernel hacking  --->                                  * *
* *            ---                                                   * *
* *            Load an Alternate Configuration File                  * *
* *            Save Configuration to an Alternate File               * *
************************************************************************
************************************************************************
*                    <Select>    < Exit >    < Help >                  *
************************************************************************
```

There are times, however, when you will not have this choice. One of these involves the storage options which include drivers for SCSI (Small Computer Systems Interface) and IDE (Integrated Drive Electronics). If the kernel is loaded from a SCSI drive, the driver for the SCSI controller *must be available* to the kernel, or the system will not boot because it does not know how to manipulate the SCSI hardware. The best way to prepare a kernel for a SCSI system, therefore, is to compile the driver for the SCSI controller directly into the kernel image. This is not a reasonable solution, however, for the generic kernel provided by the installation process. In this generic kernel, the SCSI drivers are provided as *modules,* since drivers compiled directly into the kernel would make the kernel image extremely large. If the modules are stored on the SCSI hard drive, a chicken-and-egg situation develops. The generic kernels use an *initial ramdisk* to solve this problem. The `initrd` image holds copies of all the SCSI modules. It is loaded by LILO (or whatever loader is in use) and is available as the kernel boots. In any case, `initrd` images are inconvenient and it is best if custom kernels do not rely upon them.

In addition to a basic inability to access the hard drive, a few other configuration mistakes will result in a system that will not boot. Failure to provide support for `ext2fs` (Second Extended File System) will clobber a system quite handily, since `ext2fs` is the native file system used in Red Hat Linux at this time (this situation may change with the inclusion of the XFS journaling file system in the anticipated Linux 2.4 kernel). Improper device configuration options passed as arguments to the kernel can also commonly lead to a quick death at boot time. It is not difficult to come up with a long list of things that can go wrong, so ensure a contingency plan is in place (relating to LILO and an emergency boot diskette).

Before building a kernel, you should decide on an approach to modules. When building a kernel to be used on a large number of machines, you will probably find it very convenient to disable modules and (carefully) select drivers for all required hardware to compile directly into the kernel. Afterwards, you can copy the kernel as a single file to a remote system, run LILO, and reboot in the new kernel environment. If you do use this static kernel approach, it's a good idea to comment out the single `crontab` entry in `/etc/cron.d/kmod`. Otherwise, hourly status messages will be generated by cron concerning module manipulation failures. In any case, static kernels are much more convenient from an administration standpoint than kernels that use modules. There are size limitations on the kernel binary image, however, and some features *must* be compiled as modules. If circumstances demand it, use modules and be glad for them.

Before beginning a kernel configuration, it might be appropriate to examine the output of the `lsmod` command. `lsmod` will list all loaded modules in the active kernel image. Such a list will confirm both planned kernel features and list hardware drivers that might have been neglected or forgotten. Obviously, `lsmod` will fail if a static kernel is in use.

Not every kernel configuration option can be covered here. Being aware of the specific problem areas, the administrator must build a kernel, boot with it, then test to see if all required functionality is still available. If something important doesn't work anymore (e.g., network routing, the CD-ROM drive, etc.), it is likely that the kernel wasn't built with everything it needs.

Now, a brief synopsis of the options in `make menuconfig` (help is available on any option through the menus):

Code maturity level options

This menu allows for experimental drivers and incomplete code to be included in the build. Unless you like to live on the wild side, leave this switched off. However, the kernel-based NFS server (now the supported NFS server for Red Hat Linux) is classed as an experimental feature, so this option must be turned on to provide NFS server support.

Processor type and features

Select the type of processor for which the kernel is being built. If the kernel obtained from this process will be used on a variety of machines, build for the least common denominator. For example, if the processor lacks the "math coprocessor" (the 386, 486sx, and NexGen processors do not include them, but all Pentiums do), be sure to enable *math emulation.* If the system has multiple processors, enable Symmetric Multi-Processing (SMP). Otherwise leave it off.

Loadable module support

If this option is enabled, extra kernel code will be stored under `/lib/modules`, and kernel features that support it can be loaded as dynamic modules. If modules are enabled, enable the kernel module loader (so the old `kerneld` module loader isn't required). If modules aren't enabled, remember to comment out the entry in /etc/cron.d/kmod. Otherwise hourly status messages will be generated by cron concerning module manipulation failures.

General setup

Basic networking, PCI bus controls (PCI is a hardware standard used in most modern PCs), the format of program binaries, and System V IPC are configured here. Make sure that most of these features are on. Inter-Process Communication (IPC) is used by many applications, especially the Apache web server.

Plug and Play support

Try to avoid plug and play hardware but, if you've got it, enable this feature.

Block devices

The IDE disk and CD-ROM support should probably be enabled, even if the system is SCSI-only, since IDE equipment is so cheap and plentiful. If the IDE chipset can be verified, set it here specifically (turn off the checks for the buggy CMD640 and RZ1000 if they are not needed). If this kernel will be used to write CD-ROMs, it will be useful to enable the loopback device. The **mkinitrd** command also requires the loopback device, so it is best to include support for it in any kernel you build.

Networking options

Major networking parameters including routing, firewalls and masquerade can be configured within this menu (masquerade only appears if "Network Firewalls," "TCP/IP Networking," "IP Firewalls," and "always defragment" options are set).

SCSI support

Support for SCSI configurations is available here. CD recorders require SCSI generic support. Individual SCSI adapters can be selected from the SCSI low-level drivers menu at the bottom. If your root file system is on a SCSI controller, compile the driver for the controller directly into the kernel— not as a module—or an initrd image will be required.

Network device support

Drivers for networking hardware will be found here, including Ethernet, Token Ring, fddi, etc. Support for PPP is also configured within this menu.

Amateur Radio support

Configure Linux support for amateur radio here.

IrDA subsystem support

If you have wireless infrared devices on your computer equipment, configure them here.

ISDN subsystem

If you have an Integrated Services Digital Network adapter, configure it here.

Old CD-ROM drivers (not SCSI, not IDE)

If you have a really old CD-ROM drive, which is not based on the SCSI or IDE interfaces, do us all a favor and buy something newer. IDE CD-ROM drives can be found for under $50. If you absolutely must have support for one of these older drives, configure it in this menu.

Character devices

The console and virtual terminal options in this menu probably shouldn't be changed. If you have a supported multi-port serial board, a driver for it can be configured here. Pseudo-terminal devices are also configured here. Pseudo-terminals are consumed by telnet connections, xterms, and other terminal-like services. The default is a maximum of 256 devices; increase this limit if necessary. Bus mice and PS/2 mouse support is included in this menu, as well as QIC tape support.

File systems

The critical entry here is the Second extended fs support. This is the native file system for Red Hat Linux 6.0. Without it, the system will not boot. CD-ROMs cannot be read without the ISO 9660 file system support. DOS file systems will commonly require FAT support, plus one of the DOS file system types (such as MSDOS or VFAT). Support for the `/proc` file system is virtually required—its absence will break many programs. NFS client and server support can be found under the Network File Systems menu—NFS server support requires experimental driver support in the Code Maturity menu.

Console drivers
These include drivers for basic VGA, plus the new frame buffer.

Sound
Sound cards are configured here.

Kernel hacking
The option in this menu is only used in debugging the Linux kernel. Unless you are actively modifying code in the kernel, it is safe to leave this option unset.

Load/Save alternate configuration file
It is possible to save the kernel configuration to a file. This file can then be moved to another machine and loaded into a separate kernel build environment. The kernel configuration from the Red Hat kernel source packages is stored in `kernel/redhat.config` on the CD-ROM included with this text. It can be loaded with the above menu options. This configuration requires an `initrd`, so modify the SCSI configuration to compile a driver for your SCSI controller directly into the kernel if possible.

When all options have been properly configured, exit the menu. A prompt will ask if the changes to the kernel configuration should be abandoned. Answer "No" if everything is correct.

Compiling the Kernel

Once the kernel configuration is complete, run the following two commands to clean the source tree and generate the dependency files:

```
make dep
make clean
```

At this point, one way to generate a new kernel is with the following command:

```
make zlilo
```

This command will generate the files `/vmlinuz` (the zipped kernel image) and `/System.map` (a table of symbols from the kernel). Because Red Hat Linux installs the kernel in the `/boot` directory, however, this new kernel will not boot. One way to use this new kernel is to modify LILO to boot from `/vmlinuz`. Below is an example of a stock `/etc/lilo.conf`, which is configured to boot a kernel in the "Red Hat Way." This LILO configuration is from an IDE system, which does not use an `initrd`.

```
boot=/dev/hda
map=/boot/map
install=/boot/boot.b
prompt
timeout=50
image=/boot/vmlinuz-2.2.5-15
      label=linux
      root=/dev/hda5
      read-only
other=/dev/hda1
      label=dos
      table=/dev/hda
```

The above `/etc/lilo.conf` file can be modified to boot `/vmlinuz` (as shown below). The *label* describing the kernel in the boot directory is renamed `linuxold`. (The label is the keyword typed at the LILO boot prompt that selects the operating system to boot.) Then a new image *stanza* is added, describing `/vmlinuz`.

```
boot=/dev/hda
map=/boot/map
install=/boot/boot.b
prompt
timeout=50
image=/vmlinuz
      label=linux
      root=/dev/hda5
      read-only
image=/boot/vmlinuz-2.2.5-15
      label=linuxold
      root=/dev/hda5
      read-only
other=/dev/hda1
      label=dos
      table=/dev/hda
```

Once the file is reconfigured, run **/sbin/lilo** to reconfigure the LILO boot manager with the new kernel.

Some other operating systems place the kernel image in a completely separate file system, such as `/stand`. Refrain from this behavior in Red Hat Linux.

There are two main reasons why you might not want to use `make zlilo`, as described above. Either you want to follow the Red Hat convention of placing the kernel image in the boot directory, or the `make zlilo` fails, complaining that the kernel image is too large.

If the image is too large, it can be compressed further by using **make bzImage**, which uses the `bzip2` compression format. You should first make certain that all unnecessary drivers, however, have been removed from the kernel image.

After a successful run of **make bzImage**, a copy of the compressed kernel will be stored in `/usr/src/linux/arch/i386/boot/bzImage`, and a `System.map` will be placed in `/usr/src/linux`. Move these files to the desired positions (either the root directory or `/boot` and reconfigure LILO accordingly).

Do not reboot the system until the modules and the `initrd` (if required) are installed. After booting and satisfactory testing of the new kernel, the generic kernel in `/boot` can be removed. Use caution, and do not delete the files required by LILO. Do not touch `boot.b` or `map` in the `/boot` directory.

Compiling the Modules

If modules are enabled in the kernel configuration, they must be generated in a procedure separate from the kernel preparation. Enter the following command from `/usr/src/linux`:

make modules

Once the modules have been compiled, they can be installed with:

make modules_install

This command installs the modules under `/lib/modules` in a directory that has the same name as the kernel release. When moving the kernel to another Linux system, this set of directories must be moved as well and placed in the same location on the target system.

Creating the initrd

If you are using a SCSI system, and you have made the (unwise) decision to prepare support for your SCSI adapter as a module, an `initrd` will be required. Generate it with the following command:

mkinitrd initrd 2.2.12

Below is an example `/etc/lilo.conf` demonstrating the use of an `initrd`. Note that the generic kernel put down by the Red Hat installer has been preserved:

```
boot=/dev/sda
map=/boot/map
install=/boot/boot.b
prompt
timeout=50
image=/vmlinuz
      label=linux
      root=/dev/sda1
      initrd=/initrd
      read-only
image=/boot/vmlinuz-2.2.5-15smp
      label=linuxold
      root=/dev/sda1
      initrd=/boot/initrd-2.2.5-15smp.img
      read-only
image=/boot/vmlinuz-2.2.5-15
      label=linux-up
      root=/dev/sda1
      initrd=/boot/initrd-2.2.5-15.img
      read-only
```

Using an Errata Kernel

If you don't want to go to the trouble of building your own kernel, you can apply errata kernels that are posted by Red Hat. At the time of the publication of this text, the latest version of the kernel that Red Hat would like you to use is 2.2.5, build 22. This version replaces 2.2.5, build 15, which has a bug that allows remote users to crash it.

In previous Linux distributions, Red Hat's Linux installation included a single kernel RPM compiled for an 80386 processor. Starting in Red Hat Linux 6.0, Red Hat now includes several kernels for different types of machines. Following are the kernel packages in the errata:

kernel-2.2.5-22.i386.rpm
For i386, i486 and other non-Pentium systems

kernel-2.2.5-22.i586.rpm
For Pentium and most Pentium-class CPUs

kernel-smp-2.2.5-22.i586.rpm
For Pentium SMP boxes

kernel-2.2.5-22.i686.rpm
For i686 (Pentium II, Celeron)

kernel-smp-2.2.5-22.i686.rpm
For i686 SMP

Red Hat provides a long list of steps to upgrade your kernel, but it really isn't that hard. For this exercise, we will assume that a uniprocessor Pentium system is to be upgraded. Enter the following set of commands:

```
/sbin/modprobe loop.o
rpm -ivh kernel-2.2.5-22.i586.rpm
/sbin/mkinitrd /boot/initrd-2.2.5-22.img 2.2.5-22
```

If you are really brave (or crazy), you can use the "Uvh" option of RPM instead. It will destroy your present kernel and prevent LILO from booting the system unless it is reconfigured:

```
/sbin/modprobe loop.o
rpm -Uvh kernel-2.2.5-22.i586.rpm
/sbin/mkinitrd /boot/initrd-2.2.5-22.img 2.2.5-22
```

The "Uvh" option is probably more realistic for IDE users rather than SCSI users. If, for some reason, the loopback device is not available, the `mkinitrd` will fail.

In either case, before you attempt either of these command sets, make sure that you have your boot disk handy. Lost your boot disk? You can create another, *before* your upgrade, with the following command:

```
mkbootdisk --device /dev/fd0 2.2.5-15
```

If I have to tell you that `/dev/fd0` is the A: drive on your PC, you probably aren't ready to be doing a kernel upgrade. You should also be advised that if you use the "Uvh" option to the RPM kernel upgrade command, the `loop.o` kernel module won't be available on your boot disk (if the system crashes). You can get it out of an older RPM, though. Don't use the "Uvh" option, unless you're *sure* that you can get it right the first time. You might set aside a copy of `loop.o` from your old kernel before you start. (It lives in the `/lib/modules` directory.)

The above **mkinitrd** command isn't really that important on IDE systems, but it is *deadly* important on SCSI systems. Without the kernel modules in the `initrd`, the system will not boot.

Once the new kernel is installed, the system is in a precarious state. LILO should be reconfigured *immediately.* A reboot between the kernel upgrade and LILO reconfiguration could range from inconvenient to disastrous. Upgrades for an IDE system are usually as simple as changing the name of the kernel image in `/etc/lilo.conf`, as shown in Listing 10.2.

Listing 10.2 *Modifying* `/etc/lilo.conf` *for an errata kernel.*

```
boot=/dev/hda
map=/boot/map
install=/boot/boot.b
prompt
timeout=50
image=/boot/vmlinuz-2.2.5-22
     label=linux
     root=/dev/hda5
     read-only
other=/dev/hda1
     label=dos
     table=/dev/hda
```

Alternately, if the "Uvh" option was not used, the old kernel could be set up as a backup:

```
boot=/dev/hda
map=/boot/map
install=/boot/boot.b
prompt
timeout=50
image=/boot/vmlinuz-2.2.5-22
     label=linux
     root=/dev/hda5
     read-only
image=/boot/vmlinuz-2.2.5-15
     label=linuxold
     root=/dev/hda5
     read-only
other=/dev/hda1
     label=dos
     table=/dev/hda
```

This alternate configuration lets LILO boot the new kernel if **linux** is entered at the prompt, and the old kernel if **linuxold** is entered instead (in addition to the DOS entry).

A SCSI system is a bit trickier, as the `initrd` must also be set:

```
boot=/dev/sda
map=/boot/map
install=/boot/boot.b
prompt
timeout=50
image=/boot/vmlinuz-2.2.5-22
        label=linux
        root=/dev/sda1
        initrd=/boot/initrd-2.2.5-22.img
        read-only
image=/boot/vmlinuz-2.2.5-15
        label=linuxold
        root=/dev/sda1
        initrd=/boot/initrd-2.2.5-15.img
        read-only
```

Once the new `/etc/lilo.conf` file has been written, don't forget to run the following command:

/sbin/lilo

Forgetting to rerun LILO before the reboot is a *major* cause of terror for Linux administrators, and it nabs IDE and SCSI users alike.

If I haven't frightened you away at this point, the odds are that you are about to change your kernel. Good luck! Make sure your boot disk is good, and may your LILO never fail you!

11

Recording Compact Discs

Software for writing CD-Recordables under Linux has been available for some time. The `cdrecord` utility, one of the preeminent tools for writing CDs, is very stable despite its current alpha status. Two important companion utilities, `mkisofs` and `cdda2wav`, have recently been included in the `cdrecord` distribution. With these utilities, `cdrecord` is now all you need to prepare and write CD-Recordables under Linux.

cdrecord is maintained by Jörg Schilling. The home page for the utility is *http://www.fokus.gmd.de/research/cc/glone/employees/joerg.schilling/private/cdrecord.html.*

The current release when this text was written was cdrecord-1.8a24. A copy of this distribution is on the CD-ROM included with this text in the /cdrecord directory. However, you should examine the web site to determine if a newer version is available.

On Linux, cdrecord works with the SCSI generic devices (/dev/sg?). However, there are several important things to note. For one, support for these devices must be enabled in the kernel. For another, cdrecord uses SCSI emulation to address IDE devices. Finally, cdrecord requires Inter-Process Communication facilities (IPC) to be enabled in the kernel. The standard Red Hat distribution kernels laid down by the installer contain all the support for these features that is required. Your kernel is fine as is, but the SCSI emulation must be configured through the LILO interface, which will require a reboot. For non-x86 architectures (which are not really addressed in this text), it may be necessary to raise the default shared memory size, which is documented in the README.linux file contained in the distribution.

Jörg Schilling complains bitterly in the documentation for cdrecord about the quality (or lack thereof) of the SCSI implementation in the Linux kernel. Let's hope that this issue is soon resolved to the satisfaction of all concerned.

Configuration

Before cdrecord can be used, the Linux kernel must be properly configured to address a CD-Recorder. Extra kernel functionality will be required if you are using an IDE CD-Recorder.

SCSI Considerations

SCSI CD-Recorders are ideal for use with cdrecord. The kernel will require support for the SCSI generic devices, and the /dev/sg? devices must exist. Also, if cdrecord will be used with an IDE recorder, SCSI emulation must be configured for the drive.

If the device files in the /dev directory have been damaged, they can be rebuilt with the MAKEDEV script that is itself in the /dev directory. In this case, the correct syntax to rebuild the SCSI generic devices is **MAKEDEV sg**.

The kernel will also require basic Inter-Process Communication (IPC) services. Loopback device support is also recommended as it allows you to test CD images on the hard drive before they are burned on the CD-ROM.

All of this support is available in the Red Hat distribution kernel. For information on kernel options, see Chapter 10, "Rebuilding the Linux Kernel."

IDE Considerations

Starting with Red Hat Linux 6.0, there is no longer a need to build a specialized kernel to use an IDE CD recorder (oh joy!). All required functionality is available under the standard Red Hat distribution kernel with LILO and kernel modules.

IDE CD-Recordable drives must use the `ide-scsi` kernel module to emulate a SCSI CD-ROM drive with the SCSI generic devices. This is accomplished through LILO and the `modprobe` utility, but a quick review of the IDE device names under Linux is in order.

As a Linux administrator ought to know, there are usually two IDE channels on PC motherboards. Each IDE channel can host up to two IDE devices, one master and one slave. The `/dev` entries for these devices are shown below:

Primary Channel Master	`/dev/hda`
Primary Channel Slave	`/dev/hdb`
Secondary Channel Master	`/dev/hdc`
Secondary Channel Slave	`/dev/hdd`

In most modern PCs, the hard drive is installed as the master on the primary channel (`/dev/hda`), while the CD-ROM (read-only) drive is normally installed as the master on the secondary channel (`/dev/hdc`). It can be disconcerting to have a CD-ROM drive referred to as "Hard Drive C," and there is ample reason to install a soft link from `/dev/cdrom to /dev/hdc`. This is not only for clarity; some programs, such as audio CD players, require this link. Normally, a CD-Recordable drive is installed in addition to the read-only drive as the slave on the secondary channel (`/dev/hdd`), since

CD-Recordable drives are much slower at reading CD-ROMs than the read-only drives. Some CD-Recordable drives work better if they are installed as IDE master devices. However, in this section, we will assume that the CD-Recordable drive is installed as a slave on the secondary channel.

Given the above configuration, with the CD-Recordable drive as the slave device on the secondary channel (`/dev/hdd`), the first step in configuring the drive with SCSI emulation is to pass `hdd=ide-scsi` as an argument to the kernel at boot time (if `/dev/hdd` is not the CD-Recordable drive, substitute another device name). This is normally done through LILO (unless another bootloader is in use, such as `loadlin`, `MILO`, or `SILO`, but these configurations are not covered in this text). Below is an example `/etc/lilo.conf` that passes this argument:

```
boot=/dev/hda
map=/boot/map
install=/boot/boot.b
prompt
timeout=50
other=/dev/hda1
      label=dos
      table=/dev/hda
image=/boot/vmlinuz-2.2.5-22
      label=linux
      root=/dev/hda5
      read-only
      append="hdd=ide-scsi"
```

This example LILO configuration boots a DOS variant by default, but when Linux is booted, the `hdd=ide-scsi` string is passed as an argument to the Linux kernel (with the `append` option on the last line of the file). This is not the only step required to convert the IDE drive into a SCSI-emulated drive. After booting Linux with the new kernel argument, root must issue the following command to complete the emulation:

modprobe ide-scsi

The kernel will then report the status of the SCSI initialization as it probes SCSI IDs and LUNs (Logical Unit Numbers). It should identify the manufacturer and model number of the IDE drive as the probe progresses.

Creating/Duplicating Data Discs

Simple data discs are composed of a single data track. The data is held in the ISO9660 file system format. ISO9660 supports only 8.3 filenames (i.e., up to 8 characters, optionally followed by a dot and up to 3 additional characters), but longer filenames can be implemented by using extensions to ISO9660. These extensions also permit the use of soft links and permissions that are common to UNIX file systems.

Compiling and Installing cdrecord

The home page for `cdrecord` can be found at the following website: *http://www.fokus.gmd.de/research/cc/glone/employees/joerg.schilling/private/cdrecord.html*

It is suggested that the latest version be downloaded and installed from this location. Should this be impractical, a copy of `cdrecord-1.8a24` can be found in the `cdrecord` directory on the CD-ROM included with this text (which will most likely be outdated by the time that this chapter goes to print). Use the following commands to install the older version:

```
tar xvzf cdrecord-1.8a24.tar.gz
cd cdrecord-1.8
./Gmake.linux
make install
```

The steps for installing later versions may be different; you may be required to improvise.

Using dd to Create CD Images

If a soft link is created from `/dev/cdrom` pointing to the appropriate CD-ROM device (which is usually `/dev/hdc or /dev/scd0`), a copy of a CD-ROM data disc (called `cdimage.raw`) can be sent to the hard drive with the following command:

```
dd if=/dev/cdrom of=/tmp/cdimage.raw
```

CD-ROM images can be very large; make sure there is enough space in the target file system to hold the image with which you are working. Use the `df` command to check the space available in all mounted file systems. Examine the output for lines corresponding to the CDROM as well as the target file system.

Warning The above command will write the image into the root file system, unless `/tmp` was declared as a separate file system at installation time.

One of the author's IDE drives does not properly size tracks and causes `dd` to emit `dd: /dev/hdc: Input/output error` messages each time it is used. While these errors are not fatal and result in no corruption of data, the errors are suppressed by using the SCSI-emulated CD-R drive to read the track.

The image created in the previous step can be tested by mounting it as a separate file system using the loopback device, as is done in the following command:

mount /tmp/cdimage.raw -r -o loop /mnt

We can omit the `-t iso9660` option to the mount command above since this filesystem type is automatically detected. However, some configurations might require this option.

After the mount, the `/mnt` directory should appear to be an exact duplicate of the source CD-ROM.

Sometimes, `dd` will fail to properly create an image. This failure is related to the "track at once" mode. This problem is documented in the `README.copy` file contained in the `cdrecord` distribution, which advises that the `scgskeleton` program be used in lieu of `dd` if problems arise.

Using mkisofs to Create CD Images

The `mkisofs` utility, written by Eric Youngdale, is used to prepare data images of an active file system which can be written to a blank CD-Recordable disc. `mkisofs` is part of the `cdrecord` distribution, and these tools are compiled and installed together. Do not use older versions of mkisofs as they may be buggy.

The `mkisofs` command is analogous to `tar`, in that it prepares an uncompressed "archive" of files in the ISO9660 format. This archive can then be burned directly to a blank CD-Recordable disc.

A simple invocation of `mkisofs` follows:

/opt/schily/bin/mkisofs -o /tmp/cdimage.raw .

This command stores the current directory, and all of its subdirectories, in a binary ISO9660 image that is suitable for writing to a CD-Recordable. The following command mounts the ISO9660 image on the `/mnt` directory so that it might be examined and verified (the kernel must include loopback device support):

mount /tmp/cdimage.raw -r -o loop /mnt

If the output file is mounted in this manner, it will soon be discovered that long file names have been trimmed. The ISO9660 format supports only 8.3 filenames (8 characters, followed by a dot, followed by an optional 3 character extension, just like the old days of DOS). The method described above is perfect for creating CD-ROMS for use under DOS. However, longer filenames can be accurately stored within an ISO9660 image by using "Rock Ridge" extensions with the `-r` parameter to `mkisofs`. A new image using these extensions can be created after the old image is unmounted.

umount /mnt
/opt/schily/bin/mkisofs -r -o /tmp/cdimage.raw .

The above command works well if a CD-ROM is to be used exclusively under Linux, but all DOS and Windows variants will trim the file names to 8.3. The best set of options to properly record the attributes of long file names and other UNIX filesystem particulars in a way which is more visible to other operating systems is a `mkisofs` with the `-T` and `-J` parameters in addition to `-r`. The `-T` option records additional directory information in a `TRANS.TBL` file in each directory, and `-J` generates `Joliet` directory entries, which are useful on Windows platforms.This might not be ideal for a CD-ROM made exclusively for Linux as the `TRANS.TBL` files will be added to each directory on the disc. A sample command with the added parameters is:

/opt/schily/bin/mkisofs -r -T -J -o /tmp/cdimage.raw .

A volume label can be added to the CD image with the `-V` parameter as shown below.

```
/opt/schily/bin/mkisofs -r -T -J -V "Personal Files" -o /tmp/cdimage.raw .
```

A CD-Recordable can even be made "bootable" on i386 systems with the additional `-b` and `-c` arguments as shown in this command:

```
/opt/schily/bin/mkisofs -r -T -J -V "Personal Files" -b boot/boot.img \
  -c boot/boot.catalog -o /tmp/cdimage.raw .
```

The `boot/boot.img` file is an image of a bootable floppy that can be generated with `dd`. The `boot/boot.catalog` file is created by `mkisofs` within the source file system. (Be careful: it will overwrite any existing file with the same name and location.) This bootable CD format, called the "El Torito" extension, requires BIOS support. (That is, older PCs with i386-family processors will probably not be able to boot off such CDs because the BIOS is too antiquated to support El Torito.)

Burning a data image to a CDR with cdrecord

A data image, obtained from either `dd` or `mkisofs`, can be *tested* for burning by using a command similar to the following:

```
/opt/schily/bin/cdrecord -dummy -v speed=2 dev=0,0,0 /tmp/cdimage.raw
```

The `dev=0,0,0` option above indicates the SCSI bus number, SCSI ID, and the LUN of the CD-Recorder. If the recorder at ID 5 on the third SCSI controller is desired, its dev specification would be 2,5,0. IDE drives will probably use device 0,0,0 if no other SCSI peripherals are configured in the Linux environment. The kernel will also report the address used by the drive(s) when the SCSI drivers are loaded (i.e., when the **modprobe ide-scsi** command is executed, when the module for a SCSI controller is loaded, or, at boot, when a SCSI driver that is compiled into the kernel is initialized.) Check `/var/log/messages` if there are doubts as to the location of the CD-Recordable drive. The `speed=2` option above indicates the speed that data should be written to the blank CD-R; use the maximum speed of which your drive is capable unless you have problems.

When the above command is run, `cdrecord` will simulate a complete write to the CD-Recorder, which will probably take a long time (everything is done except the actual firing of the laser). Do not be alarmed at the countdown; the disc will not be recorded. Output similar to Listing 11.1 should appear.

Listing 11.1 *A dummy run of* `cdrecord`.

```
Cdrecord release 1.8a24 Copyright (C) 1995-1999 Jörg Schilling
TOC Type: 1 = CD-ROM
scsidev: '0,0,0'
scsibus: 0 target: 0 lun: 0
atapi: 1
Device type    : Removable CD-ROM
Version        : 0
Response Format: 1
Vendor_info    : 'MITSUMI '
Identifikation : 'CR-2801TE
Revision       : '1.06'
Device seems to be: Philips CDD-522.
Using generic SCSI-3/mmc CD-R driver (mmc_cdr).
Driver flags   : SWABAUDIO
Drive buf size : 409600 = 400 KB
FIFO size      : 4194304 = 4096 KB
Track 01: data   73 MB
Total size:      84 MB (08:21.08) = 37581 sectors
Lout start:      84 MB (08:23/06) = 37581 sectors
Current Secsize: -1
ATIP info from disk:
  Indicated writing power: 5
  Is not unrestricted
  Is not erasable
  ATIP start of lead in:  -11325 (97:31/00)
  ATIP start of lead out: 336225 (74:45/00)
Disk type: Cyanine, AZO or similar
Manuf. index: 22
Manufacturer: Ritek Co.
Blocks total: 336225 Blocks current: 336225 Blocks remaining: 298644
RBlocks total: 345460 RBlocks current: 345460 RBlocks remaining: 307879
Starting to write CD/DVD at speed 2 in dummy mode for single session.
Last chance to quit, starting dummy write in 1 seconds.
Waiting for reader process to fill input-buffer ... input-buffer ready.
Starting new track at sector: 0
Track 01:  73 of  73 MB written (fifo 100%).
Track 01: Total bytes read/written: 76961792/76961792 (37579 sectors).
Writing  time:  255.390s
Fixating...
WARNING: Some drives don't like fixation in dummy mode.
Fixating time:    0.006s
/opt/schily/bin/cdrecord: fifo had 2349 puts and 2349 gets.
/opt/schily/bin/cdrecord: fifo was 0 times empty and 2211 times full, min fill was 97%.
```

An important point to make about the process of writing CD-R discs is the FIFO (First-In, First-Out) buffer. The CD-R drive has a small amount of memory which is used as a buffer as it writes to the blank CD-R. The buffer is filled as the computer writes data to the drive, and emptied as the drive writes the data to the CD-R. The buffer *must not* be allowed to go empty until the disc is completely written; if the FIFO empties prematurely, the disc will be wasted. For this reason, it is imperative that the Linux system be lightly loaded while the recording of the blank CD-R is taking place. If `cdrecord` is forced to compete with other system processes for access to the CPU or the I/O system, the CD-R media may be wasted (instant coaster!). `cdrecord` augments the buffer on the CD-Recordable drive with another FIFO in system memory, but it is advisable not to tempt fate by using `cdrecord` on a system that is too busy.

It is also not normally safe to burn an image that is mounted on an NFS file system, also for fears of a FIFO underrun. Options are available that will control the FIFO, which may allow slower file systems to perform acceptably.

A data image can be written to a CD-Recordable disc by omitting the `-dummy` option to `cdrecord`. Do not write the image until a successful test run of `cdrecord` is achieved. An example that will perform a write follows:

```
/opt/schily/bin/cdrecord -v speed=2 dev=0,0,0 /tmp/cdimage.raw
```

There are many more options to `cdrecord` (more than there are to `ls`, as the author has pointed out). Refer to the online manual page and the distribution notes for further information.

Creating/Duplicating Audio Discs

This section relies upon the `cdda2wav` companion utility in the `cdrecord` distribution. `cdda2wav` was written by Heiko Eissfeldt. It is compiled and installed at the same time as `cdrecord`.

`cdda2wav` makes an exact digital copy of the data on an audio CD. Both the right and left channels are sampled at 44.1 kHz with 16-bit linear quantization which, according to the Nyquist Sampling Theory, gives a useful audio bandwidth of 20kHz without aliasing and allowing for high-end filter roll-off. (I guess that I didn't get that electrical engineering degree for nothing.)

Preparing WAV Images of an Audio CD with cdda2wav

`cdda2wav` normally encapsulates audio data from a CD in the WAV format (a format in common use on the Windows platform). `cdda2wav` can use a number of other formats. Conversion between the formats is often simply an exercise in the options to `dd`. In this text, we will work with WAV.

`cdda2wav` is called slightly differently if it is used on IDE equipment, rather than SCSI. The following command will copy each track on an audio CD from a SCSI CD-ROM into separate WAV files (with filenames proceeding up from `audio_01.wav`) in the current directory:

/opt/schily/bin/cdda2wav -D 0,0,0 -S 8 –B

If the `-B` option above is omitted, the data is stored in one big WAV file, rather than in separate files (in other words, you will almost always want to use `-B`). The other options, although similar to those for `cdrecord`, are not identical. The argument to `-D` is the SCSI Bus:ID:LUN as before. `-S` specifies the speed that should be used (the drive used in this case is an 8-speed read, 2-speed write). The alternate invocation for IDE drives follows:

/opt/schily/bin/cdda2wav -I cooked_ioctl -D /dev/hdc -S 36 –B

Above, the `-Icooked_ioctl` option has been added, and the parameter to the `-D` option now points to the device file for the drive.

If SCSI host adapter emulation has been established for the CD-ROM as well as the CDR, use the SCSI syntax rather than the cooked_ioctl option.

Rather than reading the entire disc, it is sometimes useful to read only a few tracks. This is accomplished with the `-t` option:

/opt/schily/bin/cdda2wav -I cooked_ioctl -D /dev/hdc -S 36 -B -t 3+5

The above command reads tracks 3 through 5 only. Listing 11.2 on page 270 is the output that should be expected.

Listing 11.2 *A run of* `cdda2wav`.

```
724992 bytes buffer memory requested, 4 buffers, 75 sectors
#Cdda2wav version schily0.6_linux_2.2.5-15_i686_i686 real time sched.
     soundcard support
AUDIOtrack pre-emphasis  copy-permitted tracktype channels
      1-24            no               no      audio    2
Table of Contents: total tracks:24, (total time 69:13.30)
  1.( 1:51.53),  2.( 2:39.65),  3.( 1:07.10),  4.( 4:31.15),  5.( 0:36.72)
  6.( 1:16.38),  7.( 2:39.22),  8.( 0:48.15),  9.( 1:20.65), 10.( 2:23.70)
 11.( 1:30.00), 12.( 2:05.70), 13.( 2:08.45), 14.( 3:53.40), 15.( 5:53.60)
 16.( 1:53.55), 17.( 3:43.18), 18.( 3:58.62), 19.( 4:45.65), 20.( 3:51.18)
 21.( 4:39.12), 22.( 2:10.48), 23.( 3:00.10), 24.( 6:20.45),
Table of Contents: starting sectors
  1.(      32),  2.(    8410),  3.(   20400),  4.(   25435),  5.(   45775)
  6.(   48547),  7.(   54285),  8.(   66232),  9.(   69847), 10.(   75912)
 11.(   86707), 12.(   93457), 13.(  102902), 14.(  112547), 15.(  130062)
 16.(  156597), 17.(  165127), 18.(  181870), 19.(  199782), 20.(  221222)
 21.(  238565), 22.(  259502), 23.(  269300), 24.(  282810), lead-out(  311355)
CDDB discid: 0x47103718
CD-Text: not detected
CD-Extra: not detected
samplefiles size total will be 66201876 bytes. 3 audio tracks
recording 375.02933 seconds stereo with 16 bits @ 44100.0 Hz -'audio'...
overlap:min/max/cur, jitter, percent_done:
 1/ 1/ 1/      0  18%  track  3 successfully recorded
 1/ 1/ 1/      0  90%  track  4 successfully recorded
 1/ 1/ 1/      0 100%
  track  5 successfully recorded
```

If a single numeric argument is passed with `-t`, the digital transfer of audio data begins with the track number specified and proceeds to the end of the disc. If two numeric arguments are passed, the transfer begins at the track of the first argument and concludes with the track of the last argument. The tracks are numbered starting at 1. The `-t 3+5` option above starts recording at track 3 and ceases at the conclusion of track 5.

`cdda2wav` will also record information about the CDDB entry for the CD. All audio CDs have a unique serial number. An international Internet database exists that contains album titles, artists, and track titles for a majority of the audio compact discs that have been released. A `perl` script is included with `cdda2wav` called `tracknames.pl`. This script can be used to give useful names to the WAV files produced by `cdda2wav`. It will write a small shell script that can be used to rename the audio tracks. However, before it will run, the command interpreter in the first line of the script must be changed to `/usr/bin/perl`. Obviously, scans of this type will work only if your Linux system is connected to the Internet. Listing 11.3 is an example run of `tracknames.pl`.

Listing 11.3 *A run of* `tracknames.pl`.

```
# tracknames.pl us.cddb.com 8880 < audio.cddb
cddb query 47103718 24 182 8560 20550 25585 45925 48697 54435 66382 69997
     76062 86857 93607 103052 112697 130212 156747 165277 182020 199932
     221372 238715 259652 269450 282960 4150
Connected.
201 cddb1.cddb.com CDDBP server v1.4.1b14PL1 ready at Sun Aug 22 23:21:33 1999

cddb hello root localhost.localdomain billo-scan 0.1
200 Hello and welcome root@localhost.localdomain running billo-scan 0.1.

cddb query 47103718 24 182 8560 20550 25585 45925 48697 54435 66382 69997
     76062 86857 93607 103052 112697 130212 156747 165277 182020 199932
     221372 238715 259652 269450 282960 4150
200 classical 47103718 Modest Mussorgsky / Maurice Ravel /
     Pictures at an Exhibition / Ma Mhre l'Oye / Rapsodie Espagnole

cddb read classical 47103718
210 classical 47103718 CD database entry follows (until terminating `.')

Modest Mussorgsky / Maurice Ravel / Pictures at an Exhibition / Ma Mhre
Maurice Ravel
Modest Mussorgsky
l'Oye / Rapsodie Espagnole
Rapsodie Espagnole
l'Oye
Track match Rapsodie_Espagnole-01-Promenade
Track match Rapsodie_Espagnole-02-Gnomus
Track match Rapsodie_Espagnole-03-Promenade
Track match Rapsodie_Espagnole-04-Il_vecchio_castello
Track match Rapsodie_Espagnole-05-Promenade
Track match Rapsodie_Espagnole-06-Tuileries
Track match Rapsodie_Espagnole-07-Bydlo
Track match Rapsodie_Espagnole-08-Promenade
Track match Rapsodie_Espagnole-09-Ballet_des_Petits_Poussins_dans_leurs_Coques
Track match Rapsodie_Espagnole-10-Samuel_Goldenberg_und_Schmuyle
Track match Rapsodie_Espagnole-11-Limoges__Le_Marchi
Track match Rapsodie_Espagnole-12-Catacombae__Sepulchrum_Romanum
Track match Rapsodie_Espagnole-13-Cum_mortuis_in_lingua_mortua
Track match Rapsodie_Espagnole-14-La_Cabane_de_Baba-Yaga_sur_des_Pattes_de_Poule
Track match Rapsodie_Espagnole-15-La_Grande_Porte_de_Kiev
```

```
Track match Rapsodie_Espagnole-16-Pavane_de_La_Belle_au_Bois_Bormant
Track match Rapsodie_Espagnole-17-Petit_Poucet
Track match Rapsodie_Espagnole-18-Laideronnette,_Impiratrice_des_Pagodes
Track match Rapsodie_Espagnole-19-Les_Entretiens_de_la_Belle_et_la_Bjte
Track match Rapsodie_Espagnole-20-Le_Jardin_Fierique
Track match Rapsodie_Espagnole-21-Prilude_`_la_Nuit
Track match Rapsodie_Espagnole-22-Malaguena
Track match Rapsodie_Espagnole-23-Habanera
Track match Rapsodie_Espagnole-24-Feria
quit
230 cddbl.cddb.com Closing connection.  Goodbye.

mv 'audio_01.wav' 'Rapsodie_Espagnole-01-Promenade.wav'
mv 'audio_02.wav' 'Rapsodie_Espagnole-02-Gnomus.wav'
mv 'audio_03.wav' 'Rapsodie_Espagnole-03-Promenade.wav'
mv 'audio_04.wav' 'Rapsodie_Espagnole-04-Il_vecchio_castello.wav'
mv 'audio_05.wav' 'Rapsodie_Espagnole-05-Promenade.wav'
mv 'audio_06.wav' 'Rapsodie_Espagnole-06-Tuileries.wav'
mv 'audio_07.wav' 'Rapsodie_Espagnole-07-Bydlo.wav'
mv 'audio_08.wav' 'Rapsodie_Espagnole-08-Promenade.wav'
mv 'audio_09.wav' \
     'Rapsodie_Espagnole-09-Ballet_des_Petits_Poussins_dans_leurs_Coques.wav'
mv 'audio_10.wav' 'Rapsodie_Espagnole-10-Samuel_Goldenberg_und_Schmuyle.wav'
mv 'audio_11.wav' 'Rapsodie_Espagnole-11-Limoges__Le_Marchi.wav'
mv 'audio_12.wav' 'Rapsodie_Espagnole-12-Catacombae__Sepulchrum_Romanum.wav'
mv 'audio_13.wav' 'Rapsodie_Espagnole-13-Cum_mortuis_in_lingua_mortua.wav'
mv 'audio_14.wav' \
    'Rapsodie_Espagnole-14-La_Cabane_de_Baba-Yaga_sur_des_Pattes_de_Poule.wav'
mv 'audio_15.wav' 'Rapsodie_Espagnole-15-La_Grande_Porte_de_Kiev.wav'
mv 'audio_16.wav' 'Rapsodie_Espagnole-16-Pavane_de_La_Belle_au_Bois_Bormant.wav'
mv 'audio_17.wav' 'Rapsodie_Espagnole-17-Petit_Poucet.wav'
mv 'audio_18.wav' 'Rapsodie_Espagnole-18-Laideronnette,_Impiratrice_des_Pagodes.wav'
mv 'audio_19.wav' \
     'Rapsodie_Espagnole-19-Les_Entretiens_de_la_Belle_et_la_Bjte.wav'
mv 'audio_20.wav' 'Rapsodie_Espagnole-20-Le_Jardin_Fierique.wav'
mv 'audio_21.wav' 'Rapsodie_Espagnole-21-Prilude_`_la_Nuit.wav'
mv 'audio_22.wav' 'Rapsodie_Espagnole-22-Malaguena.wav'
mv 'audio_23.wav' 'Rapsodie_Espagnole-23-Habanera.wav'
mv 'audio_24.wav' 'Rapsodie_Espagnole-24-Feria.wav'
```

Fans of classical music will immediately recognize a small problem with the database entry for this CD; discs with multiple works may have inappropriate track titles (tracks 1–15 of this disc have absolutely nothing to do with Ravel's *Rhapsodie Espagnole*).

In any case, `tracknames.pl` has left a small script called `backup.sh` in the directory containing a set of commands. Listing 11.4 shows its contents for this disc.

Listing 11.4 *The result of* `tracknames.pl`.

```
mv audio_01.wav Rapsodie_Espagnole-01-Promenade.wav
mv audio_02.wav Rapsodie_Espagnole-02-Gnomus.wav
mv audio_03.wav Rapsodie_Espagnole-03-Promenade.wav
mv audio_04.wav Rapsodie_Espagnole-04-Il_vecchio_castello.wav
mv audio_05.wav Rapsodie_Espagnole-05-Promenade.wav
mv audio_06.wav Rapsodie_Espagnole-06-Tuileries.wav
mv audio_07.wav Rapsodie_Espagnole-07-Bydlo.wav
mv audio_08.wav Rapsodie_Espagnole-08-Promenade.wav
mv audio_09.wav \
Rapsodie_Espagnole-09-Ballet_des_Petits_Poussins_dans_leurs_Coques.wav
mv audio_10.wav Rapsodie_Espagnole-10-Samuel_Goldenberg_und_Schmuyle.wav
mv audio_11.wav Rapsodie_Espagnole-11-Limoges__Le_Marchi.wav
mv audio_12.wav Rapsodie_Espagnole-12-Catacombae__Sepulchrum_Romanum.wav
mv audio_13.wav Rapsodie_Espagnole-13-Cum_mortuis_in_lingua_mortua.wav
mv audio_14.wav \
     Rapsodie_Espagnole-14-La_Cabane_de_Baba-Yaga_sur_des_Pattes_de_Poule.wav
mv audio_15.wav Rapsodie_Espagnole-15-La_Grande_Porte_de_Kiev.wav
mv audio_16.wav Rapsodie_Espagnole-16-Pavane_de_La_Belle_au_Bois_Bormant.wav
mv audio_17.wav Rapsodie_Espagnole-17-Petit_Poucet.wav
mv audio_18.wav Rapsodie_Espagnole-18-Laideronnette,_Impiratrice_des_Pagodes.wav
mv audio_19.wav Rapsodie_Espagnole-19-Les_Entretiens_de_la_Belle_et_la_Bjte.wav
mv audio_20.wav Rapsodie_Espagnole-20-Le_Jardin_Fierique.wav
mv audio_21.wav Rapsodie_Espagnole-21-Prilude_`_la_Nuit.wav
mv audio_22.wav Rapsodie_Espagnole-22-Malaguena.wav
mv audio_23.wav Rapsodie_Espagnole-23-Habanera.wav
mv audio_24.wav Rapsodie_Espagnole-24-Feria.wav
mv audio_01.wav Rapsodie_Espagnole-01-Promenade.wav
mv audio_02.wav Rapsodie_Espagnole-02-Gnomus.wav
mv audio_03.wav Rapsodie_Espagnole-03-Promenade.wav
mv audio_04.wav Rapsodie_Espagnole-04-Il_vecchio_castello.wav
mv audio_05.wav Rapsodie_Espagnole-05-Promenade.wav
mv audio_06.wav Rapsodie_Espagnole-06-Tuileries.wav
mv audio_07.wav Rapsodie_Espagnole-07-Bydlo.wav
mv audio_08.wav Rapsodie_Espagnole-08-Promenade.wav
mv audio_09.wav \
     Rapsodie_Espagnole-09-Ballet_des_Petits_Poussins_dans_leurs_Coques.wav
mv audio_10.wav Rapsodie_Espagnole-10-Samuel_Goldenberg_und_Schmuyle.wav
mv audio_11.wav Rapsodie_Espagnole-11-Limoges__Le_Marchi.wav
mv audio_12.wav Rapsodie_Espagnole-12-Catacombae__Sepulchrum_Romanum.wav
mv audio_13.wav Rapsodie_Espagnole-13-Cum_mortuis_in_lingua_mortua.wav
mv audio_14.wav \
     Rapsodie_Espagnole-14-La_Cabane_de_Baba-Yaga_sur_des_Pattes_de_Poule.wav
mv audio_15.wav Rapsodie_Espagnole-15-La_Grande_Porte_de_Kiev.wav
mv audio_16.wav Rapsodie_Espagnole-16-Pavane_de_La_Belle_au_Bois_Bormant.wav
mv audio_17.wav Rapsodie_Espagnole-17-Petit_Poucet.wav
mv audio_18.wav Rapsodie_Espagnole-18-Laideronnette,_Impiratrice_des_Pagodes.wav
```

```
mv audio_19.wav Rapsodie_Espagnole-19-Les_Entretiens_de_la_Belle_et_la_Bjte.wav
mv audio_20.wav Rapsodie_Espagnole-20-Le_Jardin_Fierique.wav
mv audio_21.wav Rapsodie_Espagnole-21-Prilude_`_la_Nuit.wav
mv audio_22.wav Rapsodie_Espagnole-22-Malaguena.wav
mv audio_23.wav Rapsodie_Espagnole-23-Habanera.wav
mv audio_24.wav Rapsodie_Espagnole-24-Feria.wav
```

Execute permissions are not set for this script, so the simplest method to run it is with:

sh rename.sh

This script will fail for all but tracks 3 through 5, causing many error messages.

If you intend to immediately write out these WAV files to a CD-R, you may not want to run this script. `tracknames.pl` does not move the `.inf` files that are associated with each WAV file. The `.inf` files contain pre-gap information that can be used when writing the blank CD-R.

Future versions of the `cdrecord` distribution will most likely feature enhanced CDDB functionality. The programs contained within the `cdrecord` distribution will soon use *www.cdindex.org,* since the CDDB database is not free. Support will most likely have changed by the time you have read this.

Burning an audio image to a CDR with cdrecord

A collection of WAV files (recorded at the proper frequency of 44.1 kHz with the proper attributes) can be burned to a blank CD-R with a call to `cdrecord` of the following form:

**/opt/schily/bin/cdrecord -v speed=2 dev=0,0,0 -pad -useinfo \
-audio *.wav**

You should probably test the recording by using the `-dummy` option before committing to a write. The `-useinfo` option above will not work unless you have preserved the `.inf` files that were generated by `cdda2wav`. The `-pad` option above ensures that the audio tracks are padded to a multiple of 2352 bytes, as is required for storage on an audio CD.

The `-useinfo` option above has not been tested under "track at once" (TAO) mode. The author of `cdrecord` suggests `-useinfo` only under "disk at once" mode, although TAO mode can make limited use of the `.inf` files created by `cdda2wav`. The proper invocation of `cdrecord` for DAO mode is:

```
/opt/schily/bin/cdrecord -v speed=2 dev=0,0,0 -pad -dao -useinfo -audio *.wav
```

Unfortunately, the author's drive (a Mitsumi 2801) does not support DAO mode. Perhaps `-useinfo` will someday have better support for TAO mode.

Some Linux implementations also suffer from a "read ahead bug" which can corrupt CDRs written in TAO mode. This problem is solved by using DAO mode instead. The issue is discussed in the `AN-1.8a18` file included in the `cdrecord` distribution; the problem can also be corrected by the use of padding.

A data track can also be included, in addition to the audio tracks, in a "mixed-mode" CD. The single data track is specified first:

```
/opt/schily/bin/cdrecord -v speed=2 dev=0,0,0 /tmp/cdimage.raw \
-pad -useinfo -audio *.wav
```

Afterword

You've come to the end of the first edition of my little text on Red Hat Linux 6.0. I hope that with this work I've answered more questions than I've raised. However, it is likely that you will require additional documentation resources as your experience with the environment grows.

Start with the Red Hat manuals in the `/doc` directory on the CD-ROM included with this text. They offer simple installation instructions for a variety of configurations not addressed here. These manuals are equivalent to the printed material that you will find in the Red Hat Linux retail boxed set.

As you progress beyond installation, you might find the following Internet sites to be helpful:

- *http://kernelnotes.org*
  (Kernel information and HTML-formatted `HOWTOs`)
- *http://tunelinux.com*
  (Suggestions on tuning your Linux system for better performance)
- *http://freshmeat.net*
  (New software for your Linux system)
- *ftp://metalab.unc.edu/pub/Linux/docs*
  (One of the more widely used FTP repositories for Linux)

I have set up a web site, *http://rhadmin.org,* where you'll find information about administration of Red Hat Linux, along with the latest updates to this text and comments from readers.

Most RPM packages usually leave documentation in the `/usr/doc` directory on your system as they are installed. You can look there if you have questions about installed packages. Also located there are RPM distributions of the `HOWTO` files and translations of these `HOWTOs` in several languages.

And with these last bits of advice, our little tour of Linux is done. If you have dedicated yourself to the study of this text, then it is certain that you will go beyond it soon. You will soon begin many more significant excursions into Linux that will make our little journey seem positively pedestrian.

Be assured, however, that I am profoundly grateful for the opportunity to act as your guide throughout these pages. As you now take your leave, understand that you disembark with the best wishes of success from all who have participated in the production of this book.

Good luck.

A

Xconfigurator Monitor List

This list includes all the monitors whose scanning rates are contained in the Xconfigurator utility. See "Pre-installation Concerns with X11" on page 11 for information on how to access the scanning rates.

ADI DMC-2304

ADI Duo

ADI MicroScan 17

ADI MicroScan 17X

ADI MicroScan 2E

ADI MicroScan 3E+

ADI MicroScan 3E

ADI MicroScan 3V

ADI MicroScan 4A

ADI MicroScan 4G

ADI MicroScan 4GP

ADI MicroScan 5G

ADI MicroScan 5P/5P+

ADI MicroScan 5T

ADI MicroScan 5V

ADI MicroScan 6P

ADI MicroScan G70

ADI MicroScan P55

ADI ProVista 14

ADI ProVista E30

ADI ProVista E40

ADI ProVista E66

AOC 4N Series

AOC 4V & 5E Series

AOC 5V & 5G Series

AOC 7G Series

AOC 7V Series

AOC 9G Series

AOC-15

AT&T 14 in. Color Economy

AT&T 14 in. Color Value

AT&T 14 in. Mono

AT&T 15 in. Color

AT&T 17 in. Color Professional

AT&T 17 in. Color Value

AT&T CRT-365

AT&T CRT-395

Acer AcerView 11D

Acer AcerView 15P

Acer AcerView 33

Acer AcerView 33D

Acer AcerView 33DL

Acer AcerView 33s

Acer AcerView 34T

Acer AcerView 34TL

Acer AcerView 34Ts

Acer AcerView 34e

Acer AcerView 35

Acer AcerView 35c

Acer AcerView 54e

Acer AcerView 54s

Acer AcerView 55

Acer AcerView 55L

Acer AcerView 55c

Acer AcerView 55e

Acer AcerView 56L

Acer AcerView 56c

Acer AcerView 56e

Acer AcerView 56i

Acer AcerView 56is

Acer AcerView 56s

Acer AcerView 7015

Acer AcerView 76N

Acer AcerView 76c

Acer AcerView 76e

Acer AcerView 76i

Acer AcerView 76ie

Acer AcerView 76is

Acer AcerView 76t

Acer AcerView 77is

Acer AcerView 78i

Acer AcerView 78ie

Acer AcerView 79t

Acer AcerView 98i

Acer AcerView 99D

Apollo 1280x1024-68Hz

Apollo 1280x1024-70Hz

Axion CL-1566

CTX 1451

CTX 1451ES

CTX 1451GM

CTX 1462GM

CTX 1551

CTX 1562

CTX 1562ES

CTX 1562GM

CTX 1565

CTX 1565GM

CTX 1765

CTX 1765GM

CTX 1785

CTX 1785GM

CTX 2085

CTX 2185

CTX CPS-1460

CTX CPS-1560

CTX CPS-1750

CTX CPS-1760

CTX CPS-2160

CTX CPS-2180

CTX CVP-5439

CTX CVP-5468

CTX CVP-5468NI

CTX CVP-5468NL

CTX CVS-3436

CTX CVS-3450

CTX Multiscan 3436

CTX-1561

Chuntex CTX CPS-1560/LR

Compaq 1024 Monitor

Compaq 151FS Monitor

Compaq 171FS Monitor

Compaq P110 Monitor

Compaq P1610 Monitor

Compaq P50 Monitor

Compaq P75 Monitor

Compaq Qvision 172 Monitor

Compaq Qvision 200 Monitor

Compaq Qvision 210 Monitor

Compaq TFT450 Monitor

Compaq TFT500 Monitor

Compaq V50 Monitor

Compaq V75 Monitor

Compaq V75

Compaq V90 Monitor

Compudyne KD-1500N

Cornerstone - Color 20/70

Cornerstone - Color 20/77

Cornerstone - Color 21/75

Cornerstone - Color 40/95

Cornerstone - Color 45/101sf

Cornerstone - Color 50/101sf, 21/81

Cornerstone - c1000, c1001, Color 50/95

Cornerstone - c900

Cornerstone - p1400

Cornerstone - p1500

Cornerstone - p1600, Color 50/115sf, 50/115

Cornerstone - p1700

Cornerstone - v300

DEC PCXBV-KA/KB

Dell 1024i-P/1024i-Color

Dell 1024i

Dell Eizo 9080i

Dell GPD-16C

Dell GPD-19C

Dell Hewitt

Dell Super VGA Colour

Dell Super VGA DL 1428 I/L

Dell Super VGA Jostens

Dell Super VGA

Dell UGA DL 1460 NI

Dell Ultrascan 14C-E

Dell Ultrascan 14C-EN

Dell Ultrascan 14C

Dell Ultrascan 14ES

Dell Ultrascan 14LR

Dell Ultrascan 14XE

Dell Ultrascan 15ES/15ES-P

Dell Ultrascan 15FS-N/15FS-EN

Dell Ultrascan 15FS/15FS-E

Dell Ultrascan 15LR

Dell Ultrascan 15TE

Dell Ultrascan 17ES

Dell Ultrascan 17FS-ELR

Dell Ultrascan 17FS-EN

Dell Ultrascan 17FS-LR

Dell Ultrascan 17FS-N

Dell Ultrascan 21FS

Dell Ultrascan 21TE

Dell Ultrascan V17X

Dell V15X

Dell V17X

Dell VC15 Colour

Dell VGA 800

Dell VGA Color/Color Plus

Dell VGA Monochrome

Dell VS14/15

Dell VS17

Dell VS17X

Dell Vi14X

Digital 14 in. Color (FR-PCXBV-PF)

Digital 14 in. Color (FR-PCXBV-SA)

Digital 15 in. Color (FR-PCXBV-PC)

Digital 15 in. Color (FR-PCXBV-SC)

Digital 17 in. Color (FR-PCXAV-EC)

Digital 17 in. Color (FR-PCXBV-KA)

Digital 21 in. Color (FR-PCXAV-HA)

EIZO FlexScan 9080i

EIZO FlexScan FX-B5

EIZO FlexScan FX-C5

EIZO FlexScan FX-C6

EIZO FlexScan FX-E7

EIZO FlexScan T660

EIZO FlexScan TX-C7

EIZO FlexScan TX-C7S

EIZO FlexScan TX-D7S

ELSA GDM-17E40

ESCOM MONO-LCD-screen

Gateway CrystalScan 1572FS

Gateway CrystalScan 1776LE

Generic Monitor

Generic Multisync

GoldStar LG StudioWorks20i

GoldStar LG StudioWorks56i

GoldStar LG StudioWorks56m

GoldStar LG StudioWorks74m

GoldStar LG StudioWorks76i

GoldStar LG StudioWorks76m

GoldStar LG StudioWorks78T

GoldStar LG StudioWorks78i

HP D1187A 20-inch Display

HP D1188A 20-inch Display

HP D1192A VGA Monochrome 14-inch Display

HP D1193A Ultra VGA 17-inch

HP D1194A SVGA 14-inch Display

HP D1195A Ergo-SVGA 14-inch Display

HP D1196A Ergo Ultra VGA 15-inch Display

HP D1197A Color VGA 14-inch Display

HP D1198A SVGA 14-inch Display

HP D1199A Ultra VGA 1600 21-inch Display

HP D1815A 1024 Low Emissions 14-inch Display

HP D2800A Ultra VGA 1600 21-inch Display

HP D2801A VGA Monochrome 14-inch Display

HP D2802A SVGA 14-inch Display

HP D2804A Super VGA and 1024i 14-inch Display

HP D2805A Ergo 1024 14-inch Display

HP D2806A Ergo Ultra VGA 15-inch Display

HP D2807A Ultra VGA 1280 17-inch Display

HP D2808A 1024 Low Emissions 15-inch Display

HP D2814A Super VGA and 1024I 14-inch Display

HP D3857A Multi Media 15-inch Display

HP D3858A Multi Media 14-inch Display

Highscreen LE 1024

Hitachi 20-AP

Hitachi 20-APF

Hitachi 20-AS

Hitachi 21-AP
Hitachi Accuvue GX17L
Hitachi Accuvue GX20
Hitachi Accuvue GX20H
Hitachi Accuvue GX21
Hitachi Accuvue UX4717
Hitachi Accuvue UX4721
Hitachi Accuvue UX4921
Hitachi Accuvue UX6821
Hitachi CM1587M
Hitachi CM1711M
Hitachi CM1721M
Hitachi CM1786M
Hitachi CM2011M
Hitachi CM2096M
Hitachi CM2110M
Hitachi CM2111M
Hitachi CM2112M
Hitachi CM2198M
Hitachi CM2199M
Hitachi CM500
Hitachi CM600
Hitachi CM611
Hitachi CM620
Hitachi CM630
Hitachi CM701
Hitachi CM751
Hitachi CM800
Hitachi CM801
Hitachi CM802
Hitachi CM803
Hitachi HM-5219
Hitachi HM1764
Hitachi HM1782
Hitachi HM4020
Hitachi HM4021
Hitachi HM4721
Hitachi HM4820
Hitachi HM4821
Hitachi HM4921
Hitachi HM6421
Hitachi HM6821
Hyundai DeluxScan 14S
Hyundai DeluxScan 15 Pro
Hyundai DeluxScan 15B
Hyundai DeluxScan 15G+
Hyundai DeluxScan 15G
Hyundai DeluxScan 17 Pro
Hyundai DeluxScan 17B+
Hyundai DeluxScan 17B

Hyundai DeluxScan 17MB/17MS

Hyundai hcm-421E

IBM 2116 MM55 Multimedia

IBM 2128 MM75 Multimedia

IBM 2235 C50

IBM 2237 C71

IBM 6540 G42

IBM 6541 G51

IBM 6546 G52 & G54

IBM 6547 G72 & G74

IBM 6549 G94

IBM 6556 P72

IBM 6557 P92

IBM 6558 P202

IBM 8507

IBM 9514-B TFT Panel

IBM 9514-B TFT Panel

IBM 9514-B TFT Panel

Iiyama A101GT, VisionMasterPro 501

Iiyama A102GT, VisionMasterPro 502

Iiyama A701GT, VisionMasterPro 400

Iiyama MF-8221E/T, VisionMaster

Iiyama MF-8515G, VisionMaster

Iiyama MF-8617E/T, VisionMaster

Iiyama MF-8617ES, VisionMaster

Iiyama MF-8721E, VisionMaster

Iiyama MT-9017E/T, VisionMasterPro

Iiyama MT-9021E/T, VisionMasterPro

Iiyama MT-9221, VisionMasterPro

Iiyama S101GT, VisionMaster 501

Iiyama S102GT, VisionMaster 502

Iiyama S701GT, VisionMaster 400

Iiyama S702GT, VisionMaster 400

Iiyama S901GT, VisionMaster 450

Iiyama TXA3601GT, Prolite36

Iiyama TXA3602GT, Prolite36

Iiyama TXA3811/3821HT, Prolite38

Impression 7 Plus 7728D
LCD Panel 1024x768
LCD Panel 640x480
LCD Panel 800x600
Lite-On CM1414E
MAG 410V2
MAG 510V2
MAG 710V2
MAG 720V2
MAG AX1595
MAG AX15FG
MAG AX1795
MAG AX1795E
MAG AX17FG
MAG D410
MAG DJ530
MAG DJ700
MAG DJ700E
MAG DJ702
MAG DJ702E
MAG DJ704
MAG DJ707
MAG DJ707E
MAG DJ710
MAG DJ717
MAG DJ800
MAG DJ920
MAG DX1495
MAG DX1595
MAG DX1595N
MAG DX1595V
MAG DX15F
MAG DX15FG
MAG DX15N
MAG DX15T
MAG DX1795
MAG DX1795E
MAG DX17F
MAG DX17FP
MAG DX17Fe
MAG DX17N
MAG DX17S
MAG DX17SA
MAG DX17SP
MAG DX17T
MAG DX500AV
MAG DX500T
MAG DX700T
MAG DX715T
MAG MX15F

MAG MX17D

MAG MX17F

MAG MX17FP

MAG MX17S

MAG MX17SA

MAG MX17SG

MAG MX21F

MAG MXE1595

MAG MXE17S

MAG MXP17D

MAG MXP17F

MAG MXP17FE

MAG MXP17S

MAG VEI17

MAG XJ500T

MAG XJ530

MAG XJ700T

MAG XJ707

MAG XJ717

Magnavox MB4010 (14inch/CM1300)

Magnavox MB5314 (15inch/CM1200)

Magnavox MB7000 (17inch/CM6800)

Magnavox MV5011 (15inch/CM1300)

MegaImage 17

Mitsubishi Diamond Plus 100 (TFW1105)

Mitsubishi Diamond Plus 70 (TF-7700P)

Mitsubishi Diamond Plus 71 (TFV6708)

Mitsubishi Diamond Plus 72 (TFV8705)

Mitsubishi Diamond Pro 1000 (TFX1105)

Mitsubishi Diamond Pro 1010 (TUX1107)

Mitsubishi Diamond Pro 14 (FW6405)

Mitsubishi Diamond Pro 14 Plus (SD45xx)

Mitsubishi Diamond Pro 15FS (SD56xx)

Mitsubishi Diamond Pro 17 (TFS6705)

Mitsubishi Diamond Pro 17TX (TFG8705)

Mitsubishi Diamond Pro 20 (HL7955)

Mitsubishi Diamond Pro 20X (FR8905)

Mitsubishi Diamond Pro 21FS (FFL7165)

Mitsubishi Diamond Pro 21T (THZ8155)

Mitsubishi Diamond Pro 21TX (THN9105)

Mitsubishi Diamond Pro 26H (HJ6505)

Mitsubishi Diamond Pro 26M (HC3505)

Mitsubishi Diamond Pro 37 (XC3725)

Mitsubishi Diamond Pro 67TXV (TFV6705)

Mitsubishi Diamond Pro 700 (TFK9705)

Mitsubishi Diamond Pro 87TXM (TFM8705)

Mitsubishi Diamond Pro 900 (NFJ9905)

Mitsubishi Diamond Pro 91TXM (TFW9105)

Mitsubishi Diamond Pro SVGA (SD43xx)

Mitsubishi Diamond Pro VGA (SD41xx)

Mitsubishi Diamond Scan 15FS (SD55xx)

Mitsubishi Diamond Scan 15HX (SD57xx)

Mitsubishi Diamond Scan 15VX (SD58xx)

Mitsubishi Diamond Scan 17FS (FFY7705)

Mitsubishi Diamond Scan 17HX (FFF8705)

Mitsubishi Diamond Scan 20 (HL6945/55)

Mitsubishi Diamond Scan 20H (FR8905)

Mitsubishi Diamond Scan 20M (HC3925)

Mitsubishi Diamond Scan 21 (FFL7165)

Mitsubishi Diamond Scan 37 (XC3715)

Mitsubishi Diamond Scan 50 (SD5904)

Mitsubishi Diamond Scan 70 (SD7704)

Mitsubishi Diamond Scan 90e (FFT9905)

Mitsubishi LCD 40 (LXA420W)

Mitsubishi LCD 50 (LXA520W)

Mitsubishi MegaView 29 (AM2752)

Mitsubishi MegaView 33 (XC3315)

Mitsubishi MegaView 37 (XC3716)

Mitsubishi MegaView 37 Plus (XC3717)

Mitsubishi MegaView Pro 29 (XC2930)

Mitsubishi MegaView Pro 37 (XC3730)

Mitsubishi MegaView Pro 42 (AM4201)

Mitsubishi Precise Point 5800

Mitsubishi Precise Point 8705

Mitsubishi Precise Point 8905

Mitsubishi SpectraView 1000

Mitsubishi SpectraView 700

Mitsubishi The Big Easy 1281 (VS1281)

Mitsubishi The Big Easy G1A (LVPG1A)

Mitsubishi VS1280 Projector

NEC LCD1280

NEC LCD1280

NEC LCD200

NEC LCD300

NEC LCD300

NEC MultiSync 2V

NEC MultiSync 3D

NEC MultiSync 3FGe

NEC MultiSync 3FGx

NEC MultiSync 3V

NEC MultiSync 4D

NEC MultiSync 4FG

NEC MultiSync 4FGe

NEC MultiSync 50

NEC MultiSync 70

NEC MultiSync A500+

NEC MultiSync A500

NEC MultiSync A700+

NEC MultiSync A700

NEC MultiSync A900

NEC MultiSync C400

NEC MultiSync C500

NEC MultiSync E1100+

NEC MultiSync E1100

NEC MultiSync E500

NEC MultiSync E700

NEC MultiSync E750

NEC MultiSync E900+

NEC MultiSync E900

NEC MultiSync FP1350

NEC MultiSync FP950

NEC MultiSync LCD1500M

NEC MultiSync LCD1510

NEC MultiSync LCD1510V

NEC MultiSync LCD1810

NEC MultiSync LCD2000

NEC MultiSync LCD2010
NEC MultiSync LCD400
NEC MultiSync LCD400V
NEC MultiSync M500
NEC MultiSync M700
NEC MultiSync P1150
NEC MultiSync P1250+
NEC MultiSync P750
NEC MultiSync XE15
NEC MultiSync XE17
NEC MultiSync XV14
NEC MultiSync XV15+
NEC MultiSync XV15
NEC MultiSync XV17+ (-2)
NEC Multisync 5FG
NEC Multisync 5FGe
NEC Multisync 5FGp
NEC Multisync 6FG
NEC Multisync 6FGp
Nanao F340i-W
Nanao F550i-w
Nanao F550i
Nokia 300Xa
Nokia 400Xa
Nokia 417TV
Nokia 445G
Nokia 445M
Nokia 445R
Nokia 445X
Nokia 445Xav
Nokia 445Xavc
Nokia 445Xi
Nokia 445XiPlus
Nokia 445Xpro125
Nokia 445Xpro
Nokia 446XS
Nokia 446Xpro
Nokia 446Xt
Nokia 447B
Nokia 447DTC
Nokia 447E
Nokia 447K
Nokia 447KA
Nokia 447KC
Nokia 447L
Nokia 447M
Nokia 447S
Nokia 447V
Nokia 447W
Nokia 447X

Nokia 447XS
Nokia 447Xa
Nokia 447Xav
Nokia 447Xavc
Nokia 447Xi
Nokia 447XiPlus
Nokia 447Xpro
Nokia 447Za
Nokia 447Zi
Nokia 447i
Nokia 449E
Nokia 449M
Nokia 449X
Nokia 449Xa
Nokia 449XaPlus
Nokia 449Xi
Nokia 449XiPlus
Nokia 44BS
Nokia 500Xa
Nokia 800Xi
Optiquest Q100
Optiquest Q41
Optiquest Q51
Optiquest Q53
Optiquest Q71
Optiquest V115
Optiquest V115T
Optiquest V641
Optiquest V655
Optiquest V773
Optiquest V775
Optiquest V95
Panasonic C1491
Panasonic C1591E
Panasonic C1591EA
Panasonic C1791E
Panasonic C1791Ei
Panasonic C1792P
Panasonic C2192P
Panasonic E15
Panasonic E21
Panasonic P15
Panasonic P17
Panasonic P21
Panasonic PF17
Panasonic PM15
Panasonic PM17
Panasonic Panamedia-15
Panasonic Panamedia-17
Panasonic S15

Panasonic S17

Panasonic S21

Panasonic SL70

Panasonic TX-1713MA series

Panasonic TX-D1562F series

Panasonic TX-D1562NMF

Panasonic TX-D1563P series

Panasonic TX-D1731 series

Panasonic TX-D1732 series

Panasonic TX-D1733 series

Panasonic TX-D1734 series

Panasonic TX-D1734F series

Panasonic TX-D1751 series

Panasonic TX-D1752 series

Panasonic TX-D1753 series

Panasonic TX-D2051 series

Panasonic TX-D2131 series

Panasonic TX-D2131P series

Panasonic TX-D2151 series

Panasonic TX-D2162 series

Panasonic TX-D2171 series

Panasonic TX-D4L31-J

Panasonic TX-D7P53 series

Panasonic TX-T1562CJ1

Panasonic TX-T1562P series

Panasonic TX-T1563F series

Panasonic TX-T1563PT1

Panasonic TX-T1565P series

Panasonic TX-T1567P series

Philips 104B (14inch/CM1300)

Philips 105B (15inch/CM1200)

Philips 105B (15inch/CM1300)

Philips 105S (15inch/CM1300)

Philips 107B (17inch/CM6800)

Philips 107B (17inch/CM6800)

Philips 107S (17inch/CM1300)

Philips 107S (17inch/CM6800)

Philips 1764DC

Philips 200B (20inch/CM5600)

Philips 200T (20inch/CM0700)

Philips 201B (21inch/CM0770)

Philips 201B (PRODUCT ID 21B58...)

Philips 7BM749

Philips Brilliance 105(15inch/CM2200)

Philips Brilliance 107 (17inch/CM8800)

Philips Brilliance 107 (PRODUCT ID 17A58...)

Philips Brilliance 109 (PRODUCT ID 19A58...)

Philips Brilliance 201 (21inch/CM1700)

Philips Brilliance 201 (PRODUCT ID 21A58...)

Philips Brilliance 201CS (21inch/CM0900)

Philips Brilliance AX4500 (14.5 LCD MONITOR)

Philips Brilliance AX4500 (14.5 LCD MONITOR)

Princeton Graphic Systems Arcadia AR2.7

Princeton Graphic Systems Arcadia AR2.7AV

Princeton Graphic Systems Arcadia AR3.1

Princeton Graphic Systems Arcadia AR3.1AV

Princeton Graphic Systems C2001

Princeton Graphic Systems EO14

Princeton Graphic Systems EO15

Princeton Graphic Systems EO17

Princeton Graphic Systems EO2000

Princeton Graphic Systems EO40

Princeton Graphic Systems EO500

Princeton Graphic Systems EO50

Princeton Graphic Systems EO70

Princeton Graphic Systems EO710

Princeton Graphic Systems EO72

Princeton Graphic Systems EO74/74T

Princeton Graphic Systems EO75

Princeton Graphic Systems EO76/76T

Princeton Graphic Systems EO900

Princeton Graphic Systems EO90

Princeton Graphic Systems Ultra 14

Princeton Graphic Systems Ultra 14ni

Princeton Graphic Systems Ultra 15

Princeton Graphic Systems Ultra 17+

Princeton Graphic Systems Ultra 17

Princeton Graphic Systems Ultra 20

Princeton Graphic Systems Ultra 40

Princeton Graphic Systems Ultra 41

Princeton Graphic Systems Ultra 50

Princeton Graphic Systems Ultra 51

Princeton Graphic Systems Ultra 70F

Princeton Graphic Systems Ultra 71

Princeton Graphic Systems Ultra 72

Princeton Graphic Systems Ultra 80

Quantex TE1564M - Super View 1280

Relisys RE1564

Sampo alphascan-17

Samsung SyncMaster 15GLe

Samsung SyncMaster 15GLi

Samsung SyncMaster 15M

Samsung SyncMaster 17GLi

Samsung SyncMaster 17GLsi

Samsung SyncMaster 3

Samsung SyncMaster 3Ne

Samsung SyncMaster 500b/500Mb

Samsung SyncMaster 500p/500Mp

Samsung SyncMaster 500s/500Ms

Samsung SyncMaster 700b/700Mb

Samsung SyncMaster 700p/700Mp

Samsung SyncMaster 700s/700Ms

Samtron 5B/5MB

Samtron 5E/5ME

Samtron 7E/7ME/7B/7MB

Samtron SC-428PS/PSL

Samtron SC-428PT/PTL

Samtron SC-528MDL

Samtron SC-528TXL

Samtron SC-528UXL

Samtron SC-726GXL

Samtron SC-728FXL

Sony CPD-100ES

Sony CPD-100EST

Sony CPD-100GS

Sony CPD-100GST

Sony CPD-100SF

Sony CPD-100SFB

Sony CPD-100SFT

Sony CPD-100SX

Sony CPD-100VS

Sony CPD-101VS iGPE

Sony CPD-110GS/110EST

Sony CPD-120AS

Sony CPD-120VS

Sony CPD-15ES2

Sony CPD-15ES

Sony CPD-15SF2

Sony CPD-15SF8

Sony CPD-15SF9

Sony CPD-15SX1

Sony CPD-17C1

Sony CPD-17ES2

Sony CPD-17GS

Sony CPD-17MS

Sony CPD-17SF2

Sony CPD-17SF8

Sony CPD-17SF8R

Sony CPD-17SF9

Sony CPD-200ES

Sony CPD-200EST

Sony CPD-200GS

Sony CPD-200GST

Sony CPD-200SF

Sony CPD-200SFT

Sony CPD-200SX

Sony CPD-201VS iGPE

Sony CPD-20SF2

Sony CPD-20SF2T5

Sony CPD-20SF2T

Sony CPD-20SF3

Sony CPD-210GS/210EST

Sony CPD-210SFB

Sony CPD-220AS

Sony CPD-220GS/17GS2

Sony CPD-220VS

Sony CPD-300SFT5

Sony CPD-300SFT

Sony CPD-420GS/420GST/19GS2

Sony CPD-520GS/520GST/21GS2

Sony CPD-L133

Sony CPD-L150

Sony GDM-17SE2T(NEW)

Sony GDM-17SE2T5

Sony GDM-17SE2T

Sony GDM-200PS

Sony GDM-200PST

Sony GDM-20SE2T5

Sony GDM-20SE2T

Sony GDM-20SE3T

Sony GDM-20SHT(NEW)

Sony GDM-20SHT

Sony GDM-400PS/400PST/19PS

Sony GDM-500PS/500PST/21PS

Sony GDM-F400

Sony GDM-F500

Sony GDM-W900

Sony VMU-1000

Sun 17-inch 447Z

TARGA TM 1710 D

TAXAN 875

Tandberg ErgoScan 21c

Tatung CM14UHE

Tatung CM14UHR

Tatung CM14UHS

Unisys-19

ViewSonic 14E

ViewSonic 14ES

ViewSonic 15

ViewSonic 15E

ViewSonic 15ES-2

ViewSonic 15ES

ViewSonic 15EX

ViewSonic 15G-2

ViewSonic 15G

ViewSonic 15GA-2

ViewSonic 15GA

ViewSonic 15GS-2

ViewSonic 15GS-3

ViewSonic 15GS

ViewSonic 17

ViewSonic 17E

ViewSonic 17EA

ViewSonic 17G

ViewSonic 17GA-2

ViewSonic 17GA

ViewSonic 17GS-2
ViewSonic 17GS
ViewSonic 17PS-2
ViewSonic 17PS
ViewSonic 1
ViewSonic 20
ViewSonic 20G-2
ViewSonic 20G
ViewSonic 20PS
ViewSonic 21
ViewSonic 21PS-2
ViewSonic 21PS
ViewSonic 29GA
ViewSonic 2
ViewSonic 3
ViewSonic 4
ViewSonic 4E
ViewSonic 5+
ViewSonic 5
ViewSonic 5E
ViewSonic 6
ViewSonic 6E
ViewSonic 6FS
ViewSonic 7
ViewSonic 7E
ViewSonic 8
ViewSonic E40
ViewSonic E41
ViewSonic E51
ViewSonic E641-2
ViewSonic E641
ViewSonic E651
ViewSonic E655-2
ViewSonic E655-3
ViewSonic E655
ViewSonic E71
ViewSonic E771-2
ViewSonic E771
ViewSonic EA771
ViewSonic EA771B
ViewSonic G653-2
ViewSonic G653
ViewSonic G655
ViewSonic G771
ViewSonic G773-2
ViewSonic G773
ViewSonic G790
ViewSonic G800
ViewSonic G810-2
ViewSonic G810

ViewSonic GA655

ViewSonic GA771

ViewSonic GS771

ViewSonic GT770

ViewSonic GT775

ViewSonic GT800

ViewSonic MB110

ViewSonic MB50

ViewSonic MB70

ViewSonic MB90

ViewSonic P655

ViewSonic P775

ViewSonic P810-3

ViewSonic P810-A

ViewSonic P810-E

ViewSonic P810-ER

ViewSonic P810-MR

ViewSonic P810

ViewSonic P815

ViewSonic P817

ViewSonic PJ1000

ViewSonic PJ800

ViewSonic PJ820

ViewSonic PJL802

ViewSonic PS775

ViewSonic PS790

ViewSonic PT770

ViewSonic PT771

ViewSonic PT775

ViewSonic PT810-2

ViewSonic PT810-3

ViewSonic PT810

ViewSonic PT813-1

ViewSonic S6E

ViewSonic VP140

ViewSonic VP150

ViewSonic VPA138

ViewSonic VPA145

ViewSonic VPA150

Index

Symbols

Numerics

A

D

G

H

I

O

P

T

W

X

Y

Z

About the Author

Charles Fisher is Systems Analyst at a national media company based in the Midwestern United States. Under the UNIX platform, he has served as Webmaster, system administrator, and developer. Mr. Fisher has a degree in electrical and computer engineering and is a past contributor to UnixWorld Online.